UNLOCKING
THE
CAGE

MARK TULLIUS

VINCERE
P R E S S

Published by Vincere Press
65 Pine Ave., Ste 806
Long Beach, CA 90802

For my wife who understood,
my children who motivated,
my friends who encouraged,
and all the athletes who shared.

UNLOCKING
THE
CAGE

"What one has, one ought to use:
and whatever he does he should do with all his might."

– MARCUS TULLIUS CICERO

CONTENTS

PROLOGUE

January 10, 1999

Sunday's my only day off. No bodyguarding, no bouncing. No running, sparring, or hitting the heavy bag. I'm recovering from a late night, stretched out on the floor of my sparsely furnished one-bedroom apartment, killing creatures on PlayStation.

My cell phone rings in the kitchen. I'm not expecting any calls, so I almost don't answer it. The phone's beside the oatmeal and protein powder, just about the only food in the place. I don't recognize the number, but, for some reason, I answer anyway.

It's the promoter of a local No Holds Barred (NHB) show. On their last card, I'd managed to squeak by with a win, fortunate not to be matched against Ricco Rodriguez or Tito Ortiz. I ask what I can do for him.

"You got anything going on today?"

"Nothing until tonight."

"Want to do me a huge favor, and make some money?"

I don't care about the favor, but could use the cash. "Doing what?"

"How'd you like to fight? I could really use you."

I laugh. "Sorry, I'm afraid I can't. I gave it up."

"But you've been training."

He'd talked to someone, probably my old coach. "I haven't rolled in like two months, only been boxing," I tell him. "Turning pro soon."

"That's great," he says, sounding way too happy. "You're in great shape then. Come on. I got a guy from out of town who needs an opponent. He wants a shot at your belt."

All the ref did was raise my hand. This was the first I'd heard of a belt. "I promised my boxing coach I wouldn't fight in the cage again."

"Why's he got to know? Come on. It's two hundred bucks, three if you win."

I don't want him thinking I'm chicken, but I can't take the fight. "I've got a date at seven," I say, leaving out that I also swore to my girlfriend that I was done with the cage.

"Doors open at five. I'll put you on first. You'll be fine."

I look around my sorry apartment, searching for an excuse. Suddenly I'm not so sure I want one. All I can come up with is, "I don't have a cup."

"Not a problem. I'll have one for you. Just get down here soon as you can."

He'd have an answer for everything. It was either yes or no. I'm smart enough to know it'd be dumb to take the fight. I'm stupid enough to say, "Alright. I'll be there."

Well, my day just got way more interesting. I fix a little food and gather my stuff; throw a pair of jeans and a button-down into my gym bag since I'll have to go straight to the date.

In the car, I blast Slayer to block my thoughts, and jump on the freeway. I don't call my friends or brothers, even though I suppose it'd be nice to have a corner. I don't call my boxing coach to tell him I'm breaking his rule. I don't call my girlfriend to tell her I'm breaking hers, too. Odds are she'll figure it out when she sees me.

I don't care about my body, but hope my face doesn't get all messed up. That happened 5 months ago when I fought Bobby Hoffman at Extreme Challenge 20 in Iowa. The first 11 minutes of the fight were fine, but the last 50 seconds hadn't been fun, hammerfist after hammerfist straight to the face, making it so everyone on that flight knew I got my ass kicked. My mom cried when she saw me.

But it didn't really hurt. Bruises fade and a broken nose is no big deal. That's not how I should be thinking, though. I have to stay positive. I got lucky and won my last 2 fights, barely taking any punishment. Maybe this guy wouldn't be any good. Maybe the boxing had improved my striking. Shit, maybe I could actually win and get that extra hundred.

The parking lot is already getting full. This building looks far better than the dirty warehouse they'd thrown a cage in for the last event. I'm not sure if the fight is legal, but that's not a real concern. Truth is, I wish the cops would show up and shut it down, that they'd hurry up and do it in the next half hour.

Inside I find the promoter, throw on the cup and a pair of tight shorts. Just as he promised, I'd be up first in 20 minutes.

All the other fighters are with friends or teammates. I find a quiet corner and start to stretch. I don't see any heavyweights around. Maybe my guy won't show.

I'm new to NHB, with 5 fights in my single year of training, and I've never been first on a card. As one of the bigger guys, I'm usually one of the last, sitting in the back and watching guys come back bloodied and broken. Not today. I've got 15 minutes.

The static stretching isn't exactly warming me up, so I do a dozen up-downs. I'm shocked how winded I get. Not good.

The team I'd been with for my last 3 fights has guys on the card. Most of them are cool with me and understand why I gave up NHB for boxing. I thought my ex-coach hadn't been happy with my decision, but he doesn't mention it when he walks over. He even offers to work my corner, tells my old teammates to warm me up.

Holy shit, I'm in trouble. What should have been easy drills just wiped me out. The guys ask if I've been training at all, if I'm ready.

I never should've answered the phone, shouldn't have taken the fight. But I did, so none of that matters. I've got 10 minutes to calm my heart rate and get my head straight.

My buddy points out a guy shooting double-leg takedowns. He's easily just as big and strong as I am, so there goes any advantage I might've had. He's wearing wrestling shoes. His shadowboxing's better than mine. Goddamn it. This is going to suck.

I tell the guys I'm warm enough and walk to the water fountain. I grab a drink, tell myself to stop being a little bitch. It's just a fight, no different from what could happen any night at work. But those guys are usually drunk and not trained athletes.

They call us to the cage. I wonder what kind of advice I'll get from my corner. I feel like a complete coward when I tell my old coach, "I don't give a shit about this fight. Throw in that towel if I'm getting my ass kicked. I'm not even supposed to be here."

He says sure thing, but I question if he will. I get in the cage and try to look tough, like I belong in there. The *Rocky* music in the background isn't helping.

The announcer says Tim Lajcik is undefeated, an All-American wrestler, but my hearing's all fuzzy. All I know is he looks solid. And determined. He's staring right through me.

The cage door clangs shut. The lock slides into place.

The voice in my head drowns out everything else. *What the hell is wrong with me?*

CHAPTER ONE

January 14, 2012

A lot had changed in the 13 years since the Lajcik fight. I got married, divorced, married again, and became a stay-at-home dad about to launch my career as an author. In August I would turn 40, an age I never imagined I'd reach. Overall, I was content with how life had played out and considered myself very fortunate.

That one-bedroom apartment had transformed into a house filled with toys. The PlayStation got upgraded to an Xbox 360 with Kinect so I could jump around with my 3-year-old daughter, Olivia. That was practically the only exercise I was getting since I'd ruptured my Achilles tendon 6 years before.

I never accomplished anything as a fighter and ended both my short boxing and Mixed Martial Arts (MMA) careers with losing records. My last fight was in 2004 when I suffered a concussion severe enough to scare me.

Although a lot of my friends were huge MMA fans, I didn't follow the sport and rarely watched fights. When we went to my buddy's house to watch Ultimate Fighting Championship (UFC) 142, I spent most of the time playing with the kids until my friend asked me why I wasn't hanging out with the adults. I grabbed a beer and plopped down on the couch. There were some good fights and part of me enjoyed it, but another part wanted to change the channel. I wrote it off as regret that I never made it as a fighter. Or maybe I'd gone soft from being surrounded by women. Could have been that I hated to hear fans screaming for blood. Whatever it was, I no longer cared to watch two people hurt each other.

One of the wives turned to me and said, "I can't believe you ever did this stuff."

"Never on a big stage like this."

"You don't seem like a fighter." Like she really wanted to know, she asked, "Why'd you do it?"

That was the question everyone always asked, the one I could never answer. I fell back to my usual response and said, "Don't know, guess there's something wrong with me."

We headed home, but the question kept nagging. What had been the draw back then? What led me to fight, and why'd I stick with it as long as I did? I had spent most of my life steering clear of fights and breaking them up. Why would I pour so much time and energy into a sport I was unsuccessful at? A punishing sport with so little reward.

I'd spent 7 years rattling my brain playing high school and college football. Between that and fighting, it wasn't surprising that my memory sucked. I racked my brain trying to remember who I had been back then. I had a good childhood, my parents were still married, and somehow I managed to earn an Ivy League degree. Fighting didn't make sense.

I would have let the question slide, but I was a little concerned about my daughter. She loved to punch and kick and trap me in triangle chokes. Was she going to follow my path and wind up in a cage? Is the urge to fight hereditary? Did the games we play push her in that direction?

My wife, Jen, met me after my fighting days so she couldn't offer much insight. I told her about the study I had devised back when I first began fighting. Developing a survey to find out why guys fight was the only time I used what I had learned in my sociology classes. I figured that if I could discover why others fought maybe I'd understand my own reasons. Unfortunately, I never got around to handing the survey out at events.

"So do it now," Jen said. "MMA is only getting bigger and there'll be no shortages of fighters for a survey. You could write a book on it. Why do they fight and what do they have in common?"

All my friends agreed with Jen and pushed me to do it. If I trained with the fighters it would be a great opportunity to get back in shape, but I was comfortable where I was. I didn't want to take a break from writing fiction, and this would require a huge commitment to do the project the way I'd want to. Also, how could I commit to a sport I didn't even care to watch?

The self-doubt was overwhelming. What a dumb idea. I hadn't been a good fighter. I'd never written nonfiction or conducted an interview. Anything I might have learned about sociology was long forgotten. I was a painfully shy introvert, who preferred to remain inside the house all day. Plus, who really cared to discover why people fight? It seemed most fans only appreciated the violence.

I spent a few weeks watching fights and thinking that maybe the study wasn't a bad idea. I checked what else had been written on the subject and ordered Sam Sheridan's books, *A Fighter's Heart* and *The Fighter's Mind*. Sam's a Harvard grad who found his way into fighting. I hoped that reading his books would answer my questions and put this project to rest.

I devoured both books within the week, but they led to more questions. I emailed Sam and he was nice enough to meet for lunch. He told me not to worry about the similarities between our projects and gave me some great advice.

The next day I signed up at a local MMA gym and quickly discovered how out of shape I really was. Also how unmotivated; one or two workouts a week was all I could manage.

Still on the fence about committing to the project, I called Brown University's Sociology department for advice. I was prepared to explain what MMA was and then get laughed off the phone and told to stop wasting their time, but Karl Dominey, the academic coordinator who answered the phone, is a huge MMA fan and thought my project sounded incredible. He put me in touch with two professors, one who researches professional wrestlers, and the other who teaches a course on the sociology of martial arts.

I was all out of excuses. I made a modified commitment, at least for one trip to the East Coast so I could stop by Brown. My wife was incredibly supportive and gave me a 17-day travel pass. My daughter begged me not to leave. I lined up a handful of gyms in the New England area, hoping I'd find others while I was there. I had no idea who I'd talk with, how they'd react to me, or what I'd discover.

It was time to find out.

CHAPTER TWO

May 1, 2012

The red-eye to Boston was rough. I landed anxious and exhausted, having had only about an hour of sleep. It was a miserable morning outside and I hoped the downpour wasn't a warning of what lay ahead.

I trudged through the airport, the ridiculous weight of my luggage reminding me of my first move to Brown, all my belongings stuffed in 2 duffle bags. I'd felt like a fraud back then, out of my league. Crazy how little had changed in 20 years.

The rain stayed with me the whole drive to Providence, RI, and continued to pour as I settled in. I was running on fumes, ready to crash when I reached Black Diamond Mixed Martial Arts. The guys there were friendly and helpful, but the school emphasized Brazilian Jiu Jitsu (BJJ) and only had two fighters available with any experience. One gave up MMA after suffering a severe concussion in his first fight, the other dreamed of competing in the UFC despite only having won half of his fights.

Although they were interesting, both interviews lacked depth and were more of a learning experience. In addition to getting a quick tutorial from a student on how to use my camera, I picked up some valuable lessons: Never do interviews on one hour of sleep. Always ask if the radio can be turned down. Don't ask a question if I don't care about the answer.

The next night I headed to an industrial area of Pawtucket, RI. I double-checked the address and spotted the tiny sign on the massive brick building, the type of place where people aren't afraid to get a little dirty. I rolled up the windows and locked my rental, checking it twice before heading upstairs. Tri-Force MMA was located at the back of an old-school boxing gym. This was a place to put in work, not to look pretty. And they had a cage. This was what I wanted.

The co-owners, brothers Pete and Keith Jeffrey, both professional fighters and coaches, made me feel very welcome and said I could jump in with the dozen fighters already training. Although I was terribly out of shape, it felt good to get on the mat, practice some techniques, and pretend I knew what I was doing. After a few light rounds, Pete called out it was time to spar.

I took a few deep breaths, walked over to my bags, camera in one, training gear in the other. I considered gearing up, even though I promised my wife I wouldn't be that stupid. The following night I was scheduled to do a reading at Brown and I really didn't want to do it with a black eye or slurred words.

So I bowed out and felt like the biggest coward. I grabbed my camera so at least I had an excuse not to spar. That turned out to be a great decision because now I was no longer just thinking of myself and the person in front of me. I took in the entire scene, felt an intensity that I hadn't been around in quite some time. From behind the camera I could watch how people worked with one another. Which guys backed off after hurting their partner, which ones attacked? Who was aware of the camera, turning it up a notch if it zoomed on them? Who was so focused that the camera didn't exist?

There was so much to take in. A guy half my size, always moving forward. The only woman in the group, firing back just as hard as her male partners. Keith and a heavyweight trading leather in the boxing ring, while another heavyweight rotated through partners in the cage. A middleweight in a green shirt getting fired up when his nose became bloodied.

It was late when practice ended and I figured everyone would want to hurry home for food and a shower. I was pleasantly surprised when 5 of the fighters lined up to do interviews, but now the challenge was fitting them all in an hour. A mere 10 minutes to discover why each of them fought.

I brought out my notepad and questions, and video recorded each interview so I wouldn't forget what was said. The heavyweight was an experienced pro who'd grown up poor and began fighting to make money to get his brother out of jail. The clean-cut finance manager fought at the amateur level because he loved the challenge and missed his competitive days of college football. The 135-pound childcare worker who'd been wrestling since eighth grade, stressed how MMA made him a better person. The carpenter described being in the cage as a perfect moment of peace.

Then there was Andre Soukhamthath, the Asian Sensation, who had replaced his drenched and blood-spattered green shirt with a clean yellow one. The calm, soft-spoken 23-year-old was not what I had expected. Immediately I was interested in Andre because, even though he came from a family of Muay Lao fighters and enjoyed watching fights, he didn't train in the martial arts until after high school. His father, William, Tri-Force's striking coach, wanted more for his son and pushed him away from training, encouraging Andre to focus on basketball and soccer, the sports Andre enjoyed.

Andre was a very good athlete and was offered a scholarship as a soccer goalie. Before he began college, however, Andre's girlfriend became pregnant. Andre gave up his dream and began working full time to provide for his new family.

The lack of physical activity made Andre feel like he was missing something. At the suggestion of a friend, he tried out an MMA class and enjoyed it. Shortly after, his son, LeAndre, was born and they discovered the boy had a severe form of a rare skin disease. Working at a job he didn't like while caring for his sick son took its toll on Andre, and he poured more of himself into MMA, using it as outlet for his emotions.

Andre paused a moment before continuing his story. LeAndre passed away at 9 months.

I was at a loss for words, imagining how devastating it would be to lose my daughter.

Andre said that MMA played a huge role in helping him work through the grief. The outlet became his sanctuary and developed into a passion. The competitive urge he'd always had to be the best and test his skills landed him in the cage. He had a "real" job working at a Boys and Girls Club to pay his bills, but he was determined to improve his 1-1 record and become a full-time, successful fighter.

After the interview, Andre and his fiancée, Jamie, locked up Tri-Force and walked me to my car. As difficult as it'd been hearing about their loss, it was inspiring to learn that they were expecting another boy in a few months. Both of them were fighters.

* * *

The next day I returned to Brown, once again the dumb jock bumbling about campus, this time there for fighting instead of football. The rush of memories caught me off guard. Not ready to deal with them, I concentrated on the task at hand and headed for the Sociology department, considering what questions I would ask the professor.

Although I must have walked by the enormous inscription on the side of the library hundreds of times as a student, this was the first time it meant anything to me: "Speak to the past and it will teach thee."

Was this the real reason I started my project in Rhode Island instead of back home where there was always an MMA gym within throwing distance? If I was going to understand why I fought I'd have to look at my college years because it was that angry, insecure young man who'd fallen into the sport a few years after graduating.

I kept walking to my meeting, but instead of blocking out the memories and denying the nostalgia, I welcomed the flood. There was the Ratty where I ate nearly every meal because that's all I could afford. The dorms I'd blacked out in countless times. The classrooms I avoided whenever possible.

The bar I'd been banned from was no longer standing. Same went for the place I said a final goodbye to a dear friend who died a year later. But the memories were still there and that's what I needed.

I reached Maxcy Hall and pulled myself out of the pity party. After a fantastic talk with Karl, the academic coordinator/MMA fan, I met with Professor R. Tyson Smith, who was wrapping up his research on professional wrestlers. I explained what I hoped to accomplish with my study and how I planned to do it. Inspired by my experience at Tri-Force, I shared my new goal. If I asked enough people the right questions in a well-thought-out survey, in addition to conducting one-on-one interviews, I could discover not only why they fight, but also who they are as individuals. Professor Smith's questions and insight helped me see both the limitations and potential of the study. Most importantly, the talk reassured me the project would be a worthwhile endeavor. MMA is a growing part of our culture that warrants a close examination. Showing how it impacts our society is beyond the scope of this book, but perhaps it might help with the discussion.

It would have been great to have more time with the professor, but it was time to do a reading from my novel, *Brightside*, at Brown's bookstore. At least one thing had changed; my deathly fear of public speaking was a thing of the past.

Friday morning I returned to Tri-Force for the no-gi jiu jitsu class taught by middleweight Keith Jeffrey. The muscular 30-year-old impressed me as he took us through a dynamic warm-up. These weren't just a couple of random stretches Keith threw together. He had more than a decade of training in jiu jitsu, Muay Thai, boxing, and wrestling. He had studied the body and the most efficient and safest ways to put it through a hard workout. By the end of 5 minutes, I was ready to bow out and Keith hadn't even broken a sweat.

Keith was very thorough, demonstrating techniques and walking us through them. I enjoyed the way he taught and would have learned a lot more if I hadn't been completely exhausted. After I cooled down, I set up the tripod to interview Keith, grateful to have more time to hear his story.

It seemed that the best way to understand someone is to see who they were and where they came from. Keith took me back to his early years and what it was like being the youngest of 3 brothers. For him, and everyone he was close to, it was always about being the toughest, being the strongest, and who could take out whom. He constantly roughhoused with his 2 older brothers, and was usually on the losing end as the little kid. The desire to be just as tough and strong as them pushed Keith to become very competitive, and at a very young age, he vowed he'd be a champion one day.

In his quest to become the toughest, Keith practiced Tae Kwon Do for a few years before focusing on strength and conditioning and then boxing. He found his true love in BJJ and hadn't thought about fighting MMA until he was 23 and a coach asked if he was interested. Although he had limited training and didn't know much about the sport, his coach's confidence was enough to get Keith to commit. He talked about how addicting the experience was and what it felt like to perform in front of an audience. "It's the biggest thrill ride, and I wanted that feeling again."

Fighting to him is competition. Instead of viewing it as violence, Keith sees only the beauty. When he's in the cage, he's fighting for honor, and not out of a desire to injure his opponent. He said, "It's just business. It's no different from any other sport."

Although Keith still dreamed of being a champion, he completely understood how difficult it would be to make that happen. Because of injuries and having to find time to train while running a business and being a coach, Keith only had 10 fights in 7 years.

"When you mature and you become a man, that's when you really know if you're going to be a fighter or not," Keith said, pointing out how much easier it is to pursue the sport when you're a teenager or young adult with relatively few responsibilities. Once you have your own bills to pay, you realize you're spending much more money than you've made. And as all the other responsibilities pile on, it gets much harder to justify the selfish and challenging lifestyle of a fighter.

Keith wasn't done fighting, but life had reshaped his priorities. Tri-Force and his fighters had to come first.

* * *

Instead of sleeping in Saturday morning, I drove with my cousin, Rob Levesque, to a nearby gymnasium for a North American Grappling Association (NAGA) tournament. The guys at Tri-Force had said it'd be a good place to meet fighters and line up interviews. I had zero endurance and the limited skills I once had were long forgotten, but I said to hell with it and signed up. It was just grappling and not an actual fight. It wasn't like I'd get injured.

Although I felt foolish, I wasn't worried about competing and welcomed the distraction. My anxiety level around crowds made it difficult to be in the gymnasium, and the thought of getting my butt kicked was much more appealing than what I'd been doing, approaching strangers to ask if they were fighters and would they like to do an interview.

I had limited success with this approach until I met Matt Perry, an eighth-grade science teacher and pro fighter out of Lauzon MMA in Bridgewater, MA. Matt appreciated what I was trying to do with the study and texted Joe Lauzon, setting it up for me to visit the gym on Tuesday. Feeling much better about the following week, I stretched a bit and jumped into the matches, quickly getting destroyed by the real experts and tearing the cartilage between my ribs in my match against former fighter and BJJ black belt Mat Santos.

With no time to even shower, Rob and I jumped in the car and headed to Plymouth, MA, to check out Cage Titans FC, the first MMA event I'd attended since my last fight in 2004. The pain in my ribs only got worse, and by the time we hit the venue I was in a terrible mood, afraid I'd just ruined the rest of my trip because training was out of the question.

Cage Titans held its fights at the historic Plymouth Memorial Hall. At first it seemed like a strange location, but with the cage in the middle of the two-story venue, there wasn't a bad seat in the house. Thanks to a last-minute press pass from the promoter, we had full access and took advantage of it, heading backstage to get the entire experience. Some fighters were getting their hands wrapped, while others warmed up, one stretching while reading a book. The announcer called out the first fighter and I was hit with the old surge of adrenaline mixed with anxiousness, dread, and anticipation. The idea of knowing you're up soon and well past the point of walking away, the fabled point of no return.

The first fight finished quickly. We left backstage and walked around the packed hall, finally settling on a spot in the highest section where we could take in a panoramic view. Since it hurt to raise my hand, Rob was kind enough to take over camera duties, his focus split between fighters and ring girls.

The beer was flowing and the fans were loud, the energy contagious. Although I might have turned the channel if I were watching the fights on TV, I was glued to my seat, soaking in all the action, a good mix of amateur and professional bouts, the majority going to the third round. Although I was enjoying the fights, my ribs were killing me and I wished for more first-round finishes. Fifteen fights on one card made for a long night, and we were 6 hours in before we got to the main event—Johnny "Cupcakes" Campbell vs. Tateki Matsuda.

All desire for an early finish went out the window. Matsuda, who trains out of the famous Sityodtong Muay Thai academy, delivered one brutal kick after another, purpling Campbell's legs early on. Campbell, out of South Shore Sports Fighting, kept coming forward, pleasing the crowd with his athletic display and unorthodox attacks. Matsuda seemed unstoppable, but Johnny kept firing back no matter how many brutal leg kicks he ate. At the end of the five-round battle, Johnny lost a close decision but gained a great deal of respect.

Less than a week into the project and I'd once again become a fan of the sport.

CHAPTER THREE

May 6, 2012

Sunday was a much-needed—and heavily medicated—day of rest. Fortunately, I hadn't scheduled any interviews, and the only thing I had planned was to spend time with Rob's family, as in my college days, my family away from home. Spending time with them was great, but it made me miss mine. I'd never been away from my daughter for more than a day, and she wasn't handling it well.

Now that I couldn't train with the teams, I had an excuse to return home early. Even though I enjoyed the fights and had been inspired by the Tri-Force guys and Professor Smith, not being able to train took away half the fun. I checked my airline ticket info and saw an email from Sam Sheridan. He'd just sent me the phone number of Kirik Jenness, owner and founder of *The UnderGround*, an extremely popular MMA forum hosted on his website *mixedmartialarts.com*. Kirik is also the Association of Boxing Commissions' official record keeper for the sport of MMA, an MMA coach, and a fighter. Certainly one of the most knowledgeable men in the sport.

I made the call and spoke briefly with Kirik, giving him a quick rundown on my project. He was incredibly nice and invited me to stay with him on Wednesday, an opportunity I couldn't pass up. I called my wife and told her it'd be another 10 days before I saw them.

The pain in my ribs made it hard to sleep and continued all day Monday, so I didn't bother taking gym gear that night to South Shore Sports Fighting (SSSF) in Norwell, MA. I assumed Johnny Campbell wouldn't be back in the gym so soon after the battle I'd witnessed Saturday night, but I was interested in talking with co-owner, coach, and fighter Bill Mahoney, whom I'd met backstage at Cage Titans.

SSSF was a no-nonsense type of gym; there was no room for fun and diversions. Every foot of the giant building was being used, everyone training hard whether they were children, adults, or actual fighters. The intensity with which these individuals trained almost made me grateful for my injury. There was no way I'd be able to keep up. Bill proudly pointed out that SSSF was one of the only schools around dedicated exclusively to MMA, instead of being a Brazilian Jiu Jitsu or kickboxing school that offered MMA classes. They'd been voted the best fight team in New England 6 of the last 7 years, amassing a 43-8 record in 2011.

As at Tri-Force, each of the fighters I talked to had a different story. A semi-pro football player that missed competition and preferred the personal responsibility of fighting over being on a team. A guy who got experience on the streets of Brockton, MA, where fighting was commonplace. A lifelong hockey player who grew up fighting, MMA making him less like a volcano waiting to explode. A quiet wrestler who turned to MMA to stay busy and found himself fighting 3 months later.

Although 42-year-old Bill Mahoney came from the same rough area as the others, his childhood was very different from theirs. He was unable to play sports because he was a small and sickly kid who suffered from Crohn's disease. With the thud of heavy bags in the background, Bill spoke openly about growing up without a father and being constantly abused by an older brother. He only attended high school for 21 days, long enough to destroy his already poor self-esteem. In front of the entire class, his gym teacher asked him, "Why are you so weak and your brother's so strong?"

Bill wanted to be strong and tough like his brother and all the boxers he saw on TV, but knew that wasn't his reality. He said that in Brockton, "Everyone knew the pecking order, everyone fought. I knew the one kid I could beat, the hundred and thirty-six that would beat me."

A week after seeing the first UFC, and recovering from a rough stay at the hospital, Bill decided to test himself and went to a Jeet Kune Do (JKD) academy that offered BJJ. "I was a tremendously slow learner, tremendously weak, uncoordinated," Bill said. "I literally was the worst fighter at the school for two years, tapped by first-day guys."

What Bill lacked in athleticism, he compensated for with the toughness and persistence he learned as a kid. He kept at the sport, learning each day, his confidence growing. After the JKD academy, he moved on to judo and Sambo, and 6 years into training he still had no thoughts of fighting. That was until a coach made a snarky comment that none of his fighters would be competing in an upcoming MMA event. Bill took it as a challenge and spoke right up, said he would fight. Over the next 11 years he competed in another 17 fights and coached countless others.

Some people might assume that without a high school education and after all the years of fighting, Bill wouldn't be very bright. His shaved head, goatee, and Full Contact Fighter tank top might solidify their opinion. But they'd be dead wrong. Bill is very insightful and it was obvious he'd spent much of his life examining not only himself, but also those around him.

He'd given a great deal of thought to fighting and believed that MMA attracts both the best and the worst types of people. He'd even broken down the reasons for fighting into categories. Some guys fight for supplemental income; others are chasing unrealistic goals of fame and fortune. Too many guys do it to get girls, look cool, and impress; a rare few are sociopaths who enjoy hurting others. The ones doing it for personal reasons, such as testing oneself, he described as being "generally the coolest people I know."

I'd already kept Bill from training for half an hour, but wanted to hear what other theories he might have. He shared his opinion on whether fighting was primal—a resounding "Yes" in his book. He pointed to evolutionary psychology. "People that fought in history were rewarded and were the ones who survived. We are driven to fight. Everything else is conscious rationalization."

Due to Bill's age, it was getting incredibly hard for him to get licensed. His voice tinged with sadness when he said, "All I can really say is, boy, you really miss it when it's gone. I can't even think of my motivation to train when it's gone. That few seconds in the cage, it's just…it's so real."

* * *

Besides giving me some great theories to test, Bill also gave me Johnny Campbell's phone number. I called him and he agreed to an interview. Tuesday afternoon I headed back to Plymouth, the area getting nicer the closer I got. I'd never been to Brockton or the rough neighborhoods the other fighters came from, but I was sure this was not the same. The house was beautiful, the neighborhood pristine.

A clean-cut young man opened the front door. With his black eye, I could have mistaken him for a frat kid who'd gotten into a scuffle. However, the soft-spoken 25-year-old's legs were battered a deep purple, and he walked with a serious limp when he led me into his parents' house.

We set up at the kitchen table, no buzzers, no heavy bags, no extra ears or eyes paying attention. I wondered if his parents hated him fighting just as mine had. He said they supported him and had been to all his fights in the last 2 years, but his father believed Johnny was wasting his potential and didn't see the upside.

After a few minutes of talking with Johnny, I completely understood his father's point. Here was a well-spoken, respectful, intelligent, good-looking kid who must have had opportunities to do something that would make him more money, not take up so much time or leave him limping and potentially brain damaged. I didn't want any of that for my kid.

So what happened with Johnny? What put him on this path?

He began seriously playing hockey at 7, taking a beating those first couple of years because he didn't like the physical part of the game. He smiled when he remembered what it was like finally to be allowed to check others, where he could be the hammer. Spurred on by the gasps and cheers from the crowd, Johnny loved launching his body and laying out other players.

Winning was also very important to Johnny and he was competitive at everything, whether it was video games, horseshoes, or Monopoly. Since he was a kid, he liked proving to others that he was good at what he did. As an adult, he realized this probably stemmed from having low self-esteem.

The low self-esteem also explained why he struggled with anger, punching walls and anything else around him. That was something I'd dealt with and I wondered if Johnny shared any of my perfectionist traits.

Johnny said, "I'm slowly getting away from that. My ego has been a very powerful thing for a very long, long time and it's always driven me to try to be perfect or to beat myself up. I've definitely been kind of getting better at just letting everything be, and it's made me a little bit better person, and definitely just makes me better at everything that I do."

MMA had humbled Johnny, got him to the point where he could take an honest look at himself and work on the things he didn't like. He'd been reading a lot of self-improvement books and highly recommended *The Power of Now* by Eckhart Tolle, stating how much his life had improved once he became more aware of being present instead of dwelling on the past and worrying about the future.

Awareness of the present was one of the reasons he loved being in the cage. "There is just so little time for thinking. It almost sucks you into the now. You're forced to be this conscious creature that is acting on instinct alone."

Although Johnny understands fighting isn't for everybody, he said it's something everyone should try. "It's definitely one of the most unique experiences that you could possibly have," he said. "It's extremely liberating and extremely freeing."

Johnny spoke of his goal to be in the UFC and is highly motivated by his mother's battle with breast cancer. The strength with which she's handled adversity is a quality he tries to apply in his own life.

It can be difficult for a young fighter to talk about dreams, especially after a loss, but Johnny has a great attitude. "I think that we have one chance at this life," he said. "I want to be one of those people that, when I die, I want to look back on life and know that I just gave everything my one hundred percent."

I was a little surprised by Johnny's other reason for fighting. He'd given a lot of thought to life and death, and said he's fighting so he's never forgotten. This would be his way of becoming immortal.

After spending an hour with Johnny, it was time for me to hit the road. I left inspired, hopeful I'd find others like Johnny and Bill who'd spent time analyzing themselves and why they fight. It'd make my job much easier.

* * *

That night I went to Lauzon's MMA in Bridgewater, MA, the front area a wide-open room with white mats, natural light falling through the windows. Matt Perry, the science teacher I'd met at the grappling tournament Saturday, walked me up a short staircase. You had to earn a special invitation to train in this part of the gym. This was where the fight team trained.

Matt introduced me to Chris Palmquist, a former fighter who now coached and trained alongside the fighters. I explained what I was trying to do, and Chris was awesome, sending one fighter after another to be interviewed.

To talk with as many guys as possible and not ruin anyone's workout, I kept the interviews short. I discovered an undefeated, non-confrontational security officer hooked on the adrenaline rush; a construction worker and self-described nerd who enjoyed reading and writing nearly as much as competing; and a college grad working to become a police officer, fighting because he loves it, most certainly not for money. Matt, the lifelong martial arts fan, whose love of Bruce Lee, Van Damme, and WWE professional wrestling pushed him into MMA his senior year of high school.

After every interview, I'd walk out with the fighter to watch a few minutes of training and snap some photos. The fighters were going hard but controlled, coaches on top of the action. Matt pointed out a South Korean working with Joe Lauzon. He said I would want to talk to him.

The round finished and Andy Aiello, a 28-year-old who worked at the gym, came into the back room to share his story.

Andy was adopted at a very young age and had a difficult time growing up in Bridgewater, a predominantly white area. Feeling like he didn't fit in, Andy became angry and got into a lot of trouble. In eighth grade Andy went to a local MMA fight and watched Lauzon MMA head coach Joe Pomfret in action. Andy thought it was the coolest thing in the world and wanted to fight from that moment on and began training, even switched sports from soccer to wrestling because he wanted to get better at takedowns.

Just like his earlier years, high school was not enjoyable for Andy; wrestling and MMA training were the only things that got him through it. He described himself as antisocial, withdrawn, not at all comfortable with who he was. When he turned 18, Andy began fighting at the amateur level and racked up 4 wins. His nickname "The Crasian," short for crazy raging angry Asian, clearly indicated that he had some issues to work on.

When Andy got to college, his anger and self-esteem issues got the best of him and he began drinking. "Overnight," he said, "I became somebody. All of a sudden I had friends, I was meeting girls, and I thought alcohol made me that."

Up until that point Andy's life had been training and fighting, but now he had something else. Soon, partying on the weekend wasn't enough and he found himself drinking, smoking, and eating all the time, visits to the gym seemingly a thing of the past. Drinking took over Andy's life and he became an alcoholic, consuming some form of alcohol or other from the time he got up until the moment he passed out. The next 8 years of his life were wasted. During that time, he would walk out of the room if fights were on. "I just couldn't watch it because it broke my heart. It killed me."

Andy finally decided to change his life and entered detox. When he finished rehab, he returned to the gym, training hard, dieting, and losing 70 pounds in 4 months. He also began to strip away much of his deep-seated anger.

Fighting and Alcoholics Anonymous saved Andy's life and made it worth living. MMA gives Andy something constructive to do with his addictive personality. When he starts something, he said, "There's no 'I'm kinda gonna do it.' It's either I do it one hundred and ten percent or I don't do it at all."

To him, MMA is a healthy addiction, and the brotherhood it's created is unbeatable. The people in the gym are more than just friends. Joe Lauzon and the others are family and Andy would do anything for them.

Andy had just won his first fight since returning to MMA and was one month out from his next. When asked why he was doing it, he said, "We're not your normal crowd. We're all a little different to do what we do. There's just not a better feeling in the world, hands down, than winning a fight. Winning is the most addicting feeling in the world. Nothing can compare to it. You can't put it into words; it's something you have to experience. I've been bungee jumping and trying to do all these adrenaline things, and there's simply nothing better."

At the end of the interview Andy became emotional and I didn't doubt an ounce of his sincerity when he said, "I spent eight years when I was drinking wasting my life. I'm not going to waste my life. It's a gift to be alive, and I'm going to make the most of it. If I make it, awesome. If I don't, at least I frickin' tried as hard as I possibly could to do it."

Practice was winding down after the fifth interview, guys getting cleaned up to go home. I thanked Chris for his help and asked if I could come back the next day, possibly to train, maybe get another interview or two. Joe Lauzon, the co-owner of the gym, was sitting nearby and asked if I wanted to interview him. Of course I wanted to; I just hadn't wanted to bother him. Joe had more than 30 fights, 10 in the UFC. I assumed he must be tired of telling his story and especially wouldn't want to after a hard workout.

Although I had watched a lot of Joe's fights, I hadn't listened to any of his interviews and knew very little about him. It only took a few minutes to be impressed.

That's also how long it took for my camera to stop recording. My memory card was full and I didn't have a backup.

The next morning I was back at the gym half an hour before training started, grateful Joe had gone out of his way so we could finish the interview.

Joe, who was a few weeks away from his 28th birthday, recounted tales from his childhood. He'd been a promising baseball player who started with T-ball and played until his junior year in high school when his eyesight began to affect his ability. He suspected it was probably from all the video games he'd played.

Giving up baseball was easy because that was the year Joe witnessed a martial art demonstration put on by Joe Pomfret, the same person who'd turned Andy on to the sport. Joe and his friends were already huge WWE fans who reenacted moves on a trampoline or anywhere else there was something semisoft to land on. Like most kids, they had grown bored with matches and moves that were predetermined, and had made things more competitive, the wrestling more real. Having always been a bit smaller than average, Joe understood the jiu jitsu Pomfret demonstrated could be used to tap out all his friends.

Joe was a good student and very disciplined. While other kids were out drinking, Joe would take a train to his classes at Wentworth Institute of Technology during the day and spend his nights learning the art of jiu jitsu, perfecting technique, and satisfying his super-competitive side.

One of the best lessons Joe learned from baseball was that the teams that practiced the most would be the most successful. He said, "If you're going to do something, you should go do it. You shouldn't kind of jump in. You should jump in one hundred percent, put all of your energy and effort into it." Joe applied this to his life and jiu jitsu, arriving early to class, leaving late, and going every day.

This attitude paid off and Joe was very successful in the grappling tournaments he entered. Unlike many of today's fighters that jump into MMA because they want to fight in the UFC, Joe had no plans to fight. He was the training partner for Chris Palmquist's brother, Jay, who was doing well on the local level. This gave Joe confidence, and he scheduled a fight to challenge himself.

One week after turning 18, Joe found himself in his first fight. There were last minute changes made on the card and Joe agreed to fill in on the main event. His opponent was nearly twice his age and had a martial arts school and hundreds of supporters. Too inexperienced to be nervous, Joe went out and got the upset with a heel hook, the first in a long line of future submissions.

Although Joe enjoyed fighting, it was simply a hobby, a way to test his skills, be competitive, and make a few bucks. In his first 4 years, he fought 24 times, all while getting his degree in computer science and working a decent paying job in the technology industry.

While a contestant on *The Ultimate Fighter Season 5*, Joe realized he had a very limited window, and that if he wanted to be successful as a fighter, he had to do it full time. He said, "I can always go back to computers, but I couldn't go back to fighting. Once you're passed, you're passed." This and the fact that he could make more in one night of fighting than in a year behind a desk, helped Joe dedicate himself to the sport. A decision he wouldn't change if given the chance.

Joe has had a good deal of injuries spread over 12 years, but guessed he'd only suffered 6 concussions. Even though he'd recently been knocked out, Joe wasn't worried about head trauma. At Lauzon MMA, the coaches take care of their fighters and are very cautious after head injuries, whether from a blow in a fight or during training.

Joe argued that MMA was much safer than boxing and team sports like football. On top of all the stats, Joe recalled being in fights where neither he nor his opponent was struck in the head. He said, "MMA is a sport with a ref there to protect you when you can't protect yourself, and, thanks to not having a standing eight-count, fights end before too much damage is accumulated."

It was time to practice so we wrapped up the interview talking about the large number of people who think they want to fight versus the few who get in there and test themselves. Joe said, "Not everyone is meant to be a fighter. Everyone's going to react to stress differently. That's what it comes down to. It comes down to stress."

I put away my camera and taped my ribs together. They were still sore but I wasn't going to pass up the chance to train with one of the slickest submission specialists in the UFC. Unfortunately, the tape didn't help at all, and I screamed like a little girl on the first roll. Training wasn't going to be part of this trip, but I was okay with that. The most important thing was to keep meeting fighters like the ones I'd been talking to.

I took photos the rest of the practice and interviewed two more guys, bringing me up to 22 fighters and one coach—not a bad start. I gathered my stuff and hit the road for a 3-hour drive to Amherst, MA, on the other side of the state. As I drove, I considered all the different people I'd talked to, searched for similarities among them and with myself.

It wasn't going to be easy to figure out all the various reasons people fight, but I was going to enjoy doing it. Although I missed my family, I was no longer worried I was wasting my time. The sport I'd turned away from was once again exciting to watch, and the fighters I met were some of the kindest, most generous and respectful people I'd come across. I was excited that I'd recorded the interviews, not because I'd forget what they said, but so I could show others who they were.

CHAPTER FOUR

May 9, 2012

New England Submission Fighting, the oldest MMA school in New England, is tucked away in the quiet town of South Amherst, MA. There were only two cars in the parking lot when I arrived, and I wondered if I'd been mistaken about the time. The door was unlocked, but the gym was dark. I heard voices in the back and walked in, watched the final few minutes of a teenager's private lesson practicing takedowns.

The instructor came over with a smile, his hand outstretched. Kirik Jenness was tall, the first guy on the trip that I looked up to. At 6'3" and well-built, Kirik looked great for 51, but if I hadn't just seen him moving on the mat, I wouldn't have pegged him for a fighter.

I walked with Kirik as he closed the gym, giving him a quick rundown on my limited martial arts experience, the project, and my goals. When I shared my doubt that I was the right person to write the book, he brushed that aside and assured me I was—kind words from a stranger and the confidence boost I needed.

Knowing I was particularly interested in speaking with guys who had begun fighting before the sport became popular, Kirik said I needed to visit Fighting Arts Academy in Springfield and speak with the owner, Jeremy Libiszewski. I headed over early the next morning, impressed with the beautiful 7,000-square-foot, well-designed gym, complete with cage.

Although Jeremy was one of the shortest and friendliest fighters I'd met, I could tell it would be a bad idea to attempt to test him. We brought 2 chairs into the cage, a silent gym the perfect setting for the hour-long interview.

Jeremy fell in love with the martial arts in first grade when his grandfather, who had been a pro boxer, would have Jeremy do pull-ups to earn his boxing lesson down in the cellar. They would pore over books containing stories about wrestlers and boxers who'd made a name for themselves. Jeremy dreamed of being tough like his grandfather, and began training karate when he turned 10. Jeremy became hooked on martial arts, going to a few schools before finding his master at a combat martial arts academy that embraced the idea of mixing techniques from various arts.

School had been a struggle for Jeremy, whose learning disability made it hard to read. Martial arts was where he could shine, where he could put all his energy and see the results. He said, "Knowing I was good at something and excelling at it made it even more special." And when kids made fun of him and called him retarded for going to a special reading class, the taunts did nothing. The martial arts had given him the confidence that he could kick the shit out of them if he wanted, and the restraint not to.

Jeremy credited martial arts with keeping him out of trouble and not winding up like many of his childhood friends who were dead or in jail. He didn't get in fights as a kid. He didn't drink, do drugs, or steal cars. He wouldn't give in to peer pressure. He wanted to be number one, and giving up even a little edge would mean weakness. He went to the gym every day after school to train for 5 hours. "My mother never had to worry about me," he said. "Martial arts gave me this path."

Jeremy always felt the need to compete. He entered the first ever NAGA tournament and won his division. He also fought in the first closed-fist contest in Massachusetts. MMA was the next logical step, what he called a natural progression. He never questioned it as violent, but instead saw it as an expression of our primal side. "People have always watched fighting. People always wants to know who's better, who's tougher, who's number one."

A self-professed dork, Jeremy admits people are shocked to learn he's a fighter. He said, "I don't look tough at all, and I never act tough."

But he's extraordinarily tough. Same with anyone that fights. Jeremy said, "Just to get in the ring takes a lot of heart, never mind even fight, just get in the ring." He explained how you need to be tough to have all those people staring at you, essentially in your underwear, with another fighter who's trained just as hard as you have, who wants to win just as badly.

The risk involved in stepping into the cage isn't just physical. "If you win, it's the best thing in the world. It's the highest of highs. It doesn't get any better," Jeremy said. "But when you lose, it's the lowest of lows. You don't want to see anybody because you're embarrassed … around your friends, your family."

Jeremy's first loss was heart breaking. He gave up 30 pounds in a last-second matchup and fought 15 minutes straight, only to lose the decision. It was interesting that even though Jeremy thought it was a bad decision, he felt ashamed and embarrassed because he believed he was the better fighter and didn't prove it.

The loss put added pressure on him because he'd done so well prior to that in all competitions. When he lost his next fight, Jeremy went into a depression. The 26-year-old trained even harder for the subsequent fight, determined to show what he was made of. Unfortunately, he never got the chance. His career ended when a much heavier training partner sprawled on top of Jeremy and popped 3 vertebrae in his neck.

Asked if he missed fighting, Jeremy said, "Every single day. I'm thirty-five now and I still every day think that well, maybe if I get something done, I can still do it."

Although Jeremy can't get cleared for a fight, he still trains with his fighters and believes his technical skills are better than they've ever been. But every time he's tried to make a comeback, he has gotten hurt. The last injury left him not being able to pick up his son, and the worry that it might become permanent was enough to make him stop. He's first a father and a husband, and then a martial artist. His commitment to his family is the only thing keeping him from trying again.

But still there is regret, a voice that asks what he might have done with the right coaching. "There isn't a day that goes by without thinking about what I could have done competing."

Jeremy has advice for young fighters struggling with a loss, advice he wishes he'd had when he was fighting. He said, "Losing, winning, it's more about the path, the journey it takes you on. Finding out about yourself. And make sure you have a backup plan, because the odds of you making it to the very, very top are pretty slim."

And the very, very top is where you must be to make a lot of money. Jeremy estimated only 1% of fighters make enough to support themselves.

But even though it's unlikely many individuals will make it to the top tier of MMA, he highly recommended competing in the sport. "Fighting teaches how to compete in life not just in the ring," he said. "Anytime you learn to compete, it makes you a stronger person. Even if you lose, you'll be a better person from it because you competed."

* * *

The 2-hour drive to American Top Team (ATT) in Danbury, CT, gave me time to think about Jeremy's interview, how much better it was when I strayed from my list of questions and followed up on the interesting answers. Every person was going to have a different story and it was up to me to figure out how I could draw that story out and what I would learn from it.

Rob Cipriano, who acted as the fight team's coach and managed several fighters, had been incredibly supportive of the project since my first email. Not only did he arrange for fighters to be interviewed and made me feel very welcome, but he also called friends from other gyms and arranged for me to visit them. I wanted to train with Rob and his team and tried taping my ribs, but it hurt too much, even shadowboxing. That worked out for the best, though, because it allowed me to conduct interviews while the class was going on.

Although Rob hadn't fought MMA, he had boxing, kickboxing, and BJJ experience, and a story like that of many fighters—always competitive, a family of boxing fans, older kids who toughened him up. We discussed the desire to fight, and discerned how a lot of people just don't have it, even those who compete in other contact sports. He also talked about fighters not being low class, contrary to a popular public perception. "Lots of fighters are great guys. They're not punks." He waved his hand at the dozen guys sparring on the mat. "Half of these guys have degrees."

The next 2 interviewees were college grads with solid careers, both of whom fought on the side. One was a childcare worker who wrestled in high school and picked up boxing before switching to MMA. The other took up MMA when college soccer was ending. He said MMA was a great stress reliever, and claimed it improved him as a husband, father, and competitor.

An amateur fighter talked about growing up on Bruce Lee and being a fan of the UFC since he was 10, but not training until 13 years later. There was a soft-spoken paramedic who wrestled in high school, but had never been in a fight before getting in the cage. The guy who worked as a correctional officer took BJJ to get back in shape, progressed to kickboxing and then to MMA, treating each sport as a hobby since he already had a career.

Saturday morning Kirik and I discussed what I'd learned so far and what lay ahead. I got out my notepad and named a state and from memory, Kirik would shoot off a list of fighters I should talk to and what gyms to hit.

I only had an hour before I had to take off, and I still hadn't heard Kirik's story. We went onto his back porch, the beautiful western Massachusetts morning spread out behind him.

Kirik, who was born in Boston, had lived all around the world, having moved 13 times by his eighteenth birthday. As a kid, he traded one obsession for another: Legos in California, comic books in Alaska, fireworks in South Africa. It was in South Africa, in the summer of 1973, that 12-year-old Kirik walked into a theater and saw a movie that changed him. "I stepped into *Enter the Dragon* one person and really left another one," Kirik said. "I wanted to be Bruce Lee." Being a martial artist is all he has wanted to do ever since. "It sent me on a path I've been on for nearly forty years now."

The next day Kirik found a Tae Kwon Do school and began learning from a high-level instructor from Korea. A few years later, Kirik moved back to the United States and began wrestling in high school, while continuing to train and compete in TKD tournaments. While attending the University of Massachusetts, Kirik added boxing, karate, and kickboxing to his arsenal, and eventually opened his own academy.

Kirik said everything came full circle in 1993 after he saw the first UFC. Although he wasn't completely swayed by it, his close friend and training partner, Dave Roy, ordered the *Gracie in Action* tapes and began training with a judo legend, Nori Kudo. A few months later, Dave rolled with Kirik and proved the effectiveness of BJJ. Despite having trained for 20 years and owning a school for 10 of those, Kirik realized he had to start all over. He went back to doing takedowns, armlocks, and neck cranks just like Bruce Lee was doing back in 1973, and he opened New England Submission Fighting with Dave.

Like Jeremy Libiszewski, Kirik felt MMA was just a natural progression, part of his path as a martial artist. He said, "It would have been weird for me not to fight." Kirik acknowledged he feared getting hurt at the start, but that threat of physical damage was nothing compared to the emotional side of fighting, which he absolutely dreaded. "Your ego and whole sense of self is on the line up there in front of hundreds or thousands of people. The emotional side was genuine, it was pretty big. You don't want to lose in front of everyone you know."

Although a martial artist for more than 2 decades, it wasn't until 1999, at 38 years old, that Kirik had his first open-hand Pancrase fight. The late start was a factor in not getting many fights. "I never stepped up to see how good I could be," he said with a tinge of regret. "I still think I have one or two more in me."

Kirik was half joking about fighting again. But why would he want to risk getting injured? What was the draw for him?

"Fighting is good for you," he said. "It makes you challenge your fears, a really good thing for humans to do. It makes you get into good shape. It develops your confidence."

Most people are shocked to find out Kirik fights, just as the average person probably believes most fighters are much more menacing and come from troubled backgrounds than is the case. "People who don't know about fighting are full of preconceived notions," Kirik said. "Fighters are like normal people, and better. They're nicer than the average lawyer I've met. They're nicer than the average postman."

While fighters are indeed trying to hurt their opponent, Kirik pointed out they are only trying to hurt them enough to make them quit, which is no different from boxing. "Everybody always hugs at the end; it's not personal." Of the 15,000 fighters Kirik has issued ID cards to and the thousands that he knows personally, he could think of only 1 or 2 that went around wanting to hurt others all the time. For Kirik, and the overwhelming majority of fighters, hurting another person is not the reason they get in the cage.

At the end of the interview Kirik himself was questioning his reason for fighting. "I think if I was completely confident then I probably wouldn't fight. Why would you? If I had 2.2 kids, and a stay-at-home wife and I worked as an architect, then I probably wouldn't want to fight. But I'm a human being. I've got doubts about myself and issues to work through. Fighting is a vehicle to address those issues and try and make them positive."

Kirik and I covered a lot of ground in 30 minutes, and some of his lessons I wasn't yet able to understand. I wasn't a martial artist like him or Jeremy, but if I spent more time around the sport maybe that'd begin to change.

After a long day of interviews and driving across Connecticut, I pulled up to Darryl MarcAurele's home in Niantic, grateful for the chance to sit down in a quiet house with no distractions or time limit. Darryl, the head coach and owner of Strike Zone MMA in Norwich, was 48, but one glance said he was much tougher than most men half his age.

Darryl credits his toughness to his dad, the biggest influence on his life. His dad was the strongest and most resilient person Darryl knew, and the man had pushed all his children to be the best they could be. The kids were taught to be competitive at everything, have fun, and never give up.

They were also taught to stand up for themselves but never to start a fight. As one of the smaller kids, Darryl was forced to play this out. He got picked on a lot, and found himself getting into a lot of scraps and even suspended from school. This changed in eighth grade when Darryl began wrestling and the bullying became a thing of the past.

Just as his father's influence shaped Darryl's younger years, it was his father's support that helped him to succeed at wrestling. With his father driving him around the country to compete at the highest level, Darryl became an All American in both freestyle and Greco Roman at Junior Nationals. Darryl wasn't ready to be done with wrestling after high school; he put together a freestyle Greco team that traveled the country for the next 17 years.

While wrestling, Darryl began training and competing in different arts, first judo, then boxing, Muay Thai, Sambo, and BJJ. "I love anything to do with that one-on-one. That's what I want to get out of it; me against someone else, it's a competition," Darryl said. "I am one hundred percent competitor. I don't have any bad intentions on anyone."

Like other fighters I had interviewed, Darryl saw MMA as the next logical step, the best way to challenge himself, the ultimate competition. He had recently opened Strike Zone MMA and wanted to put himself on the line before any of his students. Although his father didn't like him fighting, he still went to Darryl's fights and was his biggest fan.

There was a hint of irritation as Darryl told how people are usually surprised he's a fighter. "They think that because you are nice to people and polite and caring, you can't possibly do that." He said that if people would go into a gym, sit down, and watch, they would have a totally different perspective of the sport.

Darryl has immense respect for fighters, but does not like that term and would rather they be called athletes. He talked about the training regimen of top-level pro fighters. "There isn't a better athlete in the world than an MMA fighter," he said. "These athletes are not just learning to compete; they are learning discipline, desire, work ethic."

Darryl's days of competing are over, but not because of his age. In 2011 Darryl had his second spinal surgery and hasn't been able to find a doctor who will medically clear him. And it's not for a lack of trying. Darryl wants to fight and is always in shape, training alongside his team. Even at 48 he was still hoping to find a doctor who could help him fight again. "The winning becomes an addiction," he said. "If I'm going to get hurt, I want to do it fighting and not training."

* * *

Instead of resting on Sunday, I took Kirik's advice and met with Mat Santos, the guy who injured my ribs the previous weekend. It wasn't Mat's fault; I was out of shape and without skills, practically begging to get hurt entering that division. Plus, Kirik said Mat was funny and he only lived a few minutes from where I was staying.

Mat, the owner and head coach of the Team Santos Fighting Academy in Providence, was a year younger than me and about 30 pounds lighter. We had begun MMA around the same time and had similar experiences fighting. As we set up in his backyard for a very casual interview, I looked forward to seeing what other similarities I could find.

When asked about his childhood, Mat joked about how clumsy he'd been, how he even had trouble walking. His parents put Mat in different sports with hopes it would help: first gymnastics, then diving, the swim team, track, baseball, basketball, football. All the sports made him a much better athlete, but his balance remained horrible. It got so bad that his dad, who was a judo brown belt, began training Mat in the art to improve his coordination.

Mat immediately took to judo. He was a natural grappler, perhaps because he grew up in a rough neighborhood and had plenty of experience roughhousing with his nine older cousins. Being the youngest child made him more determined, tougher, and "way ballsier." He became the wild one.

Without the high school sports to keep him in shape, Mat put on weight and became a little depressed. Knowing he needed something physical in his life, Mat found a Jeet Kune Do school and it wasn't long before he entered a grappling tournament and got hooked. He said, "Within six months of training I knew I was going to do this for the rest of my life."

With very limited experience, Mat jumped into his first MMA match. "I saw something that looked like fun, and I wanted to do it." Although he enjoyed fighting, jiu jitsu was Mat's calling, and he gave up a decent living at an unfulfilling job to train and teach. He did continue to fight occasionally, but never with delusions of grandeur. He never thought he would make it to the UFC. "Back then no one gave a crap about records. I just did it out of love. I love competition."

Another factor Mat mentioned also rang true for me. He played lineman in football, a position that few fans watched. He'd never been the focus in any spectator sport, and the thought of being in the limelight was a nice change.

Mat said fighters come from all walks of life and there are numerous reasons why they compete. "You spend the first part of your life trying to create who you think you should be. If you think you should be a super badass then you take those steps to become that person." One thing he said that really struck me was, "Most fighters are running from something, I think. There's a lot of insecurity in fighters, a lot of neuroses in fighters."

This idea reminded me of what Sam Sheridan wrote in *The Fighter's Heart*: that fighters come from a damaged past. When I first read that, I grew defensive and wanted to say that wasn't true. I had a couple of fighter friends who'd had rough childhoods, but it seemed most of the fighters I knew had had normal childhoods like mine. My parents were together, we were lower middle class, good values, blah, blah, blah. I wasn't damaged.

And based on the interviews of the 35 fighters I'd done so far, I'd say only a couple, like Bill Mahoney, came from any significant damage. But what constitutes damage and what causes it? Maybe I was overthinking it. Maybe the cause didn't have to be extreme: poverty, abuse, or jail time. Maybe the damage just had to be enough to lower the self-esteem, to create a need for approval, or a craving for fame and fortune. Or perhaps Sheridan's line was a bit exaggerated and only some fighters come from damage. I'd be sure to keep an eye on this.

The afternoon with Mat would have been a perfect ending to the trip, but I was compelled to hit New York and New Jersey while I had the opportunity. Early Monday morning I drove back to Boston for my flight and landed in Newark exhausted, a torrential downpour making things infinitely worse. Instead of staying in the hotel and getting some sleep, I drove an hour to Kurt Pellegrino's MMA down at the Jersey shore.

The gym exuded intensity from the moment I walked in; Kurt and his team were sparring hard. Even if my ribs allowed me to train, there was no way I would try working out with these guys. Instead, I took photos and squeezed in four interviews before they closed. I didn't have long with each fighter, but enough to see where that intensity came from. These guys had all been high school wrestlers, were all about the grind.

One of the fighters was a police officer, another a businessman, both understanding that losses were just part of the game. The third interviewee was Frank Ursino, a striking coach who discussed how passionate fighters are. As tough as fighters are, he pointed out, they are often equally as sensitive. He believes everyone has a fighter in him, but whether it is brought out depends on the person and where his path leads him in life.

Kurt Pellegrino was a perfect example of that. The 33-year-old coach said that if he had stayed in college, there was no way he would have become a fighter. He never wanted to be a fighter; it just happened. His success in grappling tournaments led to amateur MMA fights, and over the course of the next 10 years he had 23 professional fights, a dozen of them in the UFC, before retiring.

Kurt said he was simply a high school wrestler who never stopped competing. "I truly love to compete. I don't like the label of being a fighter; I like the label as a competitor. It was always about being a competitor."

He described himself as a knucklehead, funny, the same small-time guy he was before he was in the UFC. The lights, the attention, the fighting never changed him. But despite being friendly, he was easily just as intense. He told the story of his dad asking him if he was scared to fight. Kurt told him, "Not at all. It's a scheduled street fight. It's either me or him." Kurt said he felt like he was a shark who saw what he wanted and made himself dead to the world. "When I step into that cage I am fully prepared to let anything break at this moment in my life, or break his. I'll fight until I'll die."

The following morning I headed over to AMA Fight Club in Whippany, NJ. First up was a seasoned pro who'd started wrestling in kindergarten and switched over to BJJ, then MMA. Next was a recent college grad that transitioned from wrestling straight to fighting. Following them, were a hockey player and a philosophy grad that began BJJ after being jumped by two guys.

That night I headed to Endgame Combat Sports Academy in Lodi, NJ, to speak with Eddy Rolon, another must-see on Kirik's list. Eddy was my age, had also started fighting in 1998, and both of us had children. I didn't realize it was Eddy's night off to be home with his family, and I hated cutting into that time, but we still talked for 2 hours.

Eddy had grown up without a father and was quite an athlete and student. He earned a full academic scholarship to high school, where he played football, ran track, and was on the swim team. Although he was in honors and AP classes, he gave up striving for college when his mother suffered a serious injury his sophomore year. Soon after graduating high school, Eddy fell off a building and broke bones in both feet while training for "American Gladiators," a show I'd also dreamed of being on.

In 1996, while working as a cable TV technician, he saw UFC 3 and wanted to learn more about the sport. Even while working 60-hour weeks, he would make time to train and compete and loved being physical again. Between amateur and professional grappling, boxing, and MMA, Eddy competed more than 160 times, shedding 75 pounds in the process.

MMA gave Eddy the opportunity to perform in front of crowds and showcase his art. Even though he had since given up fighting, he still liked to entertain and ended our interview by balancing and juggling on an enormous exercise ball while disco lights flashed across the darkened gym.

On Wednesday, the final day of my trip, I dropped off my rental and dragged my luggage around the jam-packed streets of New York City. As much as I hated crowded cities, the trip to the Big Apple was worth it because I had the pleasure of talking to BJJ legend Marcelo Garcia at his academy, and later with two fighters at Renzo Gracie's. One was a strip club doorman who'd transitioned from pro baseball to BJJ to MMA. The other was Rafael Natal, a Brazilian who'd learned to fight in the streets of Rio. It was his training in judo, BJJ, and Capoeira that turned him into a much calmer, more confident, and happier person. MMA gave him a positive path and an opportunity to make a living fighting in the UFC.

Finally, the trip was over with a long flight home to consider what I'd learned. In 16 days, I drove over 2,000 miles, visited 16 schools in 5 states, and interviewed 50 MMA fighters and coaches. I also attended the Caged Titans fight and participated in my first NAGA. I learned a hell of a lot from these interviews and fell back in love with the sport I had walked away from.

The trip helped me realize what I wanted to do. It wasn't necessary for me to train. I could learn from short interviews, but I'd get much more from longer ones. Thanks to the help of coaches pushing their shy fighters my way, I had hit a wide range of interviewees and gotten a glimpse at who these fighters really were. In addition, an unexpected benefit of stepping out of my comfort zone and talking with strangers was that I'd met many people I was now proud to call friends.

CHAPTER FIVE

June 9, 2012

It was 110 degrees when the family and I arrived in Las Vegas, the heat instantly sapping our sense of fun. It was hard to believe I had chosen to live here for 5 years, working as a correctional officer and then a juvenile probation officer while trying to establish a career in boxing before switching back to MMA. The 3 weeks since the last interviews had been a nice break, but I was ready for another round. While my wife and daughter got settled in at a friend's house, I took off to Xtreme Couture to meet John Hahn, the gym's manager, who also had a few amateur and pro fights under his belt.

John had been incredibly helpful, letting the team know ahead of time that I'd be visiting so interested fighters could talk outside of training periods, with at least 20 minutes set aside for each one. Counting John, there were 9 fighters on the list. I was excited to see one of them was Ryan Couture, son of the former UFC heavyweight and light heavyweight champion, Randy "The Natural" Couture.

I met John in the reception area of the gym, which contained offices and a huge pro shop. Everything was clean and professional, nothing like the places I used to train in that were lucky to have a desk. John guided me through the enormous 34,000-sq-ft building. The first room had a boxing ring and a huge cross training area that was larger than a lot of the gyms I'd visited. He took me around the corner to an even larger space that had two massive matted areas, two long lines of heavy bags, and two full-size cages.

My childhood friend, Brian Esquivel, who edited the first batch of videotaped interviews, had talked to me about their poor quality, many of them out of focus and with terrible sound. If I was going to use the videos for any kind of project, I had to do a better job with them. I mentioned this to John and he set me up in the physical therapy area, a quiet spot where I could watch guys sparring. While I waited for the first interview, UFC legend Forest Griffin was putting in rounds, preparing for his final fight with Tito Ortiz.

Before I got started, I wondered how different this group would be from the guys back east. As the fight capital of the world, Vegas attracted people from all around and could be one hell of a place to live with its extreme weather and endless temptation. It hadn't had much of an impact on me, but only because I was already 27 when I moved there. I'm not so sure how I would have turned out if I'd lived there fresh out of college.

I interviewed a wide range of fighters before sitting down with Ryan Couture. I tried to keep the interview focused on him and not be a starstruck fan asking him what it was like having one of the baddest men on the planet as a father. But I realized that I did need to find out what that was like, because the best way to understand someone is to backtrack their path. Ryan's dad being a great wrestler and UFC champ must have contributed in many ways to Ryan's development.

The 29-year-old lightweight, who was coming off a Strikeforce win that put him at 4-1 as a pro, was soft-spoken and laid-back. When asked about his earliest memories, Ryan talked about growing up on the mats with his sister, watching their father compete at the highest level of wrestling, and constantly roughhousing with him.

Although Ryan had been around the sport since he was a baby, he didn't wrestle until third grade. He said he wasn't cut out for the sport then and stopped because he preferred soccer. In seventh grade, Ryan tried out for basketball but didn't make the team. Wanting to participate in a sport, Ryan gave wrestling another shot; this time he fell in love with it.

Two years later, Ryan's dad jumped into MMA, agreeing to be an alternate in the UFC's four-man heavyweight tournament on just 3 weeks' notice. When asked if it was hard to watch his father fight, Ryan shook his head and said, "I loved being able to show my friends and thought it was the coolest thing ever." Because MMA was so new, the family didn't know what to expect, but Randy's success was life changing. Going from a sport that relatively few people watched to becoming the UFC champion brought both fame and money.

I thought this might have put pressure on Ryan to fill his father's shoes, but he insisted that was never an issue. Every year that he wrestled he grew stronger, more skilled, and more competitive. He was proud when he placed third in the state of Washington his senior year of high school.

Although Ryan had enjoyed wrestling, he was burned out on cutting weight and chose the lifestyle of a care-free college student at Western Washington University. He focused on his studies, instead of his body, graduating with a degree in mathematics in the worst shape of his life. Ryan began working at a bank, accepting that it was the start of a career. One day he ran into a former wrestling opponent who invited him to their Sunday grappling session. Although Ryan was a bit intimidated because he hadn't been physical in such a long time, he missed training and took right to it, feeling it was the release he needed from working a regular job.

As Ryan got in better shape, his desire to train grew, and soon he'd acquired a new set of skills. After a few years of training he competed in grappling tournaments, which made him question whether he should attempt an amateur fight, not as a career option but simply as a challenge. It wasn't the first time he'd asked himself if fighting was for him. Back in college, when he attended local fights promoted by his father, Ryan would question how he would match up against the guys crazy enough to get in the cage. Sometimes he'd feel confident that he would come out on top and enjoy the experience, but then he'd watch a fighter get knocked out and he'd decide that maybe he didn't have the stomach for it.

Ryan had never been in a street fight and avoided all confrontation, so he wasn't sure what to expect from his first fight. The biggest battle for him was just getting into the cage. With a fear of public speaking and always feeling awkward in front of people, the thought of walking through the crowd freaked him out. Ryan acknowledged that once he was in the cage, his fears dissipated. "Just that rush of getting out there and exchanging blows, and putting yourself out there in front of a group of people like that, there's really nothing like it that I've ever experienced." He said, "It's completely addictive; I was hooked. The fact that I could potentially make a living doing something that's that much fun, that was too hard to pass up."

Most people are surprised to find out Ryan's a fighter, and he's glad that his disposition belies their expectation. He'd been around tons of fighters through his father, the gym, and all his training partners, but insisted he couldn't generalize fighters and said, "We're all just a little weird enough to want to get hit in the face for money, but everyone comes about it from a different perspective and has a different demeanor about them."

Although Ryan had not been super competitive growing up, it was competition that drove him to MMA. He said the sport was competition at its core, a test of wit and skills. His goal is to show that he's the superior technician, not to put someone in the hospital. If an opponent suffered an injury during a fight, that was just one of the unfortunate side effects of the sport, not the focus. No different than a quarterback getting a concussion from a hard hit.

Ryan was enjoying the ride, grateful he'd made the switch back to an active lifestyle. He loved that he was making a comfortable living doing something that was so much fun he'd be doing it as a hobby anyway. He could always go back to the corporate world if he needed to, but for now he'd pursue his passion.

* * *

Xtreme Couture was slow on Saturday afternoon, only a handful of self-motivated fighters putting themselves through their workouts. I sat down with 22-year-old lightweight Jacob Swinney, his cauliflowered ears giving away that he'd been a wrestler. Although very well-spoken, friendly, and calm, the 6-2 amateur fighter had an intensity about him I hadn't noticed in the others the day before.

Jacob had struggled with anger most of his life, and understandably so. As a child, he'd lived across the western United States, moving 26 times in a 2-year period. He was a good athlete and played every sport he could. After his older brother began wrestling, Jacob gave it a try in high school. He discovered he preferred competing as an individual and taking full blame for a loss that was a result of his inability and not his teammates'. He said, "It never bothered me to lose because I always gave it my all." If Jacob gave 100% and someone still beat him fair and square, he would just chalk it up as a learning experience.

Although Jacob had enjoyed wrestling, there wasn't much else he liked about high school. He failed classes, not because he didn't do well on tests, but because he hated homework. He also got into a lot of fights. Having moved constantly, Jacob usually made friends with the kids lowest on the totem pole. Whenever someone picked on one of these friends, Jacob took it upon himself to protect them and stand up to the bullies. It wasn't that he wanted to fight, but he wasn't going to turn his back on an injustice done to a friend.

I tried to ask every fighter if they remembered when they saw their first MMA fight and their initial reaction to it. This question usually led to talk of other sports they'd been exposed to, what was allowed in the household, whether they were automatically drawn to MMA or repulsed, and other interesting avenues. Jacob clearly remembered his first taste of MMA, becoming more animated when he described the Randy Couture vs. Tim Sylvia fight his freshman year of high school. He pointed to the giant UFC Octagon canvas hanging on the wall and said that fight had been epic; the 43-

year-old Couture taking the belt lit a fire in him, and Jacob knew then that he wanted to fight.

Jacob immediately took to MMA, his success in submission grappling tournaments spurring him on. After nine months of training, he asked for his first amateur fight, and three months later he found himself in the cage.

Before every fight, Jacob said he experienced a feeling of anxiousness rather than being scared. "That nervous feeling is a feeling of being alive, and that feeling of being alive, not everybody gets to feel that," he said. "It makes me happy, makes me feel alive. I love fighting."

Jacob believed everyone is a fighter from birth, but not many people want to put their bodies through what fighters do. "They don't have the willpower to go through it." And then there are differences among the fighters themselves. There are those who can take twenty punches and keep going forward, and those that will turn their back and give up the choke.

Outside of the gym, Jacob shares many of the characteristics of other fighters I spoke with. He said he is very trusting of others and willing to help them without expecting something for himself. It's important to him to be a good person.

I appreciated Jacob's mindset and understanding of how positivity can play a crucial role in success. He talked of the importance of setting goals in life and using positive words like *will, do, yes,* and *now,* instead of *if, want,* and *try.* He said life is what you make of it and he plans to make the most of it. "You can't get anything out of life if you don't go after it."

Unlike some of the fighters I'd spoken with who were mainly fighting for personal reasons and hadn't always made the best career choices, Jacob was treating fighting as a profession. This was not a hobby for him, his goals were set. He wasn't going to start his pro career until he was prepared, and he felt confident he had coaches who would help guide him to a successful career.

The next fighter I met also fought at lightweight and had the same intensity as Jacob. The muscular and tattooed Troy Lamson was only 20, a wrestler for Michigan State University who was finding great success fighting on the amateur level during his offseason.

Troy grew up in Flint, Michigan, ranked one of the most dangerous cities in the United States and in a state of financial emergency it might never recover from. He'd been introduced to boxing at a young age by his father, an accomplished Golden Gloves boxer, but due to Troy's intestinal problems, his mother didn't want him boxing. She did allow him to wrestle, though, a move that Troy is incredibly grateful for.

Wrestling became more serious for Troy when he hit sixth grade and began competing in national tournaments. Performing on a bigger stage to showcase his skill increased his dedication. Although his focus was on wrestling, Troy preferred playing football, which was more fun and much easier. He went on to earn All-Conference as a free safety. "The only fun time with wrestling is when you get your hand raised," Troy said. "I was much better at wrestling than I ever was football. I had to take advantage of that." And by training wrestling year-round he did just that and become a state champion.

In his freshman year of high school, Troy watched his first UFC and immediately felt drawn to it. He saw how successful wrestlers were and realized his skills would transition nicely. It wasn't long after this that he discovered an assistant wrestling coach was an MMA fighter. The coach saw potential in Troy and took him to the gym. Troy loved the training and within 2 weeks he knew he wanted to fight.

One of the most powerful experiences for Troy was sparring as a 15-year-old against men twice his age. Being able to beat grown men did wonders for his confidence and he jumped into the cage when he turned 18. Fully committed to wrestling, Troy said his MMA season was limited to March through August. Each summer he traveled to Xtreme Couture for top level coaching and training partners. He managed to remain undefeated, racking up several amateur titles in two years.

As Troy had learned through wrestling, performance in MMA, or any other activity, was all about mat time, how much time and effort you could pour into it. He said, "People that are putting in the blood, sweat, and tears in the gym, those are the ones who are going to get to the next level." He promised that dedication would never be an issue for him. His goal was to finish out a successful collegiate career while polishing his skills in the cage, getting in as much experience as possible so he could fly through the ranks as a pro. With complete confidence, he said, "I'm going to be an impact player."

Speaking of MMA, Troy said, "I understood that this was my way out. I don't want to be a normal person. And I don't want to be a normal fighter." He wasn't ashamed to tell me, "Money is power. I want that money. To want that money, as shallow as it may sound, you have to be the best. If I wake up every morning, and I wanna get that money, you know what, I'm gonna get that money, and I'm gonna go to the gym and work my ass off. You have to sacrifice. If you have to leave some people in the dust to get to the top, you have to make your mind up, and I'm willing to do that."

Troy's intensity flared when asked what he was like inside the cage. "If the ref didn't pull me off, I would probably punch that guy until he died," he said. "That's just the type of person I am, and in this sport, if you want to get to the top level, you have to have that."

I thanked Troy for the interview and told him I had no doubt he was going to be successful. Unless he suffered a serious injury, I couldn't see anything sidetracking his confidence, determination, and hard work. I headed to John Hahn's office and wondered about Troy and Jacob, how dangerous and motivated this new breed of fighters was. Unlike Ryan Couture who started training at 23, these guys knew at 15 that they wanted to fight. Jacob wished he'd started in the martial arts much younger and said, "The next ultimate fighters in ten years from now, they're all going to have a MMA background since they were six. Guys that are starting in MMA now are usually blue or purple belts because they started at fifteen. The next generation will be on another level."

John Hahn was one of the most intellectual fighters I sat down with. The 40-year-old retired Marine and former FBI agent had given a lot of thought to why he and others were fighting.

Like Jacob Swinney, John had moved all over the country and attended 20 schools, which led to severe bullying, difficulty making friends, and inability to play sports. It wasn't until high school that he played football, finding success and playing two more years in college as a linebacker. After football was over John began kickboxing and boxing to stay active in college. He was working as an assistant kickboxing instructor when he watched the first UFC, and didn't think much of it. It wasn't until 2006 when he was going through the FBI academy that he watched MMA again and began learning BJJ and entering grappling tournaments.

John was very open about his main reason for fighting. He wanted a profitable career in the sport, but not as a fighter. The fighting was giving him the experience to become a better coach, promoter, and businessman. He loves the idea of leading by example, something he taught in the Marine Corp, and said it's one thing to tell people what to do, quite another to show and do alongside them. Plus, he loves to compete and said he feels just as capable now as he did at any other point in his life.

One of the things John appreciates about MMA is its rules. As someone who upheld the law, and had also been in some very unfair street fights, John dislikes cheaters and insisted there isn't a place for it in the sport. To him, MMA is laissez faire economics. "It's pure capitalism. No one's in there interfering with us," he said. "We get to go as hard as we want and there's just a tiny bit of rules."

John also made some very good arguments for why fighting wasn't necessarily primal and might have more to do with how we're raised. He thought that people with a strong sense of justice and honor tend to be the types that fight back. That made me wonder, if Ryan and Troy had not grown up on the wrestling mat, would they have become fighters? If John and Jacob had stable parents and not grown up defending themselves and others from bullying, would they have chosen to risk everything to step into the cage?

What I saw on this trip wasn't just the reasons that led fighters to MMA, but what they were doing with it. When they saw their first fight or made the decision to compete wasn't important—it was what they were doing to prepare. Were they putting in the mat time, grinding out those 10,000 hours, becoming an expert in their field, preparing their body and mind? Were they giving themselves every possible advantage instead of just taking fights to prove they were tough or demand respect? How they were conducting themselves, whether on the amateur or pro level, spoke volumes about why they were fighting and what would become of their career.

CHAPTER SIX

June 13, 2012

Three days after returning from Vegas, I got on another red-eye to Boston, a very open and unplanned 2 weeks in front of me. Based on how responsive and helpful fighters were on my first trip to the Northeast, I figured everything would work out.

Since I'd already covered Massachusetts and Rhode Island, I headed north to the quaint little town of Somersworth, NH. The co-owners of The Shop MMA, Skip Libby and Bill Jones, made me feel very welcome and invited me to join them in a workout, promising there would be time for interviews after. I'd done almost no training in the 5 weeks since I'd injured my ribs and doubted I'd be able to make it through the whole workout, but I had to try.

The striking class was a mix of fighters and regular gym members, males and females, as young as 15 and as old as me. The music was loud and the energy high and I was pouring sweat before we finished the warm-up. When we broke to get on our gloves, I seriously considered bowing out and grabbing my camera instead.

To say my performance was embarrassing is an understatement. I'd mentally prepared to be blown away in workouts by fighters, but I was the weakest link in the entire class. I was breathing heavily, my legs burning, arms shaking as I tried to hold the pads for my teenage partner. All my life I'd been very competitive and never wanted to come in last, but I could no longer to do the things I once did. I'd become lazy and out of shape. Now I just wanted to quit, use my ribs as an excuse to save face, but Bill, Skip, and the other guys pushed me through it.

The workout session gave me a good glimpse of who these guys were: hard workers who liked to joke around and keep things positive. They were a fun crew and I wasn't surprised when they all gathered around for the interviews. If the interviewee didn't mind people listening in, then I was all for it. Plus, several of the guys hadn't been interviewed on camera before, so having friends around might help ease the stage fright.

After my arms stopped shaking, I set up my camera and talked with Skip, who was a month out from his fifth amateur fight, but didn't identify as a fighter. The 30-year-old said his role as coach and friend would always be his priority. He thinks of the young guys as little brothers and tries to watch out for their best interest and help guide them. He only stepped in the cage for personal accomplishment and to push his mind and body.

There were two heavyweights in the group. The younger one said he'd been the fat kid growing up and he still held a lot of bottled up anger from being bullied. Wrestling and then MMA helped his confidence and self-image and he planned to keep fighting because it is rewarding, unlike his crappy job.

The other heavyweight was the same age as me and coming off an 8-year break. He had a fulfilling career as a correctional officer and a family of five to care for but had recently jumped back into training for one last fight. He knew it was a little selfish, but also necessary, something he needed to do for himself. Just the health benefits alone had been worth it as he'd already dropped a lot of weight.

Two of the guys were scheduled to fight in 3 days at the New England Fight Night 3 I planned on attending in Lewiston, ME. Normally I don't like to interview guys so close to a fight as they are generally in a vulnerable place due to cutting weight and stress. The absolute last thing I'd want to do is screw up someone's mindset and have them question why they were about to fight, but both guys were game.

First up was a 26-year-old bouncer who had lost all four of his professional fights in the past year but hoped he'd turn everything around Saturday. He talked about all that the martial arts had given him and why he continued training and fighting despite the losses. MMA was a much-needed outlet for his anger and energy and has been an extremely positive adventure.

The other guy scheduled to fight was a 30-year-old lightweight, his cauliflowered right ear giving him away as a wrestler. He'd had a traumatic childhood and had some major setbacks in life. His dream of being a professional wrestler didn't pan out, but MMA was giving him another shot at doing something extraordinary. It changed his life and set him on a new and positive path.

Bill Jones, the other owner, was the most experienced fighter, 33 years old with a 10-5 record. Bill was quiet and hard to read. He skimmed over his childhood, saying it wasn't very great and that there were a lot of drugs and violence in his teenage years. Also a lot of hard work. Bill began working at a young age and had been a roofer for 20 years, becoming very strong in the process.

Bill had no idea what mixed martial arts was until he went to a local fight. Two weeks later he signed up at a Tae Kwon Do academy where he trained 2 months before walking into the cage. Although he continued to put in 60 to 80 hours a week on roofs as a foreman while helping raise his three kids, Bill managed to squeeze in 15 fights over 4 years and win some local titles.

There were a couple of reasons Bill said he fought, but the main one was simply for fun. Fighting was a break from work, from the kids, from an ordinary life. Fighting was Bill's outlet, the thing he could turn to instead of drinking and drugs. Although he said he wasn't a big fan of getting hit, he was a straight brawler in the cage and said fighting was better than any high he'd had. It was the release he needed.

After we finished the interviews, Bill was nice enough to invite me to his house to hang out. The old introvert in me would have said no thanks, but I had the next 2 weeks to spend alone in hotels. Bill's house was tucked back in the woods and sat on more property than I was used to. It was awesome what he'd done with his yard, having turned it into the coolest playground for his kids. Tree houses and zip lines, an off-road track, and a nine-hole miniature golf course. Bill wanted to give them the childhood that he never had.

It was a beautiful night so we sat on the front porch. After his wife and kids called it a night, Bill and I exchanged stories. He opened up and talked in greater detail about early trauma, troubled teenage years, struggles and failures as an adult, and his new positive approach to life.

Once we'd gotten all the sobering stuff out of the way, we played a midnight game of golf. On the way back to the hotel, I couldn't stop thinking about how much Bill had revealed, all the things he'd never tell some stranger with a camera in a room full of people. How many other stories had I missed on my journey? How many important facts had been left out?

There was no telling what might have been left unsaid in other interviews, but even if I wasn't always getting the whole story from fighters, I believe overall I was given a very good sense of who these people were.

* * *

Sunday I drove up to beautiful Bangor, ME, home of my favorite author, Stephen King. It was strange spending Father's Day by myself, but it gave me time to think about sacrifice and what lots of these fighters I'd talked to were giving up to chase a dream.

Monday morning I took time out for myself and did the nerdiest thing I'd ever done by going on a Stephen King tour done by SK Tours of Maine. I've read nearly everything King has written, so as both an author and fan I enjoyed seeing all the spots that sparked his stories. Stu Tinker, the tour guide, also gave me a good look at all of Bangor, a taste of what life was like in this part of the country.

At noon I stopped by Young's MMA which had two big wins at the NEF 3 fight I attended Saturday night in Lewiston. The gym was larger than I imagined, very clean and bright, with the feel of a martial arts dojo.

I had interviewed Ryan Sanders, a 25-year-old bartender, just a few hours before his co-main event fight. The energetic, charming, and funny Ryan had told me that he'd been very competitive and athletic as a kid, but hated team sports. Although he didn't have any martial arts training, he did a lot of backyard boxing in high school and decided he wanted to become a fighter when he saw local boxing legend Marcus "The Irish Hand Grenade" Davis on *The Ultimate Fighter.*

Ryan greeted me at the front, very humble and respectful, happy things went his way Saturday. He introduced me to his training partner, Bruce Boyington, who had landed a nasty spinning back kick knock out of his opponent in the first 10 seconds. I interviewed the 33-year-old Bruce, who had started Tae Kwon Do at 7 and never stopped. The second-degree black belt had been a martial arts instructor for the Marines and described himself as a hard-nosed guy who was loyal and compassionate. He saw MMA as a lifestyle, not a sport, and said it was an incredible outlet great for all ages. With a family and full-time job, Bruce knew fighting wouldn't be easy, but he was giving it what he could.

The team's head coach, Chris Young, was also 33, but finished with his fighting career. Chris had started early and fought back when the sport was still called NHB and relatively unheard of in Maine. He described it as being back when you just hoped you wouldn't catch anything the other guy had if either you or your opponent got cut.

Chris was born and raised in Bangor, where he played a bit of baseball but wasn't big into sports. From a very young age Chris was fascinated by martial arts movies and Chuck Norris was his hero. When he turned 10 he was finally allowed to begin training at a local Kenpo Karate school.

Chris said he'd been an introvert with low self-confidence, but the training changed all that. He didn't have to worry about growing up with bullies and found he excelled at the one thing he'd always loved.

Martial arts became Chris's life and he identified as a martial artist. By high school he said, "I was known as Chris, that guy who fights. It became who I was."

And that reputation was earned thanks to his instructor. Although Chris loves the man and is grateful for all the knowledge he passed on, Chris understood that his instructor was not a great influential character. He would take the 140-pound Chris to weight lifting gyms and pit him against muscle-bound men that outweighed Chris by a hundred pounds. While most of Chris's friends were goofing off or getting into trouble, he was fighting grown men and defeating them.

Chris said if it weren't for his strong personality, he might have been molded into something completely different than what he became. As an example of his willpower and focus, Chris said he'd never touched a drop of alcohol. He never wanted to do anything where he wasn't in control. He had already adopted the martial code even though his instructor hadn't.

After high school, Chris felt like he no longer had his identity. He knew he didn't want to do a 9-to-5 and that school wasn't for him, but he didn't know where he fit in society. The only thing he felt compelled to do was continue his martial arts journey by taking the next step and get in the cage.

In the late 90s Bangor was not exactly a mecca of martial arts, so Chris ordered BJJ tapes and paid friends to let him practice moves on them. In '99 he entered the first MMA event held in New England even though he knew he'd probably lose. His philosophy was to challenge himself by going against the best, and therefore, seeing what he was made of. Although he did get choked out, he learned a lot about himself and was hooked.

While working as a preschool teacher for his main source of income, Chris continued training himself and competing. With little or no financial reward, Chris was fighting to figure out who he was. "It doesn't matter who you are in society, or who people think you are. When you strap on the gloves and you start throwing down, you find out really quick."

He said all the other crap in life becomes irrelevant. The fight is pure, it's primal, it's truth. "You find out exactly who you are, very freaking quickly," he said. "It tears you open and it exposes everything. And there's absolutely no lying."

Chris discovered who he was. He wasn't as talented as other fighters, wasn't an athlete, and wasn't training at a big school, but he had no quit. He said, "You might beat the crap out of me but I'll keep coming."

The one time he didn't keep coming back was in a fight he didn't prepare for. He felt like he wasn't there and took a bad beating, decided it should be his last fight. As hard as it was to stop fighting, he realized it was no longer for him. During the break from training, Chris discovered he loved coaching and never looked back.

Losing had never been something that seriously bothered Chris, but he understands just how devastating it can be for fighters. That's why he teaches his guys they can't be afraid to lose. A warrior can't be afraid to die. It was something to do well.

Chris said, "I'm not here training fighters, I'm here training warriors. It's about a lifestyle. That's what I push on these guys. That's who I am. I have these warrior philosophies in life."

When we finished up, Chris's wife and his 2-year-old son, Kaden, were waiting for us. His son beamed when he saw Chris, ran right up to him for a giant hug. Just as Chris said there's no lying in the cage, I believe there's no lying with kids. This was a happy child who loved his daddy.

I said goodbye and got a huge high-five from Kaden to send me on my way. I thought about the Bushido code, the way of the warrior. There are seven virtues of the Samurai: Righteousness. Courage. Benevolence. Respect. Sincerity. Honor. Loyalty. Although these traits weren't specifically discussed in any of the interviews, I sensed each of these with Chris and his warriors. It was no wonder I liked them.

* * *

That night I felt like a traitor visiting Chris Young's crosstown rival, Team Irish MMA, but that gym was the main reason I'd driven all the way to Bangor. The gym's owner, Marcus Davis, was a fighter I'd watched at least half a dozen times. There weren't any fighters who had been as successful as Marcus at both boxing and MMA. I was sure Chris would understand.

One look at Marcus and I understood why he was still fighting at 38. He was solid and intense, someone you wouldn't want to tangle with. Marcus was very friendly and said I should jump in his MMA class. There weren't going to be any fighters in class that night and he assured me it was his easiest session.

I went for it and quickly discovered that what was easy for him and the others was not easy for me. Getting through the warm-ups was a challenge, but I tried to hide that I was hurting. Next we went over armbar and triangle techniques, and I had a chance to see Marcus as an instructor. He did an excellent job of walking us through the moves, showing us why they worked, and how they would need to be modified to work in the streets. I made a mental note to ask why that was important to him.

Class would have been awesome if it had ended right there, but we finished off with conditioning. Crawling, jumping, duck-walks, push-ups, and several other stations. Everything was on fire, especially my thighs. I wanted to quit, but refused to do that in front of someone I was going to interview.

I somehow made it to the end and wobbled over to my water where Marcus and the others were standing around talking. My legs were jelly and I had to take a knee, couldn't believe they'd gone out on me like that. Everyone understood because they'd all been there, those first days back to the gym when you're trying to decide whether it's worth it.

It was already late when class ended and Marcus had his family to get home to. He was gracious and agreed to meet early the next morning for my 75th interview.

Marcus locked the door behind us and said the gym wouldn't be open to the public for another hour. We set up in the padded MMA room. I was grateful there'd be no interruptions or noises to deal with. We started with childhood, how Marcus's mother claimed he was punching before he was walking. Fighting was in his blood. Both sides of his family had boxers and his mom's father went undefeated in 60 professional bouts. Marcus's grandfather never said much as they would sit and watch boxing, but Marcus looked up to him with awe, and boxing became his passion. No one questioned Marcus would be a fighter.

For the next 20 minutes we talked about Marcus's boxing career and transition into MMA, but I wanted to know more about his childhood. I understood his initial desire to box and be like his grandfather, but what was it that made him stick it out and be successful? Not everyone responds positively to the physicality of fighting. I asked if he could think of other reasons why he was drawn to it.

Marcus is incredibly intelligent, very well-spoken, and had been quick with his answers. On this question, he started his sentence a few times, looked down like he was considering what, if anything, he should tell me, then let out a deep sigh. He said, "My father was not a good guy. My brother's father, a different man, was not a good guy." Marcus and Brad were raised by their mother, but grew up running the house with no positive male role models to guide them. The boys brawled constantly, his much older and bigger half-brother always getting the better of him. Marcus took his unbridled aggression on to the street, challenging everyone that crossed his path. "And I wasn't just fighting," he said. "I was doing everything that was wrong."

By the age of 15, Marcus had been convicted of assault 13 times. Convicted. Not went to trial for. Not arrested. This was the number of times a plaintiff was brave enough to show up in court and Marcus was found guilty. He had no direction, no one to guide him. And he ended up in juvenile detention.

The time spent locked up made Marcus value his freedom. He'd begun his amateur boxing career and dedicated himself to it. Having heard all the stories of backyard boxing, Marcus realized he could get all the boxing experience he needed right at home without getting in trouble. Every day he'd wait outside his house and yell at the customers of the store across the street. It didn't matter if they were grown men, Marcus would hold up his gloves and challenge them to a fight, never backing down. He couldn't count all the times he'd beat the crap out of someone else or how many times he'd had the piss beat out of him. "It's impossible to give you a number. This was years and years." He also developed a friendship with one guy who came over every day so they could beat the hell out of each other before running to the gate and challenging others.

With the backyard experience and a little help along the way, Marcus put together an impressive 32-2 record, beating Golden Glove champs in New England and Arizona. He said he didn't have a very amateurish style and his midget arms gave him the reach of a Cabbage Patch doll, but he hit hard and with bad intentions.

Marcus turned pro at 19 and knocked out 8 of 11 opponents during his first 2 years. Legal battles, fights being cancelled, injuries, and other mishaps crippled his career, and he began to question his path. Although his focus remained on boxing, he developed an interest in MMA and began training Jeet Kune Do while living in Boston.

Marcus continued to box and remained undefeated but wasn't making much money only fighting twice a year. In 1997, then 23, he moved back to Bangor, opened an MMA school, and went back to running a bar. Some of the doormen at the bar took Marcus's classes, and the one who stood out was 6'8", 300 plus pounds Tim Sylvia, who would go on to become the UFC champ. Three years later, a controversial call landed Marcus his only loss and he retired from boxing. When Tim decided to leave the tiny town of Bangor to train with Pat Miletech in Iowa, Marcus made the move halfway across the country soon after.

Marcus jumped into his first MMA fight before he had any real grappling experience, but he did very well. Even though he wasn't making much money in those early days, he loved the sport and preferred it over boxing, seeing it as more of a challenge with so many more elements to master. In 2005 he became a contestant on *The Ultimate Fighter Season 2*, but things didn't go his way. Not one to give up on his dream, Marcus won his next 5 fights and returned to the UFC where he went 9-5, winning several Fight of the Night bonuses and completely changing his life.

Marcus points to 2007 as the year his life became storybook, the type of life he'd always wanted but never imagined he'd have. He'd found a perfect partner with his third wife, he was finally making money doing what he loved, and he'd become much healthier as a person and a parent.

Without a doubt, a huge part of the reason for that change was MMA, but there was another part, a mental technique he'd adopted. Marcus had discovered that as he became more peaceful and okay with himself as a person, he began to lose some of his fire, some of his edge. That angry little boy who'd become The Irish Hand Grenade had his purpose, and Marcus decided he'd keep him around. He just had to keep him separate and decide when he'd let him loose.

Marcus said he knew it sounded crazy, but this self-imposed split personality was exactly what he needed to be whole as both a fighter and person. And this wasn't simply a fighter saying he flips a switch when he steps into the cage. Marcus does not let any part of The Irish Hand Grenade's life enter his home. There are no medals, trophies, photos, magazines, or anything else fight related. He doesn't talk about fighting. He doesn't have students over. One of his best friends, MMA fighter and BJJ black belt Jorge Gurgel, visited his house and turned to Marcus after 40 minutes and said, "I don't know who you are, but you need to get me out of here." He spent the night in a hotel, too freaked out by the difference.

"I just can't be that angry kid anymore." Marcus pointed around the matted room. "Only when I'm in here."

Marcus said he'd transformed from being an unapproachable person that trusted no one to someone whose main goal is to be a good person and help others. His true focus and passion are his family, but teaching others is incredibly rewarding and brings him more joy than other aspects of the sport. He said, "I don't do this [teaching] because I have to; I do this because I love it."

I was a little surprised by this, not because of anything I witnessed the night before, but because I believed most fighters would rather focus on themselves than spend their time teaching. I couldn't point to any of the places I'd been and maybe it was just an unfounded bias from before, but it wasn't true for Marcus. He was excited about teaching and was more animated talking about this than anything else we'd been over.

When he sees one of his students use something he's shown him, even if it's just in sparring, Marcus is moved. That person has shown he believes in Marcus as a teacher, that the skills they've been given will keep them safe in chaotic situations.

And Marcus is just as excited to teach non-fighters, if not more so. He strives to make them understand the difference between sport fighting and self-defense, just as he had in the previous night's workout. He said if you saw him in a real fight and then an MMA match, they would not look the same at all. People are animalistic, vicious creatures who bite, gouge eyes, head butt, and break bottles when they fight. Marcus had been on both sides of it and knew people would do whatever they could to survive a fight. He'd had four knives pulled on him and was stabbed twice. He'd been smashed in the head with pint glasses, ash trays, beer bottles, and twice with a crowbar. He'd been in situations where he easily could have died, and he likes to think he was given a second chance to pass on knowledge and be the positive male role model he never had.

His philosophy was, "We're all here, not only to better ourselves and improve ourselves, but also to impact people in some sort of way. That's the key. You need to find out what your gifts are, and you need to embrace them. You need to develop them, and you need to not hoard them. You need to share them and help other people." Marcus said, "We're here for progress. We're here to make an impact on not just yourself, but to help other people achieve their goals."

The desire to help others was a common characteristic of the men I'd met this trip: Bill Jones, a quiet leader the team looked up to, a friend offering help whenever he could; Chris Young, training his students in the way of the warrior, understanding those virtues would improve lives.

MMA allowed these men to find out who they were and helped them evolve into stronger, kinder, and calmer individuals. Each of them had a darker side, but they'd adapted, found ways to lead healthier and happier lives. Peace through violence, a new concept to consider.

CHAPTER SEVEN

June 22, 2012

Friday morning and I was back in my rental enjoying the emptiness around me, just beautiful blue skies and lush green grass as I headed to St. Albans, the Maple Syrup Capital of the World. Considering Vermont's population is less than Washington, D.C.'s, I wasn't surprised at how few MMA academies were around. Kirik Jenness had warned me there wasn't much, but he said if I did ever go that way there was one man I needed to talk with.

Because I'd never followed *The Ultimate Fighter* reality show, I wasn't familiar with Tom Murphy who'd been a contestant on the second season with Marcus Davis. I researched him the night before to see why Kirik recommended him so highly. Turned out Tom isn't your average MMA fighter. The 37-year-old is a corporate director for a railway company, a motivational speaker who fights bullying with his non-profit Sweethearts and Heroes, and he started a company that tests clients' DNA to learn more about their ancestry and physical traits. And if that wasn't enough, he also owned the Italian restaurant we were scheduled to meet.

I slowed down as I reached St. Albans' historic downtown. Everything was so pristine and peaceful, the perfect setting for a postcard. The restaurant was closed, but a crew was setting up inside. Tom greeted me with a smile and a firm handshake. It'd been two years since he'd last fought but he looked to be in great shape, the remnant of a black eye tingeing his right cheek proof he was still training. We were practically the same height and weight, both with shaved heads, and I couldn't help but think he was what I might have looked like if I trained hard, lived clean, and made some wiser choices.

Tom showed me inside the elegant restaurant where the staff quietly prepared the night's dinner. I had a special interest in Tom's side projects so we discussed those first. The DNA testing was fascinating, but Tom came alive when he talked about his anti-bullying program. I could see why kids would respond to him, a motivational speaker who honestly wanted to, and was, making a difference. Tom said, "I have a very simple philosophy in life. It's do the right thing for the right reasons, to help people."

The desire to help others was instilled into Tom when he was a young child living in Philadelphia. His parents had opened their doors to struggling people who wanted to change their lives and Tom grew up thinking that all families had homeless people living with them. There was even one time where his parents gave away Tom's bedroom and he slept in a bathtub for an entire year.

The psychology major said it was this passion to help others along with dedication and hard work that made him successful. And he credited it all to his parents, wrestling, and martial arts.

Tom doubted anyone who saw him as a young child would have predicted his success or guessed how many lives he would impact. He was a problem child and the school wanted to label him. They said he was out of control, hyperactive, had ADD and other learning disabilities. They wanted to medicate him, tame him with pharmaceuticals.

His parents refused and pulled Tom out of school. His dad said there was nothing wrong with Tom, he was just a boy with a ton of energy and they would fix it with good old-fashioned discipline. The roughhousing with dad that Tom had always enjoyed was replaced with competitive wrestling, and suddenly Tom became a different person. The ultra-competitive kid found his calling, an activity which he could pour himself into, where winning or losing was all on him.

Tom said it was wrestling that got him through junior high, high school, and finally college. He no longer got in trouble, initially because of the fear wrestling could be taken away, but later due to him becoming a focused individual who understood what he could accomplish if he set his mind to it and put in the time, dedication, and hard work.

The thousands of hours Tom put into training, all the sweating, bleeding, and hurting, shaped who he became. He began to lose the anger, that uncontrollable something he described as being similar to seeing red. He still marvels at that transformation from out of control kid to a man who can't think of anything possible that would make him hurt someone violently.

Tom was adamant about MMA not being violent and that the term 'fighting' is something he likes to stay away from. He understands fighting as using violent physical means, which is something he's never done. He said the word tarnishes what he and all these other MMA athletes do, spending a significant portion of their lives working on their skills and testing them on a stage. He said, "I'm like a basketball player, a volleyball player. Just in my sport you get a cut."

Tom became involved in MMA because he's a competitor at heart and a training nut who's not very pleasant to be around if misses the gym for a few days. MMA is simply a continuation of his wrestling and he describes it as his greatest hobby. Making money was never a factor for Tom and he gave nearly all his fight purses away to his manager, coach, and charities.

Although I was very impressed with him, Tom said he's not a great guy, not even a good guy. He's just a guy trying to make himself a little better every day. He measures his success every night with the pillow test when he lays his head down and thinks about the day. If he says, "I'm glad I did," he passes. More often than not he says, "I wish I had." But Tom points out the motivation even in failing and says that he uses that to push him to improve the next day.

One of Tom's most admirable traits is his gratitude. He appreciates where he is in life and said he could never thank enough people, that if it hadn't been for all of them, he'd be nowhere. He feels it's his turn to give it back and his unbeatable work ethic has him doing just that.

* * *

It was my first time in Canada and I was excited to train at Tristar Gym which is recognized as one of the top MMA academies in the world and best known as being the gym Georges St. Pierre calls home. That night's MMA class was taught by David Loiseau, a talented UFC vet who has been through many battles. I felt like a fish out of water, both with the striking and on the ground, but David was a friendly and patient teacher who made the class fun. He said he'd be up for an interview the next day after the pro's sparring.

Saturday morning I got up early to shop for a new pair of gloves and shin pads. If I was going to get serious about training I should look the part. I made it to the gym half an hour before practice, anxious to test myself a little more with training and get in some interviews. I introduced myself to the assistant coach who was in charge for the day. I told him what I wanted to do, but he shook his head, said he hadn't been notified.

At first I thought he was joking, but only for a second. I said I understood not being able to train, but what about photos and interviews? He explained that since I hadn't been approved none of those things could happen. I thought I had cleared it with the right people but that didn't matter. For all he knew I could be a spy. I had to leave.

Damn. I hadn't seen that coming.

The whole ride back to the hotel I might have been mumbling *Fuck Canada*, but my anger was misplaced. I should have planned better. Big name fighters have a lot to lose and not much to gain by having a stranger in their gym. My wasted day, a 4-hour drive, and the hotel were the cost of the expensive lesson.

I sat in my room, tried to figure what to do. The plan had been to travel to Ottawa the next morning but I decided the added driving time wasn't worth it. Truth is, I get pretty burned out on these trips, the positive interactions with the fighters the only thing keeping me going. When I'm on the road I eat like crap and only average five hours of sleep. My entire body aches and the pain in my ribs constantly flares up. I was tired and cranky, no different than my little daughter who'd been begging me to hurry up and come home and this time to stay forever. It was selfish for me to be out on the road. I didn't need to be doing this. I should be home taking care of her and my wife instead of embarrassing myself on and off the mat.

The pity party raged while I calculated the cost of an early flight home. Then I thought back to all the fighters I'd been talking with, that all my bitching was ridiculous when compared to what they sacrifice. Fighting is a lifestyle, probably one of the hardest you can imagine, and sacrifice is a big part of it. Whether it's family, food, fun or free time, something's going to go.

The blow to my ego got me off track, but I pulled out of it. It made no sense to dwell on Montreal being a waste of time and money, especially when I'd had so many other incredible experiences on this trip. I had an opportunity, not a problem.

The Sunday morning seven-hour drive to Boston gave me plenty of time to get refocused. Driving 2,000 miles in two weeks had taken its toll on me, but I wasn't ready to call it quits. Instead I woke early the next morning, starting the day off right with a chiropractic adjustment. I hurried over to Rivera Athletic Center for an inspiring talk with UFC veteran, Jorge Rivera, whose mission is to be a positive role model and improve people's lives. I drove straight to Wai Kru's brand new South Shore facility and watched UFC fighter John "Doomsday" Howard and his teammates have a brutal training session. After interviewing John and four other fighters, I got a quick bite and finished the day out at Lauzon Mixed Martial Arts, relearning how to do an armbar in a class taught by Joe Cushman. The day's tally: 14 hours; 3 schools; 8 interviews. A much better day.

I passed Tom's pillow test. Time to go home.

* * *

It was great being home, but two days later I was back in the gym. In the months prior, I'd already had a few easy classes at Kings MMA in Huntington Beach, but this was my first time training in the pro class. I managed to make it through the warm-ups, did okay with the striking, and was completely useless for the light sparring. Fortunately all the fighters took it easy, treating me like a grown-up version of a Make a Wish kid.

After practice I interviewed three fighters. Kory Kelley, who was getting ready for his pro debut, suggested I train with him at Mark Munoz's Reign Training Center. I said yes, before realizing I'd just signed up for a wrestling practice.

It was three days later and I was sticking to my word, regretting it the whole ride down to Lake Forest. Besides worrying about how much I had for breakfast and whether it'd be coming back up, I considered how little I knew about wrestling. And not just in terms of techniques and skill.

I'd never once been to a wrestling class and what little I knew was gathered through fighting: Tim Lajcik showing me that a real wrestler will never quit. Travis Wiuff teaching me how much it sucks when a wrestler puts you on his shoulder and slams you down, doing it multiple times to make sure the lesson stuck.

I thought back to how Kirik Jenness had described wrestling. "Wrestling is in our DNA," he said. "The jury might be out on whether or not smacking someone in the face with a closed fist is natural, but the base of fighting is wrestling, and wrestling absolutely is an innate human activity. In fact, it's an innate mammalian activity. Even protozoa probably bang together in some wrestling type way."

I pulled into the industrial center and parked in front of the massive building. Mark Munoz, who was just a week away from fighting Chris Weidman, invited me to take photos and train with the team. Before I chickened out, I changed my clothes and headed into the back, surprised by the two dozen fighters getting ready, a few who I recognized from the UFC.

I had no business trying to train alongside these guys and I felt foolish standing among them. Just as I'd made up my mind to change back and only take photos, Kory from Kings came up and introduced me to a few friends. I couldn't back out.

The warm-up kicked my ass and I was dripping sweat after five minutes. Munoz told us to partner up and like the fat kid that knows he's going to get picked last, I stepped back, hoping there was an uneven number of fighters and I'd be the odd man out. No such luck. 6'4" UFC fighter, Brendan Schaub, needed a partner and I was closest to him in size.

Munoz demonstrated the drill and then we found an open spot on the mat. As we got into position I explained I was dangerously out of shape and didn't know what the hell I was doing. Brendan told me not to worry about it and laughed when I suggested he find another partner so I didn't waste his workout.

I didn't bring it up again because I was having a hard enough time trying to breathe, let alone talk. Brendan was a great partner and taking it easy on me, but the training was brutal, drill after drill, grind, grind, grind. Get away from your opponent, get off your back, get up the wall, take him down, don't let him get up, go, go, go.

This is why I never liked wrestling. It was too hard.

I surprised myself and made it through the first half of class, but when the team was told to gear up, I could barely stand. Sparring was out of the question, plus it'd be good for me to see the team as a whole and indulge in the intensity.

The sparring was just as fast-paced as the rest of class, guys switching partners at the end of each round. Fighters took up the entire mat, some rotating through the cage to help their teammates who were coming up on their fights. There was only one female in the group. I watched her hitting the mitts, thinking how sad it was that she could kick my ass.

After the workout ended I announced to the fighters that I'd be around for interviews if anyone would like to share their story. I was glad the female fighter, Ashlee Evans-Smith, was up for it. She was just the second female I interviewed who had any MMA experience and the only one I'd watched train. A big part of why I started Unlocking was the worry that my daughter might become a fighter. Why had Ashlee gone down this path?

The 24-year-old bantamweight bunched up her long dark hair and wiped the sweat from her face, joking about running to the back to throw on some makeup. She was friendly and outgoing, very easy to talk to. We started with her childhood, how she'd been a pudgy little girl who didn't play any sports in her small hometown of Ukiah in Northern California. Instead, Ashlee had loved playing outside and gravitated towards boy stuff, identifying with the punk rock scene when she was in high school.

One of the things she'd always enjoyed was roughhousing with her younger brother and his friends, always getting the best of them. That changed her sophomore year when one of the boys came back from a wrestling camp. He told her not to feel bad about losing, that girls can't wrestle.

'Girls can't' anything is a challenge Ashlee had to take. She always believed she could do whatever she wanted, regardless of her sex. Even though there were no other girls on her high school's team, Ashlee joined the next day. Thanks to her recruitment effort, there were three other females her senior year, but Ashlee was completely fine training with the boys. Her commitment to the sport earned her a college scholarship.

I didn't equate wrestling with anger, but the punk rock music and tattoos made me wonder if there was more to Ashlee's story. I asked if she had been troubled at all as a kid, had she been reckless.

Without going into many details, Ashlee said she didn't have the best situation growing up and she had been angry at the world and rebellious. Although wrestling was a positive path, Ashlee was also out partying those first few years which led to trouble. After some soul searching, Ashlee realized she needed to wholly embrace wrestling, have it be the anchor to ground herself.

In college, Ashlee committed to living a clean lifestyle, dedicating herself to wrestling while also working on a degree in journalism and acting as the editor of the school's paper. Her senior year, Ashlee came across the photo of a female MMA fighter and was drawn to the womanly and empowering picture. Ashlee hadn't watched MMA prior to that and her only knowledge of the sport came from her friend and teammate, Carla Esparza, who was already training and planning on fighting. Although intrigued by the idea, Ashlee continued to concentrate on wrestling and academics.

Not long after graduating, Ashlee once again lost direction, something I'd heard from many college athletes, especially wrestlers. She began training MMA and it anchored her just like wrestling had. With her wrestling experience and having been on a rugby team, Ashlee wasn't worried about a little contact in the cage. Three months into training, Ashlee had her first amateur fight and earned a TKO in the second round. That year was great with four wins, but then she lost 3 fights in 3 weeks. The losses were hard to take and she considered hanging it up.

Ashlee had already made up her mind she was going to be successful so she recommitted and decided a change of scenery would be best. Even though she loved her old coach, Ashlee relocated to Southern California and after a hard six months of training she won an amateur title. Now she was getting set to fight in three days for her final amateur bout.

I asked how people reacted when they found out she fights. She said that most people are shocked but her true friends think MMA is the perfect sport for her.

Was MMA just a sport to her, no different than wrestling? Ashlee said, "It's a sport. There's technique, and there's conditioning, there's motivation, there's dedication. It's not a street fight by any means."

There were many similarities between MMA and wrestling, but Ashlee said it takes something else to be a fighter. She brought up all her wrestler friends who could never get in the cage. She said, "You do have to have a little bit of a vicious side to you to do this sport. This sport takes a bit more aggression." She laughed at the thought. "I mean, it is fighting." She said that although everyone has their own drives for fighting, one thing for certain is that the most successful fighters will have a ton of aggression to unleash.

Ashlee seemed like such a pleasant and friendly person. I wondered if she worried about losing her aggression. She smiled and shook her head. Even though Ashlee's no longer that angry little girl, she still had that fire inside. In wrestling she embraced her never quit attitude and is now stubborn, spunky, and tenacious in whatever she does in life. She said, "I don't think I'm ever going to lose my aggression."

Although Ashlee couldn't pinpoint all her drives, she knew MMA was her calling. She's taking a chance, waitressing to support herself so she can live her dream. "Nothing else feels this fun. Nothing else feels this rewarding. I just know that if I picked another sport, I wouldn't feel as happy with myself because I know it wouldn't be as tough of a sport. I really like to challenge myself in every aspect of my life. I think the reason I fight is because it's the hardest thing I can think of doing, on an athletic level at least."

I thanked Ashlee for the insight and continued the interviews with a unique group of individuals. If I was going solely by looks and had no knowledge these guys were fighters, I might have incorrectly guessed I could hang with all four of them in a street fight. But there was no doubt I'd try to avoid a confrontation with the last interviewee, Lew Polley, a solid heavyweight, each of his legs as thick as my waist.

From the few minutes we talked prior to the interview, I pegged Lew as coming from privilege, maybe an only child, perhaps he'd gone to a fancy prep school back east. But I had it all wrong. Lew's childhood had come with challenges. Lew's mother is an immigrant from the Philippines who moved to the United States with Lew's father, an African-American who was an active-duty Marine. Similar to some of the other fighters I'd spoken with who came from military families, Lew moved often.

While the moving helped Lew learn to get along with others and adapt, it was tough. The self-described nerd had been bullied because he was quiet, took AP classes, and is biracial. For much of his life he had trouble being accepted by either race.

Lew's parents stressed education and pushed him towards numerous extra-curricular activities, like band, cheerleading, and the Academics club. His dad, a college football coach, felt Lew was built for the sport, but Lew excelled at all athletics. In addition to football, he played baseball, soccer, ran track, and wrestled. He said, "Football was probably the most fun that I had, but wrestling just spoke to me. This is where I need to be, on the mats."

The work in the wrestling room earned Lew a Division 1 scholarship to Bloomsburg University. Although he said it was funny, I could hear the regret that he didn't hit his stride with wrestling until after he graduated and began competing internationally. While training, he crossed paths with some of the wrestlers who were big names in the UFC. They recognized Lew's potential and encouraged him to try MMA, but Lew didn't think much of it until his friend offered him a fight in Florida. With no MMA experience, Lew fought three weeks later, winning with a quick submission. He thought it was fun, but his life had been focused on wrestling for such a long time that he couldn't stop. Over the next 7 months, Lew's friend called and set up 3 more fights. Now that he was 4-0, Lew's friend convinced him he could make a career out of the sport if he would stop wrestling and train MMA with a real team.

"I fell in love with it," Lew said. "I felt like I was born to do it, just because of how good I felt, how natural it came to me. Pressure didn't really bother me. Fans didn't bother me. It was just another competition. So, I was like, 'I'm going to be successful at this.'"

The decision to fight always comes with a price tag. In Lew's case, his girlfriend dumped him, he gave up a great job, and had to explain to his mom and everyone else why he'd risk so much just to fight in a cage. Over the last six years, Lew had given up relationships, seeing nieces and nephews, missing funerals, a secure career, and social fun. And as much as he would love having children and a committed relationship, he understands that can't happen yet. His focus is on MMA and anyone involved with him wouldn't be getting the attention they deserve. Lew said, "I just want this so bad; I'm going to make this work. I have to. I'm at the point of no return; I've committed too much to just throw it away."

That's not to say there weren't doubts along the way. For the last two years, Lew hadn't had a fight because he couldn't find opponents, shows fell through, and guys pulled out. But Lew continued to train and refused to give up. He kept grinding and now he was set to fight in just ten more days.

When asked if there were reasons for fighting other than competition, Lew said, "I know a lot of people who fight because deep down they are insecure, they have some demons they have to battle, or they want to prove they're a macho guy. They fight for girls or attention. This is just something that chose me, and I am walking the path that was in front of me. I love what I do, I appreciate what I do. It's fun and I enjoy it, but at the end of the day, it's work."

Many fighters feel they are different from others, like there might be something wrong with them, so I appreciated Lew's perspective. "I believe that every human being has a primal nature, and people who fight or do combative sports just embrace that side of themselves a little more than the normal person." He said, "It's just another competition."

Although Lew is physically imposing, I doubt anyone would have guessed he was a fighter if they listened to him speak. Just in the short time we'd been talking he used at least five words I'd have to later look up. Already impressed by his story and accomplishments, I asked who he was outside of the cage. In the gym he was very serious because MMA is his job, but he said that changes once practice is over.

Lew said, "I'm like a lexicon of a wide range of emotions. I'm pretty eclectic, there are a lot of things people don't know about me." He likes to learn and is very cerebral, spending free time reading, watching educational shows, and balancing it by being sarcastic and silly, having fun and acting like a big kid.

His key value is work ethic, something he learned at a young age. With six brothers and sisters and not a lot of money at times, Lew clearly remembered eating MREs, rice, spam, and ramen. Both his parents had both grown up very poor and taught him through words and example that if you want something you work hard and go get it. It might take a long time but just keep applying yourself and it will happen.

This work ethic is what has kept Lew going in a sport that is anything but easy. He described it as a life grind, something that most people can't do, especially for an extended period. He sees young fighters come in who think MMA's a fun hobby that's trendy, and he asks them if it'll still be as much fun 5 years down the road when things aren't going their way. "It's a grind. I love it," Lew said. "I love it because it makes people understand what life is about. It makes people understand what wrestling is about. If you can handle wrestling in college and make it through the other side, you can handle anything in life."

We ended on that last sentence, a truth I'd finally accepted. I'd heard the sentiment many times over the last 3 months from guys like Kurt Pellegrino and his crew. Even the guys like Troy Lamson, Tom Murphy, and Lew, who also excelled at football, each viewed that sport as a fun game. Wrestling was the real deal. It was competition.

I'd feared wrestlers for their technique but not their grind and tenacity. I knew wrestling was a hard sport yet I had no understanding of the mental toughness it developed. And not only were wrestlers not meatheads, but these were some of the brightest people I'd talked with. Also some of the most driven. Whether or not they stuck with MMA, these wrestlers were going to succeed in whatever they applied themselves to. They had the drive and determination to accomplish their goals.

CHAPTER EIGHT

July 13, 2012

It was Saturday night and I was at the Samurai MMA3 fight in Culver City, CA. The auditorium was packed and the crowd anxious as the fighters warmed up in the back. There were only eight fights on the card, and the two fighters I cared about I'd interviewed at Kings MMA.

Kory Kelley, the fighter who had invited me to Reign, was the second fight of the night. This was his pro debut, the importance of which he had talked about in his emotional interview. He fought a hard three rounds but lost the decision, his dreams of a successful career off to a rocky start.

The next five fights flew by with two submissions, two knockouts, and an exciting majority draw decision. Magno Almeida, a BJJ black belt who'd recently moved to the U.S. from Sao Paulo, was next up as the main event. The tall welterweight had begun training at 13 to overcome bullying by other kids and getting beat up by his brothers. Training had given him a confidence he'd always lacked and his life improved drastically. The humble and generous 26-year-old had much to be grateful for, and even though it was his hard work and dedication that helped secure those things, he gave all credit to God and said, "I don't believe I deserve to sleep in my bed before I give thanks to God."

I could see how Magno's beliefs helped make him the kind man he'd become, but I didn't expect religion to come up when I asked why he decided to fight after 8 years of BJJ. "It's not you who chooses MMA," he said, "it's MMA that chooses you." There have been many times when he questioned why he doesn't just get a normal job like everyone else and take a much simpler path, but Magno has decided that God has plans for everybody. He believes that God wants certain people to represent him, and MMA is the arena where Magno can best do that.

At the time I didn't think much of it, but I remembered Magno's words as he calmly strode through the crowd. He hugged each of his coaches and blessed himself with the sign of the cross upon entering the cage. Halfway through the first round, Magno slapped on an armbar for the win and raised his hand to the heavens. This wasn't just an athlete thanking God for a victory; Magno drew strength from his conviction.

I usually shied away from religion in the interviews and hadn't been considering what kind of impact it could have on someone competing in MMA. I'd been raised Catholic, but as a teenager I turned away from all religion because I had too many questions. Although I said I no longer believed what I'd been taught, deep-seated beliefs, especially those that are engrained in us at a young age, often stay with us despite attempts to rationalize them away. One of the beliefs, tied to Catholicism, that I'm sure I held onto was that fighting was wrong. I'd been spanked enough times for fighting with my brothers to know that as a truth. You shouldn't fight. It was a sin to hurt other people. Violence wasn't the answer. Always turn the other cheek.

Perhaps this was part of the reason I always questioned why I was fighting. If hurting another person was supposedly wrong, what did participating in a sport where you constantly deal and receive damage say about fighters? There's no telling what influence my religious beliefs may have had on my development, but I now had plans to include it in the survey to see who was raised religious, who remained religious, and how it related to their fighting career.

Out of the 90-plus fighters I'd talked with, there had been a good number who briefly mentioned their beliefs. One guy in Rhode Island said he was a God-fearing man. A former gangbanger in Las Vegas turned his life over to God. Marcus Davis hinted at the impact religion had on him later in life, and a young wrestler confided that he didn't believe in God but knew right from wrong and made moral decisions.

Although my talk with Jorge Rivera had been brief, he shared more than the others when he focused on the camera and spoke from the heart. "All things are possible due to God," he said. "I've had struggles in my life and my ups and downs in my belief, but I've always known in my heart that there's a God, call it whatever you want. Choose to believe however you want to believe, but surrender to it and you'll find your life will become better."

The most interesting conversation about religion had occurred recently at Reign. Jason Manly was only an inch shorter than me but about 80 pounds lighter. He was one of the interviewees I might have guessed I could take if I hadn't seen him training or known he was the fifth Cesar Gracie black belt and had recently competed in the very prestigious Abu Dhabi Combat Club championship.

The 32-year-old lightweight was vibrant, happy, and full of energy, not what you'd expect from someone who'd just completed a hard training session and was 10 days out from a fight, his return to the cage after an 11-year break.

Like his teammate, Lew Polley, Jason was a natural athlete who excelled at a lot of sports. He listed them off: soccer, baseball, football, track, basketball, and even hockey, something Manly, who is African American, laughed about when he said it was uncommon. Unlike Lew, who continued playing a lot of sports in high school, Jason focused solely on track, the rest of his time devoted to martial arts, which he'd started in second grade.

Jason's desire to train in the martial arts came from his love of martial arts movies, TV shows, and professional wrestling. Over the years, he studied a variety of different disciplines, including judo, sambo, karate, ninjitsu, and Japanese Jiu Jitsu, his progress intensified by wrestling with his two older brothers, often for control of what they'd be watching on TV.

Like many other fighters, Jason watched the first UFC and knew that he had to study BJJ. He sought out Royce Gracie and earned his blue belt under him before moving up to the University of California Berkeley on a track and field scholarship. Since seeing the huge shiny gold belt awarded in a later UFC, Jason knew he would one day fight MMA; he just didn't know it would happen so soon after starting college.

A month into the semester, Jason had tried out for Cesar Gracie's fight team and was surprised when a few days later he was told he was fighting in 3 weeks. Although Jason hadn't been training to fight, he was in great shape, had competed all his life, and had a lot of experience with challenges and fights in gyms, in school, and on the street. With too little time to get nervous, Jason jumped into the cage, winning in the second round with a triangle choke.

In trying to explain what an incredible experience fighting is, Jason compared it to running the 400-meter race at all-out speed. "You want to do it, but you don't want to do it. You're dreading the start of that race," he said. "It's the same feeling for a fight, or anything competitive. I was used to that feeling."

Jason waited until after the fight before telling his family and coaches. They were happy that he won but understandably worried about his health, his studies, and his track scholarship. Jason agreed the risk wasn't worth it and promised he'd keep the martial arts in the academy. His focus earned him MVP honors in track and his bachelor's degree.

Looking at Jason and his resume, it wasn't surprising that he hadn't fought in the last 11 years. Jason is intelligent, motivated, charismatic, talented, and successful. I couldn't see the reason for him to fight again. With so little money to be made and a more than decent risk of injury, why was he going to step back into the cage?

Jason said that he always knew he'd fight again but didn't expect the break to be so long. He stayed close to the sport by being involved in the business side: management, sponsorship, producing a curriculum, fight promoter, brand manager and consultant. But trying to live responsibly and take the safe and easier path wasn't working for him.

He explained, "When God's made you with certain abilities, you won't thrive and feel complete if you don't pursue them. My entire life the one thing that's been constant has been me being an athlete and me competing. That was the missing thing for me over the years that made me feel incomplete. I wasn't living an ongoing daily life as an athlete, training and competing, and training and competing, which I had done my entire life. I finally feel balanced now, when I'm doing that." The anticipation of showing up and doing battle is something Jason embraces. He said, "As much as that feeling is nerve wracking, you're not alive without it."

When asked who he was as a person, Jason smiled and said, "I'm a Christian. That's the centerpiece of my life. That's another reason why I'm fighting and competing."

Jason's mother always told him the Bible story, the Parable of the Talents in Matthew 25. "God's given everybody different talents and gifts, some more than others," Jason said. "The moral of the story is that if God's given you a talent, he expects you to use it, even if you don't want to use it. Even if it's a talent that you don't enjoy, you have an obligation to use it." In words similar to those of Magno, Jason said, "If God's given you that ability, he's given it to you for a reason, and it's not necessarily for you. There's other people that have to be motivated and inspired by the things that you do."

The thought of God wanting people to fight didn't fit my biased belief. When asked if there was any contradiction between being a Christian and an MMA fighter, Jason said absolutely not. "MMA is a sport. It's no different than any other sport."

Jason did go on to say, though, that he has been accused of being too nice, the one thing holding him back from being a monster. He sees this in his training when he gives partners the opportunity to tap out instead of putting the responsibility on them of tapping to protect themselves. He said, "There's some people who fight and they want to hurt somebody. I want to win, I want to show my skill level, I want to show my gift to its highest ability, but I don't want to hurt anybody. But, at the same time, not wanting to hurt someone and giving them an opportunity, it sets you up for an opportunity to lose. I think it's something I could get over, and in the right circumstance, and with the right opponent, I think it's something I could easily get over. It's really a matter of thinking through it and figuring out, 'Is it the right thing to do, or is it not the right thing to do?' At the end of the day, if I lose because of that, I'm not going to knock myself for it. I'm looking at a much bigger picture than winning and losing."

I asked if this return fight was just a one-time shot to get it out of his system, an itch that had to be scratched. Jason would like to make it to the UFC but was very clear when he said, "My bottom line goal is just to use the talents that I've been given. To me, if I don't use them, then I'm not doing God's will. If I do use them, then everything else just falls into place."

* * *

It was Tuesday, 4 days since the Samurai fight, and I was getting on a plane, heading to the Midwest in the middle of summer. Perhaps all the religion talk had been preparing me for the hellishly hot tour around the Bible Belt: 6 states, 12 schools, 1 fight, 2,000 miles in 11 days. Magno and Jason's talks were inspiring, and I wished I had their kind of conviction and strength to help get me through my trip.

I landed in Kansas City, MO, and the heat was suffocating. Thanks to a tip from the guys at Knuckle Junkies, I was headed to Farmington, MO, to check out a small gym named Destruction MMA, but a few hours into the trip I realized that I was going to miss most of practice and only get in a few interviews. I was still determined though and kept at it, slapping myself to stay awake, then finally pulling over for an energy drink.

About 10 minutes later, the caffeine kicked in and the car gave out, dying on me in the middle of Missouri in the 100-plus heat. After cursing at the car and Enterprise's roadside service, I realized I had simply run out of gas, the first time I'd ever done that.

Once I was done being pissed at myself, I got out of the car prepared to walk miles to the nearest gas station. The very next second, a car stopped on the other side of the freeway on-ramp and asked if I needed help. Dan said he usually didn't pick up strangers because you never know about people, but he did it because that's what Jesus would've wanted. He even refused my money when I tried to thank him for his time and trouble. He said helping was just the Christian thing to do.

I was grateful, but bummed there was no way I was going to reach the gym in time. I rescheduled Destruction for Thursday and made my way to St. Charles, trying not to focus on the wasted day. I settled in at the hotel and did some writing, then dug into *The Power of Now* by Eckhart Tolle. Johnny Campbell from Massachusetts had said it might help me stay positive.

The next morning I went to Saint Charles MMA and met head coach Mike Rogers, who invited me to take the jiu jitsu class. I enjoyed talking with Mike, as we were the same age, both bigger guys, and had fought around the same time. The big difference was that Mike was much better suited for the sport. The Rodrigo Vaghi BJJ black belt had been an All-American wrestler in college and a two-time Golden Gloves boxing champion who won his first 10 MMA fights. After class, we talked about what I hoped to accomplish with my study. Mike told me to show up that night for the pro practice and he'd take care of the rest.

The team was warming up when I arrived. I expected to take photos during training and catch a few interviews at the end, but Mike had already explained to the team that the interview was part of the day's session. No one complained, probably due to the heat and high-intensity wrestling practice they were about to endure.

To fit in as many fighters as possible, I kept the interviews under 20 minutes. It didn't take me long to realize I'd underestimated the caliber of fighters I'd find in the Midwest. I spoke with Lance Benoist, a UFC fighter who had recently lost his twin brother in a tragic car accident; Matt Ricehouse, a Strikeforce fighter who talked about sacrifice and dedication;

decorated collegiate wrestlers and roommates Alp Ozkilic and Josh Sampo, who talked about how the sport had shaped them and would help them reach the UFC; Andrew Sanchez, another college wrestler who discussed how much both wrestling and MMA have changed him; Ashley Cummins, a college soccer player turned police officer and Invicta fighter, who echoed Ashlee Evans-Smith's statement that MMA was the toughest sport and that as a competitive person she'd always set the toughest goals.

My hundredth interview was Zach Freeman, an extremely competitive 28-year-old who'd begun his martial arts journey with wrestling at the age of 6. Just like Alp, Josh, Andrew, and Coach Rogers, Zach reinforced my beliefs about what wrestling can do for a person, both mentally and physically. "I liked soccer, I liked baseball, I liked football," Zach said. "You name it, I played it. I did bowling, I did golf, I did a ton of sports, except basketball, but the reason I loved wrestling is because whenever I would lose, there was no one I could blame but myself. I had to accept responsibility 100 percent myself. If you play baseball and you hit a homerun and a triple and your team loses, it's kind of hard to swallow. When you wrestle and you lose, it's easier to swallow because you know the only person you can blame it on is yourself."

The tall, lean lightweight wrestled until his senior year of high school, which he missed due to an injury that required 12 surgeries on his leg and 6 months in the hospital. This ruined Zach's dream of wrestling for the colleges that had already shown interest, and he ended up going to a junior college that didn't even have a wrestling program.

Zach seemed incredibly calm, collected, and very much a gentleman, so I was surprised when he mentioned he had plenty of fighting experience on the street. I knew the martial arts changed people, but I had trouble imagining Zach wanting to fight outside the cage. I wondered even more as I looked at the fight banner he stood in front of that proudly displayed his nickname, The Altar Boy.

"I never went looking for trouble," Zach said. Everything started when he dated a girl in high school who failed to mention she had a boyfriend. Zach avoided the confrontation for over a year, but the much bigger guy finally tracked him down. A strong wrestler and natural athlete, Zach beat the guy up and earned the reputation of being tough. Zach didn't want the reputation or all the challenges it brought, guys always trying to fight him to prove they were tougher. It got so bad, Zach was scared to go places.

That fear was well founded. Even though Zach wasn't the instigator, a fight he had at 19 landed him in jail and threw him off the college course. As a last-ditch effort to get his life back on track, Zach listened to a friend who said he should at least make some money off fighting. At his first MMA practice, and with no training, Zach tapped an experienced pro fighter 5 times. This gave Zach all the confidence he needed and he began training and looking for a fight. Zach smiled when he told me how at a local event he watched a nice young man have a very tough fight. Even though the guy had six fights under his belt, Zach politely asked him if he'd like to fight and they met 3 weeks later.

Zach thought about what he'd just said and laughed a little. "I do sometimes ask myself what am I doing."

That was the question I and so many other fighters were unable to answer. I asked Zach if he knew why he was fighting.

Part of it was because he missed the "competitive edge" in his life and he enjoyed the UFC, but there was a bigger, more powerful, reason. It was a spiritual conviction. Zach said. "I feel it's something I don't really have a choice over. It's what I've been given; it's the hand I've been dealt."

Zach continued. "When I do fight, I feel closer to God. When I walk out to the cage, I'm praying for the safety of me and my opponent, I'm praying that I perform to the best of my ability, not to win or anything like that."

Just as Jason Manly had explained, Zach saw no conflict between Christianity and MMA. He said, "I completely do fighting out of love, not anger. It's a passion I have for competition and the sport." He said, "I feel like I'm doing what I am supposed to be doing."

Zach's undefeated record makes that hard to argue with. In the 2 years Zach had been fighting, he finished all but one of his 4 amateur and 5 pro fights in the first round; one he won in the second. Very humble, he attributed his success to a little bit of luck, timing, circumstance, and his natural killer instinct when he goes for finishes and not points.

In just another 9 days, Zach would be once again testing his skills in the cage. He discussed the stew of emotions leading up to the fight, acknowledging it can be extremely scary, but also exhilarating. "Any time you are afraid of something and you beat it, there's nothing better than that feeling. People find that feeling every day. I found mine fighting."

I left Saint Charles MMA incredibly inspired, marveling at how much my opinion had changed about both MMA and the people involved. Although many of the fighters had a good deal of aggression inside, they were some of the most gentle and compassionate people I'd ever met. MMA was a sport and they were athletes. It had simply been my beliefs, and perhaps a distorted media, that had me looking at things from a skewed perspective.

CHAPTER NINE

July 23, 2012

It was Monday morning and I was in Little Rock, AR, halfway through my trip around the Midwest. In the 4 days since St. Charles MMA, I'd spent more time in my car than at gyms, did very little training, and I was getting anxious for the trip to be over. My visit to Destruction MMA and Memphis Judo and Jiu-Jitsu had been great, and I enjoyed interviewing Kenneth Degenhardt after watching him win at Rhino Fights in Nashville, but what I wanted was to fast forward to Sunday when I'd meet my family in the Lake of the Ozarks for a much-needed vacation.

All the wishing in the world wasn't going to change a thing. I'd finished reading *The Power of Now* and was changing my perspective, trying to stay positive. I reminded myself how fortunate I was to be doing what I was doing. I was also looking forward to visiting this next gym, Westside MMA, because I'd fought on the same SuperBrawl card 14 years before in El Paso with Matt Hamilton, one of the owners.

I parked in front of the huge building and met Matt, a BJJ black belt who had been the first Arkansan to compete at the prestigious Abu Dhabi Combat Club and one of the first in the state to fight in MMA. The Pink Leprechaun showed me around the 8,000 sq. ft. gym then took me to his office for the interview.

Matt, who has both history and psych degrees, was a real pleasure to talk with. He'd grown up the smallest kid in school and it was easy to picture him as the class comedian. I appreciated his very honest look at himself both in and out of the cage. "Man, I'm 130 some odd pounds, I have red hair, I fight in pink tights," Matt said. "I can't act like some sort of a bad ass. That's not me."

We talked about fighting back when the sport was called no holds barred and you weren't sure what to expect. He remembered his first fight, standing backstage, hearing his music, the curtain pulling open and the spotlight hitting him in the face for the first time in his life. Seeing a crowd of 2,000 people, half wanting him to lose, Matt said, "The way it felt then was kind of like the scene in *Gladiator* where the guy's pissing down his leg because you don't know what you're going into. But to even that out, you're young and dumb enough to not really care. But it was great, I wouldn't trade it for anything."

For the SuperBrawl we'd both fought on, Matt had shelled out the money to fly, while my team had rented a van and driven 10 hours from Los Angeles. All so we could each make about $400 or $500, minus all the expenses, and money not made because of taking days off work.

We touched on a lot of subjects and it was clear Matt had a good understanding of himself and why he fought. It'd been 2 years since his last fight and he didn't think there would be another. He wasn't concerned about that because he said whenever he has a bit of stress, he gets on the mat with the much younger, stronger, and faster students to rid it from his system. The bleeding, sweating, and grinding it out might make him feel like he's 58 for that short time, but it allows him to live the rest of his day feeling 28.

After our interview, Matt introduced me to Roli "The Crazy Cuban" Delgado, a 30-year-old BJJ black belt with a bushy beard and right hand in a cast thanks to breaking it in a fight 5 weeks before. A fight he had yet to be paid for.

The UFC veteran hadn't been a great athlete growing up in Philadelphia and had only been an average wrestler his first 2 years of high school. Roli was 15 when he and his mother moved to Little Rock and he was disappointed that there weren't any wrestling programs in the area. He did discover BJJ and his life began to change for the better as he became a more confident and focused young man. He loved training and 4 years later when a fight opportunity came up, Roli decided to test himself. He did this throughout his entire career, taking it one fight at a time, winning all 5 amateur bouts and going 11-6-1 as a pro.

Roli is a pretty conservative person, very analytical, and a bit more serious than Matt. Our talk covered MMA, shady promoters, healthy eating, libertarianism, and how football is way more barbaric than fighting. To Roli, MMA is simply a sport that allows a lot of expression, a way to showcase his set of skills. This was the second time he'd had surgery on his hand and although he hoped it wouldn't be the end of his career, he understood one more injury would be it. Knowing he has a lifetime of coaching ahead of him, and that he enjoys coaching even more than fighting, Roli said he'd be okay when he hangs up the gloves. But that day hadn't come yet, so he would give it his all before his fighting window closed.

When asked what kind of man he respected, Roli said good fathers like his friend Tony. Roli grew up with his father living in another state, which prevented a close relationship, but he learned from many of his fellow martial artists who had achieved the type of strong relationship Roli always desired. "The people that are selfless enough to put time into their families are the people I respect." Roli stressed that the most important thing to understand is that our children learn from our actions and not just our words. "What we say is one thing, but how we live is the instruction manual for our kids. It's important for my son to see how I treat his mother, communicate with other people, how I handle conflict. That's the blueprint for how he's going to live his life."

After the interview, Roli insisted on treating me to a delicious BBQ. We met back at 6 so I could snap photos of Roli teaching gi class with his cast, while Matt worked mitts with some fighters. With no excuse not to train, I jumped into the seven o'clock session. The class was difficult, but fortunately not too fast-paced, and I made it through thanks to my partner, Bobby Oller, pushing me along.

Bobby, a 30-year-old paratrooper who had served in both Iraq and Afghanistan, sat down with me after class to discuss why he was fighting. He had realistic goals and said he wasn't trying to be in the UFC. It was just a release for him, a much-needed therapy. The next fighter, T.J. Brown, the 22-year-old whom Matt and Roli had pointed out, had a much different mindset. T.J., who was 5-0 as an amateur, was planning to be a champion.

T.J., who had excelled at athletics his whole life, had recently given up college to focus on fighting. He'd become a father 9 months before and had already changed considerably, making better decisions to benefit his boy. T.J. didn't have a father growing up and he promised he was going to do everything in his power to make sure his son could never say that.

There were other interviewees that had children while actively fighting, but not many, maybe a dozen. I did remember Lew Polley's words, however, that he wasn't going to have kids yet because he had to focus on fighting. Lew knew they wouldn't get the attention they deserved.

I asked T.J. if that was going to be an issue for him. Was having a child going to take time and focus away from his sport, would it hurt his chances of becoming a champion? He shook his head and said, "Not at all. I'm just going to fight harder. This is how I can provide for him. I'm going to make him proud."

* * *

It was Wednesday morning and I'd just rolled into Oklahoma City. Tuesday had been rough with only 4 hours of sleep and 5 hours of driving in the blazing heat, but I wouldn't have changed a thing. Thanks to a recommendation from Bobby, Tuesday morning I had trained with and interviewed fighters at Inferno MMA, in Bentonville, AR, and then that night I dropped by The Factory MMA in Tulsa, OK, for an unannounced visit. The owner, UFC veteran Josh "The Beast" Bryant, welcomed me into the gym and shared his story. I was impressed by Josh, the number of fighters, and the level of training at The Factory, but what I most enjoyed watching was how nearly every adult on the mat, regardless of rank or fighter status, worked a round with the 9-year-old boy who trains with them.

Thanks to all the detours and changes in my schedule, I didn't have anything planned for Oklahoma City. I wanted to visit the American Top Team affiliate in town, but hadn't been able to get ahold of anyone. Their website said pro training was at eleven o'clock, so I figured I'd give it a shot.

It felt good to get out of the car after the 2-hour drive from Tulsa. I tried the gym's front door, but it was locked. I walked along the front and saw four guys wrapping their hands while they stretched, another man talking to them. I knocked on the window and the man met me at the door, said the gym was closed for pro training. Shit, Canada all over.

Before he could close the door, I gave him a rundown on my project and mentioned my visit to the ATT in Connecticut. He invited me inside and introduced himself as the head instructor, Giulliano Gallupi. Noticing the gloves and shin guards poking out of my bag, he looked me over and asked if I wanted to work out with the team. My neck was sore from grappling at Inferno, but it looked like these guys would be striking. I figured I'd be fine; they were probably going to drill technique.

Giulliano locked the door behind me and pointed out the restroom so I could change. When I came back out, the warm-up had begun. I jumped in behind the heavyweight and hoped I could keep up. My heart was pumping by the end of the warm-up, but I felt alright. Giulliano rotated me in on the mixture of striking and takedown drills, and I was reminded there was nothing I could do to stop these guys if I wanted to. Even the guys that were 80 pounds lighter than me.

Giulliano gave us a water break and told us to prepare to spar. Damn, I hadn't considered that. I didn't know how these guys worked and I had just strolled into their gym as a stranger. Because of my size, I had to keep in mind someone could consider me a threat. I was confident that by now everyone in the room could tell I wasn't a fighter, but I reminded each of them just to be safe.

We were told to start off at 30%. By the second round I realized that not everyone has the same understanding of what 30% sparring power means, especially a Brazilian who speaks very little English and is just days out from a fight. They all took it easy on me though, pulling punches and not dropping their kicks, toying with me like I was a little mouse. Giving just enough to let me know not to try anything crazy.

I was winded after a few rotations and said I needed to sit out to take photographs. I slipped off one glove and tried to keep my arm from shaking while I sucked in deep breaths. I'm sure it looked foolish trying to take photos with one hand, and the shots weren't going to be great, but there was no one else in the gym besides a young girl around 4 or 5 playing with toy dinosaurs. Plus, I needed a longer break, the camera only an excuse so I didn't look like I was wussing out.

I sat out one more round, then jumped back in for another beating. My body was going to be bruised and I could barely think, but it felt good to push myself. The gym usually closed right after practice, but Giulliano kept it open so I could interview Jonathan Gary, the lightweight who'd been taking it easy on me, exhibiting great control picking me apart without unleashing any power. I got permission to interview Jonathan from his daughter, the young girl playing with dinosaurs.

The 27-year-old lightweight, the youngest in his family, said life had been a little tough without his father in the picture. He stayed out of trouble because his mother kept him busy with band and a variety of sports, his favorite being soccer. He had dreams of playing in college, but couldn't afford it without a full scholarship.

Jonathan enlisted in the Navy to secure his education but had a hard time handling the freedom of being away from home. He began going down a bad path and was drinking a lot until a friend turned him on to Muay Thai while they were stationed in Japan. Jonathan took right to the training and found a new focus. His competitive drive and desire to be the best returned, and after testing himself with Muay Thai he began fighting in amateur Shooto, proud to go 8-1, something few Americans can claim.

Jonathan had spent the last 8 years living in Japan, fighting there and in Thailand, Korea, Hong Kong, Australia, and finally America. He said the sport that had taken him around the world was a test of heart, spirit, and mental toughness and had taught him how to be responsible and consistent. He was focused on his ninth pro fight, which was coming up the next month, but he said the most important thing was hanging out with his daughter. He looked over at her and smiled, his voice cracking when he told me he doesn't get to see her much. When he's deployed, he can be gone for 10 months out of the year; and when he is around, fighting cuts into their precious time.

He got choked up when he said, "A father will be there for their kid. They'll be a good role model. Maybe you can't be there all the time, but you really need to be there for them when they need you." He looked at his daughter as a tear rolled down his cheek. "I just want the best for her."

I got some lunch and checked into my hotel. All I wanted to do was crank the air conditioner and pass out on the bed, but I absolutely had to find a chiropractor. My neck was in bad shape and driving was difficult because I couldn't turn my head. But after a quick trip to Dr. Mills' office, I was put back in place and made my way to R1 MMA, the gym owned by UFC fighter Matt Grice.

The 31-year-old Oklahoma City police officer talked about his martial arts journey and how it began at 5 with wrestling. Although Matt was a well-rounded athlete who played a lot of sports, wrestling was always his focus. It taught him how to compete, to remain focused, to win.

While still in middle school, Matt saw the UFC and knew right then that he wanted to fight. He also knew wrestling's grueling schedule and constant grind would prepare him mentally and physically for MMA. Matt continued wrestling through high school and became a four-time state champ and the only person to win outstanding wrestler 3 times. Matt could have gone anywhere to wrestle but stayed close to home and went to the University of Oklahoma, earning a degree in sociology but having a disappointing time wrestling due to injuries on and off the mat.

The disappointments with wrestling only drove Matt closer to MMA. He would have started the sport much sooner, but he'd promised his parents he'd wait until he was finished with college. Matt began training 2 weeks before he graduated, and, as someone who would rather jump into anything with both feet, he had his first BJJ tournament the following weekend. The very next week, on the same day as his last college final, he drove down to Texas and entered the cage. He dominated the fight and was hooked. Over the next 7 years, while working as a police officer and married with children, Matt racked up 17 wins, his only four loses coming via the UFC.

When asked why he was fighting, Matt said, "I love to compete. If it wasn't MMA, it would be something else I'd want to be competing in. I love to compete and I love to challenge myself. Fighting just happens to be something that I'm good at and that I enjoy doing."

He continued. "All it is is a competition. I'm not necessarily trying to permanently hurt this guy, but for the time being I'm going to do what I need to do to win. I pray that God gives us both safety in the fight, and when we're done hopefully we can go hang out, have words, and be friends, but that 15 minutes we're in there, it's on. It's kill or be killed. I'd rather be the one doing the beating."

One of the things Matt loved about wrestling held true for MMA. "You learn your true character in a fight; whether you're going to push through or you're going to quit. There's no hiding. There's just you and another person out there, and if you haven't put in the work in the training camp, it's going to show," he said. "If you don't put the work in and do what you need to do, it's all you and you can't hide it. I love that about this sport."

Although Matt had spent his life competing and was just coming off a huge win in the UFC, something most fighters only dream of reaching, he said it wouldn't even be a consideration if he had to choose between fighting and his family. He described himself as loyal, honest, and a hard worker, but his family comes first and foremost in his life. The two best days of his life were when his kids were born healthy. Nothing else mattered.

Matt had the luxury of a stable career, and owning the gym would allow him to stop fighting if he wanted. But fighting is his passion and he's good at it, so he had to find the balance. Matt understood the importance of keeping his family and personal life in order and how it enabled him to be at his best in the cage. He had a great support system at home that allowed him to do what he needed to do.

Keeping everything in proper perspective entails sacrifice, something every fighter faces. For Matt it meant working graveyard at the station, hitting the gym, getting 4 or 5 hours of sleep, time with the kids, back to the gym, then back to work. With a smile, Matt said, "I never have free time."

I'd worked graveyard shifts at a Nevada prison and a juvenile probation center so I could fight, but I couldn't imagine trying that with kids. Matt told me the key was being present. He said, "A good father was someone that's always there for their kids; always makes time, even if he doesn't have time. That time doesn't count if you're watching TV or absorbed by your phone. You have to interact with them. Show them that they're special."

I completely agreed with Matt and called home on the drive back to the hotel. I told my wife and daughter I couldn't wait to see them on Sunday and asked Jen if there was any way she could join me for the Invicta fight in Kansas City Saturday night.

* * *

It was hard getting out of bed with just another 4 hours of sleep, but I was on the last leg of the trip. It was a 5-hour drive to Kansas City, but I broke it up with a stop at Laselva MMA in Wichita, KS. The head instructor and MMA fighter Marcio Navarro was also a full-time father who was raising his 7-month-old baby boy in the gym. He spoke of balancing fighting and family, then displayed it by holding his boy in his left hand while demonstrating correct punching technique with his right.

The break was inspiring, enough to get me through the rest of the drive. In Kansas City, I drove straight to Grindhouse MMA and took photos of their gi class. The energy of the gym was contagious and my neck was feeling much better from the adjustment, so I joined in the Muay Thai class that followed, struggling through the entire session. I wanted to crawl to my car and pass out, but there were some fighters available for interviews, including a couple of women. Female fighters were very rare and accounted for only 1 out of every 25 interviews.

One of the females, Jessica Philippus, would be making her pro debut in 2 days on the Invicta card. The tiny 29-year-old had started out as a ballerina, then a gymnast before she wrestled on a dare her freshman year in high school. The wrestling gave her a mental edge and kept her out of trouble. She said, "I would have been a crappier person had I not wrestled. It makes you dig deep."

The wrestling earned Jessica a scholarship, which she used to obtain a degree in exercise science. The lack of competition after college ate at her over the next 6 years, but it wasn't until she attended her first MMA fight that Jessica wanted to try it. Three months later she took her first fight against a seasoned fighter and lost in the second round. The loss was disappointing, but Jessica jumped back into the cage and won all 4 of her next amateur fights.

MMA was a way for Jessica to compete. "I don't do it because I want to hurt anybody," she said. "I don't do it because I have anger or animosity in my heart." She fought with the hope she could be a positive role model for other women, especially mothers. Her upcoming pro debut would be Jessica's second fight since having her second child 6 months before. She wanted to show that women could accomplish whatever they set their sights on, a lesson learned through wrestling, and that it didn't have to be all or nothing. She had her husband (who also fought and trained beside her), her children, and MMA. Each of those things would have her full attention; but on days like this leading up to a fight, she had to be a bit more selfish and rely on the support of family and friends.

Jessica had just finished a private workout and then the Muay Thai class. And she still had another 8 pounds to cut. "The next 24 hours of my life are going to be no food and water. That seems crazy to me," she said. "But when my busy thoughts stop, I hear in the back of my head, 'this is it, this is what you've been working for, this is the time.' I don't think there's anything in normal life that compares to anything like that. There's nothing that makes you dig that deep or push that hard. These next twenty-four hours are going to be horrible but it's just one whole day in the rest of my life."

Jessica was in a vulnerable place and showing who she really was. I said I could only imagine how difficult it must be, both physically and emotionally, to fight so soon after having a baby. Jessica clutched her chest and looked on the verge of tears. "Little babies, they do something to your heart, they make you soft," she said. "I feel like sometimes that's my weakness."

In her last fight, she punched her opponent to sleep, and saw the woman's eyes roll back in her head. "My heart dropped. I wasn't excited that I won. You can't take the mommy out of you; you just can't. I'm always trying to take care of somebody." She said, "One of the girls here calls me Mama Jessica because I'm always trying to take care of people. I'm very loving and I have a big heart."

I was back at Grindhouse 12 hours later for the MMA class taught by James Krause, who already had 27 fights by the age of 26. I was sore and considered just taking photos, but Joe Wooster, a MMA promoter, took over as photographer. I'm glad Joe was there because James was a great instructor and showed us some practical and efficient moves that even I could remember. It helped having a good partner, Brandon Cottrell, a Kansas City firefighter who'd played college basketball and semi-pro football before taking a shot at amateur MMA.

Most of class was spent slowly going over technique, so I was doing okay. When it was time to roll, Brandon and I stayed partners since we were the heaviest ones in the room. Nothing exciting happened between us, thanks to my ability to stalemate.

The owner of the gym, Brian Davidson, who I'd interviewed earlier that morning, asked if I'd like to roll. Brian was 36 and a hundred pounds lighter than me and had been in Tae Kwon Do since he was 9. In addition to fighting MMA for Strikeforce and Bellator, Brian still competed in TKD tournaments, had won four world championship titles and was consistently ranked in the top 10 in the world. I knew I wouldn't want to stand with him but figured with the size difference alone I would be safe on the ground.

Wrong. Ten seconds in and Brian had already passed my guard, secured side control, and completely dominated me. He was fast and had great pressure, flattening me out and keeping me on my back. I'd forgotten he was a BJJ black belt, an athlete, and a fighter who was competing to reach the UFC.

I thanked Brian for the lessons and for welcoming me at his gym. I appreciated his outlook on life and I could see why he was successful and fulfilled. He said it came down to having his priorities in order. "Outside of the gym, I'm a family man. One hundred percent." He said, "Then I'm a Christian, a martial artist, a businessman, and a coach."

Brian reminded me of Matt Grice when he talked about the quality of time he spends with his children. Performing as a mixed martial artist is just one of Brian's jobs, and he wouldn't be pursuing it or anything else that interfered with his top priority: his family. By continually putting them first, he in turn received their support, allowing him to fulfill himself on all levels.

After training, I interviewed James Krause and Brandon, the guy I'd been partnered with. Brandon was most proud that his boys look up to him and that he is a dedicated father. The fighting was a fun hobby, firefighting a career, but nothing was more important than being a good father.

I headed to my hotel trying to decide what to do next. The Invicta weigh-ins were the smart choice and easiest since they were in town, but I was also considering driving back to St. Charles so I could watch Zach Freeman, Josh Sampo, and Eric Irvin all fight for local promotion Rumble Time. The third option was driving the 3 hours to the Lake of the Ozarks and surprising my family, who were flying in from Los Angeles and would be there by nightfall.

Jen understood why it was important for me to stay on the road and had offered to meet me in Kansas City the following night for Invicta. I thought back to all the important lessons I'd learned on this trip, all the men I respected, not because they were fighters, but because they were fathers and had their priorities straight. The ones who put in the time with their families when they needed it. The ones who found the balance without letting anything suffer. The ones following their dreams and encouraging their children to do the same.

For someone who claims to take pride in being a good father, I had to admit I'd been lacking in that department. Over the last 3 months, I'd spent 7 weeks on the road, and no amount of rationalization changed that. My daughter is a trooper and understood at some level that I need to do my work, but still she didn't like it and my absence was affecting her. She'd been having nightmares I wasn't coming back. There was only one choice I could make.

I packed my bags and tallied up the last 9 days. Each day on the road I'd averaged 250 miles, 2 gyms, 4 interviews, half a workout, and 5 hours of sleep. I'd put in enough work. Now it was time for the reward.

CHAPTER TEN

August 15, 2012

It was Wednesday morning and I was headed to Kings MMA.
Besides a BJJ class the day before at Babalu's Iron Gym, my only MMA-
related activity in the two weeks since the Midwest trip was attending a UFC
with my wife. Besides babying my back and nursing my neck, I had been
spending most of my time with my daughter. Now it was time to refocus and
get ready for the upcoming trip to the Northwest.

I arrived early and took photos as BJJ black belt and 3-0 professional
MMA fighter Beneil Dariush taught a gi class. After class, Benny slipped off
his gi and began hitting mitts with Tyler Wombles, surprising me with his
swift and accurate hands. While Benny fired off combinations, pro and
amateur fighters began to stroll in. I congratulated Magno on his Samurai
victory. He pointed a finger to heaven, said he was blessed. We had half an
hour before the fighters would start training, so I sat down with Matt
Horwich, the first fighter I interviewed to have 50 fights, 15 more than the
second highest.

Matt's puffy Mohawk, beard, and red-tinted glasses set him apart
from the other fighters. As did his nickname: The Multiverse Surfing
Sabretooth Riverdolphin. Matt was a unique individual who didn't just think
outside the box; he lived outside it.

The 35-year-old described himself as being a shithead kid with
divorced parents that moved around a lot. It wasn't until he left home as a
teenager and got some real-life experience that he began to evolve. He was
17 and living on the streets of Seattle when he saw the UFC and decided he

wanted to fight. He moved to Torrance, CA, and worked odd jobs to train under Royce Gracie, still living on the street and partying as he alternated between his dreams of being a musician and a martial artist.

Although Matt had more cage experience than any other interviewee, was a UFC veteran, and had been an International Fight League (IFL) middleweight champ, the 10th Planet purple belt talked very little about fighting. He expressed gratitude and respect for Royce Gracie, Eddie Bravo, the guys at Team Quest, and everyone at Kings, but Matt said there were much more important things to talk about.

Quantum physics was one of the things more important to Matt than fighting. He described fascinating theories and philosophies. He loved to learn; art, history, science, it didn't matter what it was. When asked how long he'd been fighting, he said his concept of time wasn't that great because he was usually immersed in the moment.

Matt, who also likes to go by The Limit-Smasher, became excited as he described what a beautiful world we live in, how much there is to see. His goal was to learn what he could, share it, and make the most of it. He was an artistic freethinker, always seeking out new knowledge, and he thrived on the battle against himself, high on life whenever he broke a personal record.

Matt said he was just another person tapping into limitless potential and inspiring others. He compared himself to Evan Tanner and said he was more of an artist than a fighter. "Once you've found your dream it leads to new depths and new dreams to follow," Matt said. "We're all surfing this infinitely accelerated current of creativity, immersed in the experience."

It looked like the rest of the fighters were ready for practice so we wrapped up the interview. Matt asked if I'd be joining them. Instead of worrying about looking foolish and embarrassing myself, I decided to go with the flow. With all that positivity from Matt, I felt like I could accomplish anything. Plus, my buddy, Glenn, could take photos—no excuse there.

Master Rafael Cordeiro was out of town so Fernando Bettega, a BJJ black belt and pro MMA fighter, was teaching the class. Even without training recently, I was finally at a point where the warm-ups didn't crush me. Matt was closest to me in size and got stuck as my partner. We drilled technique for the first two thirds of class. I wasn't getting the moves down well enough to remember when I got home, but after the tenth repetition or so I had a decent understanding of what I should be doing. There were even occasional moments when I felt I'd nailed the technique, temporarily forgetting that the move only worked because Matt allowed it.

The buzzer sounded and Fernando told us to gear up for sparring. I got a drink and told Glenn I should just take pictures. He told me to stop being a sissy and get my shin guards on.

The team was ready for what they probably considered the best part of training. Benny was sweaty but didn't look like his earlier mitt session and the practice we just went through had affected him. Matt was bouncing up and down, repeating a positive phrase again and again. I had no idea how anyone could have so much energy. If I sat down I wouldn't get back up.

I waited while everyone else partnered up so I wouldn't feel as guilty wasting someone's round. There was just one guy left. He was a head shorter than me, but looked solid. I noticed his elbow pads and was grateful he didn't use them as we did little more than shadowbox.

The round ended and Fernando told us to pick up the intensity, grabbed me for his partner. Although he wasn't going very hard, he still beat me to every punch, touched me with repeated knees, took me down at will, mounted me, choked me, armbarred me with a couple variations. All in 5 minutes.

When it was time to switch partners, Matt bounced up and down and waved me over. I stuffed one takedown, but not the second. I tried to keep him in my guard, but he opened me up with light face shots, reminded me we're practicing MMA, not jiu jitsu. He passed my guard and mounted me and I couldn't do a thing. I wanted him off, for the punches to stop, but I had nothing left and covered my face, held out an arm, hoped he'd take it so I could get a few moments of air after I tapped. He continued to pepper my face just enough to let me know how utterly screwed I'd be in a real fight. I turtled up and he took my back, sunk in a choke.

I was exhausted but figured I could survive the next guy, a kid half my age who couldn't weigh more than 170 pounds. He had me on my back within 20 seconds, mounted in another 10. His pressure was just as heavy as Matt's, and I couldn't move. Whatever hope and false confidence I'd gained from recent workouts was blown away. People that have never matched themselves against another person like this might have a hard time understanding the hopelessness. This wasn't a blowout in football where I couldn't keep the other team from scoring. This wasn't basketball where my shot kept getting blocked. This was a physical contest where a teenage boy completely controlled me.

I was embarrassed and pissed at myself for not training, for listening to Glenn, for doing the stupid project. There was another round to go and I was relieved my partner was Jessica Martinez, who had a few amateur fights. Surely I could handle a woman. The round started and Jessica's jab split my gloves, knocked back my forehead. Again and again.

The round ended and I threw down my gloves. The team headed over to the heavy bags for two more rounds, but I called it quits. I couldn't remember the last time I felt that bad, physically wiped out and mentally broken.

The fighters went hard on the bags while I guzzled water. I set up my camera in the cage and interviewed Benny, Jessica, Fernando, and Tyler. I had trouble remembering my questions and concentrating on the interviews. My head was throbbing, and now that I had time to recover, I was even more upset at myself for all the days at home that I didn't do anything physical. No push-ups, pull-ups, squats, or even walks around the house. I knew I was going to be getting back into workouts, but didn't take the time to physically prepare.

I gathered my gear and headed home. Glenn's photos reminded me of Roli Delgado's description of what it's like to be a BJJ blue belt and go against someone with no training. "It's ridiculous," he said, "it's not even fun because it's like playing with a kid."

Well, now I was that kid. A 245-pound kid with a shaved head and tattoos, trying to look tough but really a soft out-of-shape man going through a midlife crisis. Either I needed to get serious with training or stop completely and focus on interviews. I had a week to decide before the next trip.

* * *

It was the following Wednesday morning, and I was on a peaceful two-hour drive from Portland, OR, to Olympia, WA. Thanks to the reality check at Kings, I hadn't missed a day of exercise and was eating a little better. Even though I had just turned 40, I felt better physically and mentally than I had in a long time.

Instead of destroying the evidence of me getting my ass kicked, I put the photos in a blog that Kirik shared on *The UnderGround*. The pictures were a testament to my laziness and lack of commitment. Even if I had been in great shape, I'd obviously have been destroyed by real fighters—trained, conditioned, mentally strong athletes—but my breaking point would've been pushed further back, and I could've been a better training partner.

Although most of my exercise had been basic, it had paid off and helped me get through a strength and conditioning session and a kickboxing class at Team Quest Gresham the night before. There were a few amateur fighters in the group I couldn't keep up with, but I was doing much better than I would have when I started in May.

There were only 2 guys in the large metal building that was Team Quest Olympia's home. The head coach, Brandon "Buzz" Alderman, a 27-year-old who had been victorious the month before in his ninth amateur fight, welcomed me inside and introduced Robbie Durant. Robbie was 10 years older than Brandon and 4 days out from his first amateur fight. Brandon explained that it was going to be a light workout, just the pair of them, more mental than anything else.

I was sore from the Gresham workouts and said an easy one was exactly what I needed. I joined them in shadowboxing and then walked through techniques, stepping out for a few seconds here and there to take photos.

Although Rob didn't have any fights yet, I wanted to hear his story. I was inspired by an older guy giving it a shot, and his commitment to this fight was remarkable. For the last couple of months, he'd been driving 200 miles round-trip to train at Olympia, and nearly double that the 2 months before when he trained at Gresham.

Rob credited training for saving his life and said Team Quest was a perfect fit and well worth the drive and cost. He had gotten to a bad place in his life and couldn't see a light in the darkness. The only thing he could do to better himself was to train. "There's a calmness in MMA for me," Rob said. "The gym satiates some of my demons and puts others to rest. When I leave the gym, I'm centered."

I asked how he felt about the fight, if there were any nerves. Rob shook his head. He had never been tested to this degree and was anxious to see how he would respond. He smiled and said, "I'm expecting to be cut loose."

After a powerful talk with Brandon about his 3 deployments to Iraq, PTSD, and MMA, I thanked them and headed north. This was my shortest trip yet, only 8 days total, so I wanted to fit in as much as possible. I stopped by West Coast Fight Team in Auburn, WA and interviewed 5 guys who had a total of 14 fights and only a single one of whom was still fighting.

Their coach, Reese Andy, a UFC veteran and accomplished wrestler, had plenty of experience and knowledge to pass on to them and he was a pleasure to talk with. When asked what kind of people he looked up to, Reese said, "A person that finishes what they started." If someone wanted to be a champion fighter or wrestler, he should be on the mat, committed to it.

His philosophy was to figure out what it is that you want to do, commit to it, and sooner or later it will happen.

I put away my gear as the team finished practice with a fun game of group dodgeball. Two hours later I rolled into Seattle, arriving just in time for fight team training at Salaverry's MMA. I introduced myself to Ivan Salaverry, a UFC veteran with nearly 2 dozen fights, who welcomed me to take photos. There were 10 or so fighters on the mat, so I squeezed into a corner with my camera and watched them get to work.

After only a few minutes, I was thanking myself for not having made the mistake of asking to train. Ivan was a drill sergeant, barking orders, pushing, demanding more from the men and women. He was smart with his instruction, using medicine balls for striking drills and requiring fighters to wear headgear during live drills, but I hadn't been around this kind of intensity in quite some time.

It was close to ten o'clock when training finished, and I was wiped out from the long day. I returned Friday, hoping I hadn't made a terrible mistake in asking to train with the team. My friend Brian Esquivel, who had been editing the interviews and was a huge MMA fan, had come along to take photos, but I worried about embarrassing myself like I had at Kings. Ivan was not the type of coach I'd ever ask for a break. With him it seemed like you better be either all in or all out.

The warm-up was thorough and woke up my body. We put on all our equipment, the first time I'd worn headgear in 12 years. We worked dirty boxing smashed against the matted wall, reversing the position, and then moved on to the next partner. The round seemed like it would never end, but finally the headgear was put away. Half of us grabbed shields so we could drill a variety of kicks. If I aimed below the waist, I felt alright. After a couple of rounds and corrections from Ivan, there was a huge improvement and I felt some of the old snap, a nice pop when my shin slammed into the bag. I had a hard time keeping up because I was winded, but I probably averaged 7 decent kicks for every 10 Ivan called out.

I was relieved when Ivan said to put away the pads and shin gear and spread out on the mat. Andy Paves led a difficult core session, following it with stretching and cool down. Again, I couldn't do every repetition, but I got through it without too much cheating.

While the rest of the team hit the showers, I interviewed Andy, an unimposing 29-year-old Filipino who began fighting 3 years earlier when he began grad school, working towards becoming a clinical psychologist. On top of the stress of graduate school and work, he had the extra pressure of MMA and training under a tough instructor. A lot of people wouldn't perform under those circumstances, but Andy seemed to thrive. Like so many other fighters I'd talked with, Andy had learned he was capable of that because of a background in wrestling.

Andy had won all 4 of his amateur fights and was 4-1 as a pro. He credited his success to dedication, the trait that'd been ingrained in him by wrestling. Fighting was important to him, so he put in the work and didn't make excuses. Without neglecting any of his other responsibilities, he busted his ass to represent himself and Team Ivan to the best of his ability. He had dreamed of being on a big stage since he'd been a little kid, first baseball, then professional wrestling, but always as a high-level athlete. MMA was his chance to live that dream, feeding a part of his ego the other parts of his life didn't.

The next day we checked out Ivan's kids' class, and then drove to Portland for Rumble at the Roseland 65. There were 20 fights on the card, but Rob Durant was up early. I had seen how badly he wanted to win this fight, heard how much he'd sacrificed. I also knew there was a good chance the 18-year-old standing across from him had been just as dedicated, just as prepared. Robbie was twice as old as his opponent, but didn't look it. The bell rang and Rob was unleashed, shooting across the cage and overwhelming his opponent, finishing him with a TKO halfway through the first round.

Brian and I didn't know any of the other fighters, so it was easy to sit back and enjoy. I thought back to what Ryan Couture had said about watching the local fights here in Oregon. That was the first time Ryan wondered whether he could compete with the guys in the cage. I found myself thinking the same thing. A couple of fighters were obviously unprepared and out of shape, some rusty or lacking skill. I thought maybe I would do okay against them if I got enough training. Maybe fighting again wasn't completely out of the question. I hated myself for thinking something so ridiculous. I knew I had absolutely nothing to gain by fighting. But I couldn't deny the thought was there.

* * *

Monday afternoon I was back at Team Quest Gresham with Brian along to help with photos and videos. That morning we'd stopped by Alive MMA in Portland and gotten in 4 interviews, but now it was time to train. Making it through Friday night's practice at Salaverry's had given me the confidence that I could make it through any practice if I pushed myself. Plus, I'd see another side of the fighters I had already interviewed, and I didn't want to miss the opportunity to train under Matt Lindland, an accomplished UFC veteran and Olympic wrestler.

There were 5 fighters, 2 of them heavyweights who I rotated in with. The first part of the session focused on takedowns, the next on submissions, everything technical, drilling again and again until even I had the move down.

When it was time to go live, my confidence was up. I wouldn't be shooting in for any takedowns, but I was hopeful I'd stay on my feet. The first round was with Jacob Mitchell, a 21-year-old college wrestler who had just won his second amateur fight. At 6'2", 245 pounds, Jacob was practically the same size as me. This would be a great test; an indicator of how things would have turned out if I had fought on Saturday.

We locked horns and fought for position. A few seconds later, Jacob took my back and launched me. I slammed onto the mat and Jacob was on top of me, secured a shoulder lock from side control, and was back on his feet. We slapped hands and did it again, with a similar outcome. Takedown, position, submission, repeat. He was only 2-0 as an amateur, but would have murdered me had I stepped into the cage with him.

Next was Brandon Pitts, a 31-year-old heavyweight with football and wrestling experience. Although he'd just won his second professional fight a few weeks earlier, MMA was only an unexpected hobby, not a career. Still, Brandon was always serious on the mat, and he manhandled me just as Jacob had, helping me up each time because he could see I was hurting.

Next up was a welterweight I hadn't met. Even with the weight advantage, I couldn't take him down. I delayed his takedown for a while, but still ended up on my back.

Cody Isaacson, a thin amateur fighter followed. We were on our feet, and he had me pressed against the wall. Cody dropped levels so quickly it was like he disappeared. He snatched my legs out from under me and slammed me down, the back of my head bouncing off the mat, everything going black for a second. Then Cody was on top of me, delivering light punches, putting on pressure until I opened up and tapped to an armbar.

The round ended and my head was killing me, but training wasn't over. Matt pointed out something he saw some of us doing incorrectly. He reviewed the technique and had us drill it. After that there was some conditioning carrying heavy dummies back and forth across the mat. My legs were jelly, and I'm not sure how I finished, but I was relieved when it was through.

I pounded some aspirin and asked Matt if he could do an interview. Normally he'd be headed home to his family, but he was incredibly generous and spent an hour talking with me about politics, parenting, wrestling, and MMA.

Matt had been involved in extreme sports since he was a kid. He loved racing dirt bikes and being an equestrian athlete doing endurance runs, steeple chases, and show jumping. He said, "I did anything where I could put myself in danger."

Although Matt started wrestling relatively late at the age of 15, he took right to the sport, dominating at the community college level before winning a Big 8 title at the University of Nebraska. Matt began coaching after graduation and trained out of the Olympic Training Center. After making the 1997 World Team in wrestling, Matt jumped into MMA, which he'd been wanting to do for several years. Although he launched his career without any real training, he won 3 fights in the first round, no easy task, especially since one of those rounds lasted more than 22 minutes.

Even though he had success and enjoyed fighting, Matt understood that the level of commitment needed to excel in MMA would interfere with his wrestling. He postponed his fight career and rededicated himself to wrestling, his efforts paying off when he earned the silver medal in the 2000 Summer Olympics Greco-Roman wrestling.

After realizing his wrestling goal, Matt co-founded Team Quest and 2 months later he was back in the cage, jumping right into the UFC where he fought a dozen times. When asked about his mindset in the cage, Matt said it varied moment to moment, but his main goal was to inflict as much damage as he could.

He described himself as a simple man who had been married 22 years to a loving wife and had 2 wonderful kids. He'd been blessed to do what he wanted to do, coaching fighters and wrestlers, helping regular people and young kids gain confidence and self-esteem. He knew what he wanted to do with his life, he committed to making those things appear, and now he was reaping the rewards.

We discussed how the martial arts can change people, and I appreciated his take on what kind of individuals will stay with training. "People either go one of two ways. They either just quit because it's too hard and they've already built that pattern or you see guys that recognize the challenge and they're willing to work through it."

Speaking of the fitness class that I had taken on Friday, Matt said, "Guys will take classes like that which help build their fortitude, their mental toughness. Every day you could push a little harder, just like at the end of practice today. It was getting tough and guys were starting to slow down."

Looking right at me, he said, "You know what, you were getting uncomfortable. Good. It's okay to be uncomfortable and push past that uncomfortable part of training." Matt said, "If we stop every time we're uncomfortable we aren't going to improve, not take it to the next level."

I hadn't heard it described this way, but it made complete sense. Matt said, "You have to constantly push that comfort zone farther and farther away and work through it. That's the best place to be, is the uncomfortable area. Be comfortable being uncomfortable, no matter where you're at." Applying it to life, Matt said, "If you're comfortable in every situation, then you're not challenging yourself."

I thanked Matt for his time, for the reminder to be present in whatever I was doing, for pushing me past my old breaking point. All the things that had been far outside of my comfort zone before the project were no longer as hard. I could walk up to strangers and ask them for an interview, take my beatings in class, fight through that feeling of helplessness. I was a better man because of it.

But now I needed to take a shower and do something about my throbbing head. I had no doubt that slam on the mat had given me a decent concussion.

The next morning I tried to get out of bed, but my upper back and neck were on fire. I took a deep breath and tried again, but the pain was too much. Brian got me some Advil and I fired off messages to fighters looking for help. One of them directed me to Wilsonville Chiropractic to see Dr. Dale Johnston who helps a bunch of the Quest guys.

By the time I left Dr. Johnston's office I could turn my head every direction, just not very far. I played it safe and asked Brian to drive us to nearby Tualatin to visit another Team Quest gym.

I didn't know much about the head instructor, Scott McQuary, other than that he was the coach of popular UFC fighter Chael Sonnen and had been working with Yushin Okami from Japan. When we walked in, Scott was in the middle of coaching a small kids' class. It was obvious that he was enjoying himself and getting satisfaction from teaching. It held true for his next class, which had 1 or 2 young fighters and several members who were there just to train.

I interviewed 3 amateur fighters and a 2-0 pro while Scott finished the class. We still had half an hour before the fight team practice, so we went into Scott's office where he shared his story.

Scott had the desire to be an athlete from a young age, but in 1969, when he was 8, he had major heart surgery. He had a lot of complications growing up, and he was told he couldn't do anything active or he'd die. Once kids found out that Scott couldn't defend himself, they began to pick on him. His parents enrolled him in martial arts, and it'd been his way of life since.

Scott talked about his reasons for fighting and the fact that now so many young kids come in with money on their mind. "A lot of these guys are under the illusion that they're going to make a lot of money at this. The reality is very few people make enough money to even pay their gym dues." He also saw a lot of guys who wanted a pro card for bragging rights, some who wanted to prove something to themselves, and finally a few who were real martial artists and wanted to test their skills. If the fighter didn't have a burning desire to reach their full potential, Scott said they couldn't be successful.

Scott also touched on promoters not caring about fighters, and how it was the responsibility of coaches and managers to guide fighters and make sure they weren't too brave for their own good. He assured me that his gym had a family atmosphere and wasn't dog-eat-dog with animosity among fighters. If I wanted to give the practice a shot, I was more than welcome to join them.

Having watched him coach, listened to the fighters he respected, and understanding how much he valued honor and integrity, I knew I could trust Scott. I told him about my neck issue and how it felt like I'd been in a car accident. He said not to worry and to go at my own pace, sit out if I needed.

It would have been easy just to shoot photos with Brian, but I embraced how uncomfortable I felt, stepping onto the mat at a new gym, not knowing what to expect. We started with light shadowboxing and then worked with a partner. Scott started me in the cage with a muscle-bound monster, his legs as big as my waist. We worked well together and I moved on to the giant 6'6", 400-pound biker, who was preparing for his first MMA match. By the end of the fourth round, I was warmed up, my neck feeling surprisingly well for all the light jabs and hooks that were knocking my head around.

Next was the real work, a two-on-one drill where you fire off a combination on the mitts while the guy next to the mitt holder unexpectedly shoots in on you for the takedown. My wrestling was weak and I was partnered against that monster. No way could I shoot a double leg on him. But Scott was watching, so I tried and got stuffed. It was close though. I got up and tried again.

It felt great throwing combinations, awkward holding the mitts, surprising when I stuffed a takedown, unbelievable when I landed my own. I was exhausted and wanted to quit, but I used the slogan on the back of Scott's Team Quest shirt to motivate me: Pain is merely weakness leaving the body. I finished the workout, and for the first time since I started this project, I wasn't embarrassed joining the circle of fighters putting their hands together to wrap up the workout.

I'd only shared 90 minutes on the mat, but I'd pushed myself as hard as I could, overcome lots of the mental weakness that made me want to sit on the sidelines. I felt like I'd earned this.

Brian and I headed back to the hotel and discussed the trip. Although he was a much bigger fan of MMA than I ever was, it had been his first time seeing this side of the fighters. It only made him more of a fan, gave him a look at those that were successful in the sport and those that never would be.

There are countless reasons why guys like me wouldn't pan out in the sport, but one of the biggest is commitment. In anything in life, a person's level of commitment is a huge predictor of success. I didn't dedicate myself to the sport and was a hobbyist, just like lots of the guys I talked with on this trip. Besides Matt Lindland, Andy Paves, and Reese Andy, only a handful of this trip's interviewees were committed to the fight game. The 9 guys with pro fights were 14-14, and several of the amateur fighters were fine with having just a few fights. Training and the occasional fight were giving them everything they needed. It kept them pushing their comfort zone and made them better for it.

Being committed doesn't guarantee success, but not being dedicated ensures failure. It was just a matter of figuring out what I wanted to do and committing to it.

CHAPTER ELEVEN

September 16, 2012

All the traveling I'd been doing was taking its toll on the family, so I had been focusing on Southern California, checking out nearby gyms and retracing my steps to get a better understanding of why I had fought. Thursday night I had visited Elite MMA in Westlake Village, interviewed 2 pro fighters and had a challenging no-gi jiu jitsu class. Now I was headed back there early Sunday morning to catch the pro training led by MMA legend, Bas "El Guapo" Rutten, my first MMA instructor.

Aside from catching Bas's television and movie appearances, I hadn't seen him in person since UFC 20 in Birmingham, AL, in 1999. I had been there to corner my teammate, Tony Petarra, who fought Wanderlai Silva. The highlight of the night was watching Bas's brutal 20-minute match against Kevin Randleman, which Bas won in a split decision, becoming the heavyweight champion.

It had been 14 years since I had trained with Bas, and that had only been for 6 months. I did not expect him to remember me at all. He couldn't recall my name, but I was shocked when he remembered I had been preparing to enter the military, something I'd nearly forgotten.

Back then I was 26 and only watched the UFC occasionally. My interest in NHB didn't develop until I took a defensive tactics class as part of my bodyguard training and was introduced to basic grappling. Because of my size, strength, and just a little bit of knowledge, I could neutralize my instructor, who had black belts in various arts. I wondered what I'd be capable of if I took training seriously and I figured it'd be the perfect way to get in shape and drop down to 215 so I could begin the Marine Corp's Officer Candidates School.

I signed up at the Beverly Hills Jiu Jitsu Club because they had MMA classes taught by UFC fighter Marco Ruas. I hadn't heard of the other instructor. All I knew about Bas was that he was from Holland and was the three-time king of Pancrase, a Japanese promotion that did not allow closed fist punches to the head. I imagined palm strikes as ineffective slaps and didn't think it sounded like a real fight. That changed after I took a "soft" strike to the chest by Bas and could barely breathe.

Most students at the club only took BJJ, so the intense MMA classes were relatively small and only one of us had any real experience. Although both Marco and Bas recommended we also take gi classes, I had limited time as I was working 50 hours a week and the gym was an hour drive each way. After a handful of BJJ classes, I entered a tournament held at the school and lost on points, realizing that wasn't the experience I was looking for. I focused on MMA and began reading up on the sport, relished the opportunity to work alongside greats like Mark "The Specimen" Kerr, Oleg "The Russian Bear" Taktarov, and Marco's prodigy, Pedro Rizzo.

With a couple months of training just a few times a week, I decided to test myself. Bas and Marco knew I was nowhere near ready for competition, so I found a fight on my own and called a friend to corner me. I drove down to a rundown San Pedro nightclub, the cage taking up the dance floor. I'd agreed to the fight because strikes to the head were not allowed and I figured it'd be a great way to ease myself in, to see if this was really what I wanted to do. It wasn't for the money because I paid to fight, my $50 going towards a winner-take-all tournament that didn't take place. I was the only one who showed up to fight the promoter's 300-pound prospect, neither of us doing much during the 8-minute match. I felt I had done more than enough to win but wasn't surprised when the decision went to their guy.

The experience was far more exciting than getting jerked around in the jiu jitsu competition, but again I wanted more. I increased my training over the next few weeks and fought alongside 3 of my teammates at a Larry Landless Submission Wrestling Tournament that used Pancrase rules. As the heaviest guy on the card, I went last, feeling brave with Bas in my corner. I was matched against a much lighter, but more skilled opponent, and we went the whole 8 minutes, fighting to a draw.

The fight had been fun and the adrenaline rush was addictive, but I wasn't satisfied with my performance and didn't like being restricted to what was allowed. It was a good warm-up, though, for the following weekend when I was to be the main event at Extreme Shoot against Jason Fairn who had been fighting 4 years and had already been in the UFC. I'd always been an introvert, the guy who'd keep his back to the wall in every social setting, but now I was the center of attention in the packed community college basketball gym, the music pounding, fans booing, cameras following me as I walked to the ring. My adrenaline surged as Bas held apart the ropes so I could duck through. I was excited, but not scared, no worries about any physical harm I might face.

I pitted my toughness against technique and landed a couple of heavy kicks and some punches, but not one came close to ending the fight. My conditioning was exposed a few minutes into the round, and when Jason took me down, there was no getting back up. That feeling of helplessness and frustration I'd felt at Kings was amplified 10 times as I was mounted. I blocked most of the punches, but a few solid ones landed, breaking my nose, blood flowing down my throat. Seven minutes in, unable to buck him off and completely spent, I gave my back and tapped to a rear-naked choke, a sign I had no business being in there. A humiliating 5-second clip made the local news that night.

But that had been a long time ago, and now it was time to get to work. There were only a few cars in the Elite MMA parking lot, the gym closed on Sunday except for the fight team training session. Bas unlocked the door and greeted me with a smile. His neck was in bad shape, and you could tell it hurt at times, but his smile rarely wavered. With his hosting job on MMA Live, his role in feature films, and his line of equipment, coaching, especially on a Sunday morning, wasn't something he needed to do. Bas was doing this because he enjoyed it.

Mike Jasper, the 5-0 pro fighter I'd interviewed on Thursday, and 4 amateurs made up the class. After a light warm-up, Bas began shouting out numbers, the team rattling off punches. I tried to make sense and follow along, but I was lost, throwing jabs and crosses to keep busy, trying to hide I was winded.

After warm-ups, we worked technique, dirty boxing, and reversals off the wall, followed by striking combinations. Throughout the class I was flooded with memories, reminded why I enjoyed training under Bas. It wasn't because he was a pioneer of MMA and considered one of the greatest martial artists ever with 22 wins in a row. Bas was a legitimately great guy, and it was obvious all the fame hadn't changed him a bit. He was still the same funny, positive, inspiring person he'd been back when he was fighting, and he still pushed his students past their limits.

* * *

It was Sunday morning, 2 weeks later, and I was heading to Valeriu MMA, a small gym a few miles from my house. Thanks to some eye-opening workouts taught by Jared Carlsten at 10th Planet Jiu Jitsu Burbank, I was enjoying the ground game more than ever and was anxious for the open mat roll.

There were only 6 of us, but that was plenty. I matched up okay against the 2-1 amateur heavyweight, but was completely controlled by BJJ black belt and MMA fighter Joe Camacho. Despite having 5 inches and 80 pounds on him, I couldn't do a thing and was submitted several times.

Joe and I were the same age and had grown up about 10 miles apart. We hadn't fought on any of the same cards, but I knew his name and reputation. He was tough as nails and would fight anyone; he practically had with his 35 documented fights plus many more there were no records of.

Joe had been raised by his single mother in a rough area of East Los Angles. Even though he was one of the smaller kids, Joe was an athlete who was usually one of the better players on his baseball and football teams. Although Joe took Tae Kwon Do for a short stint, it was the traditional sports that kept Joe out of trouble and pushed him towards bettering himself.

When the UFC came out in 1993, Joe and I had similar reactions to it. Having been raised on action movies, both of us were fans of Jean Claude Van Damme's *Kickboxer* which gave us the sense that Muay Thai was the most powerful martial art. With the early UFC's pitting style against style, Joe and I expected to see the kickboxers besting the competition. Obviously that wasn't the case, the effectiveness of BJJ undeniable. While I went on and focused on college football, Joe went to Larry Landless' gym to learn submission grappling.

Joe had been fascinated by the UFC, but he thought guys were crazy to fight bare-fisted with very few rules; never imagining it was something he would want to do. He began training BJJ in 1996, and it wasn't long before he was competing in tournaments and winning medals. Joe's instructor asked if he would like to fight in a local eight-man NHB tournament. There wouldn't be any money, only bragging rights. Joe was unsure of his ability but figured if his instructor had faith in him then he should do it. It would be an honor to represent his school. Joe represented far better than he imagined, winning all three of his fights by knockout.

When offered $200 for the next fight, Joe jumped on it. Again, representing his school was the main reason, the money just a small bonus. Now that he knew what could happen in a fight, Joe was a little more nervous, and performing in front of a larger crowd only added to the anxiety. Joe lost the fight, but he loved the experience and was more motivated to train hard and get back in the cage to avenge the loss.

Fighting was something Joe did for fun. To represent his art. To represent his school and his instructor.

Joe never imagined NHB could be a career because there was no money in fighting, it was rarely televised, and, in many places, illegal. He fought anyone he could, picking the toughest opponents.

The sport changed for Joe when fight results began being documented. Suddenly people were concerned with losses. Coaches, managers, and cautious fighters picked easy opponents. Joe's record had stayed at about 50% throughout his career, which stopped him from getting into UFC. His dream of being a champion would only be realized by the couple of championships he had in smaller organizations.

I hadn't run into many guys like Joe, and doubted there were many left like him. He'd started fighting in '97 and was still going strong, planning on having his retirement fight at 40 in a few months for Bellator. Lots of guys like me who develop a losing record early on don't stick around. Not only are the dreams of making decent money washed away, but MMA is a tough sport where fighters often spend more money fighting than they make. There comes a time when it gets too hard to justify the selfish sport, and many decide they should get a real job.

Joe had a degree in graphic design, and said he could fall back into being that kind of artist whenever he desired. "I'm not in it for the money, I'm in it for the sport," Joe said. "I continue fighting because I'm an instructor. If I'm going to send my fighters to battle, I have to be at the forefront with them. I have to represent for them."

There was that word he kept going back to: represent.

Joe wanted to prove that BJJ as a whole, and his instructor's style, were effective. I'd heard this from several fighters who trained at length in a martial art before fighting.

Although Joe felt a twinge of regret at not seeing his biggest dreams come true, it was great to hear how rewarding his decision to fight had been. Through MMA, Joe had traveled to Japan, Guam, and all over the United States. The martial arts had given him the ability to be an instructor and affect countless lives. Whether it was a fighter, an adult, a child, or a blind student, Joe loved seeing them evolve into better martial artists and people.

He'd met many quality individuals that had made him a better person. He felt like a father, a brother, a good friend to his students. By giving them his art and his knowledge and being a great role model, Joe had made a far bigger impact on the world than he would have done in graphic design.

Joe got a little emotional when he talked about another part of the reward, something I only experienced a couple times at small shows. He said that having people want to take a photo of him or have his autograph made him feel like it was all worth it. "Sometimes we go through our trials and tribulations in life and we beat ourselves up and kind of feel like a loser because we're not where we wanted to be when we set our goals five to ten years ago." The autographs made him feel like he accomplished something. He rolled his shoulders back and expanded his chest. "It's those little things that keep us up."

He said our interview had done the same. It lifted him up.

I thanked him. It had done the same for me.

* * *

I stayed in Southern California for all of October and spent a few days training with Fabiano Silva at American Top Team in Murrieta and Ian Harris at Systems Training Center in Hawthorne. I'd also learned that my wife was pregnant, leaving me with only eight more months to wrap things up.

My friend Brian recommended I check out Sityodtong LA in Pasadena to observe similarities and differences between kickboxers and MMA fighters. The gym, located just a couple miles from where I grew up, was only a few years old and much larger than I expected, complete with two rings, tons of heavy bags, and an MMA cage. Kru Walter "Sleeper" Michalowski, a respected trainer and accomplished Muay Thai fighter, introduced himself and explained that, just like their sister school I'd visited outside of Boston, they had both kickboxers and MMA fighters in the gym.

While the team wrapped their hands and geared up, I talked with Walter about his path and was surprised to hear that we had trained together at one point—the first time I'd tried a martial art. The summer I graduated from high school, I'd trained under Vut Kamnark, a small Thai fighter who had been coaching fighters in a garage just a few blocks from my house.

The memories of that sweltering hot room, the skin of my toes tearing off on the carpet, the mind-numbing deep bone bruises from banging shin to shin. Vut had been a tough, but likable coach who pushed us hard, showed me how to deaden the nerves in my leg by rubbing metal up and down, smacking them with sticks, then rubbing away the pain with a seemingly magical orange ointment. I remember walking home barefoot from practice with my little brother and bloodying the canvas heavy bag in my garage by refusing to wear gloves. I couldn't recall if I did any smokers or why I stopped training, but I knew that was the point in my life when I could no longer walk by a light post or tree and not want to kick it, a quick blast of pain to make me feel alive.

College football took me out of training, but Walter had only begun, moving to Sityodtong Thailand to learn from the elders. That journey changed his life and he's honored to carry their name, the pride shining through as he ran a disciplined class.

I took photos for the first half of the competition team's training then joined their workout, feeling pitiful hitting pads and always a second too late in the light sparring. After training, I interviewed three Muay Thai fighters, one of whom also fought amateur MMA. I didn't notice anything that set kickboxers apart from MMA fighters, but it made me question the effect of media, whether watching martial art movies and TV shows increased the odds of being involved in MMA, and how much it influenced which art someone would start with.

I was 180 interviews deep into the project, and although I hadn't asked all of them what they watched as a kid, the subject usually came up when they described their childhoods. There were guys like Kirik Jenness and Brian Davidson, whose admiration for Bruce Lee started their martial arts journey. I'd been 12 when *The Karate Kid* came out, a movie that sent thousands to local dojos. A good percentage of younger fighters, and practically everyone at Lauzon's MMA, had been huge professional wrestling fans that went straight into MMA.

The influence of media on fighters was interesting, especially when considering whether contact sports, mainly boxing and later MMA, were viewed in their households. But the visit made me think of John Johnston, a 41-year-old coach and fighter from Sityodtong, Boston, who I had interviewed on my second trip to the east coast. Just like Joe Camacho, a big part of the reason John fought was to represent.

I hadn't come across many MMA fighters who'd trained Muay Thai exclusively before switching to MMA, but John stood out. The 6'4" 260-pound giant had always been an athlete, playing football, baseball, hockey and other sports throughout his childhood. He also got into a lot of fights, so his parents enrolled him in karate, which he studied from age 11 to17, giving him the discipline he lacked.

As an adult, John was still interested in the martial arts and enjoyed watching the UFC, but he was focused on his business, a professional dog training school he opened in 1994. Then, in 2003 Mark DellaGrotte, the owner of Sityodtong and world-renowned trainer, brought his dog in. Soon after, John took private Muay Thai lessons with Mark and Kru Eric Armington. After 10 months of training, John said he wanted to fight, but it took 4 years to get one as most Muay Thai fighters are on the small side.

Shortly after John's first fight, Kru Eric died in a motorcycle accident, a tragedy that shook John. Eventually Kru Mark asked John to coach, and when John asked to fight in MMA, Mark said he wanted John as a trainer and not a fighter. After constant asking and proving his dedication in the gym, John got Mark's blessing and had his first fight in 2011. Because it had been such a long journey, John said he wasn't nervous at all for his first MMA fight, and it showed as the 40-year-old knocked his opponent out halfway through the first round.

"One of the main reasons I'm fighting is the passion I have for my camp and the sport itself," John said. "When I first started fighting Muay Thai, I wanted to represent Sityodtong. I wanted to represent Kru Mark and I wanted to represent Kru Eric." Kru Eric's death gave John more passion and desire to continue on. The man had put a lot of work into John, and as a token of remembrance John wears a black armband for his camps and fights.

"Even though you're not in the cage with your team, your team is always in there with you," John said. "Your team is what brought you to that point."

This desire to perform to his best ability to represent his team and instructors, coupled with his competiveness and dedication, transformed John into a person that would not quit. Before his second MMA fight started, John slipped on the wet mat and broke his ankle, but did not let them cancel the fight. He fought through the pain and KO'd the guy in the second round. Being 41 wasn't a factor and never an excuse. He'd fight until he no longer had the desire or until his body wouldn't allow him.

I had a feeling John would be at it for a while. Representing his art, his instructors, and his team, leading them into battle.

CHAPTER TWELVE

November 19, 2012

Monday morning, Brian and I headed down to Kings MMA. Over the last 2 weeks I had been pushing myself harder with sessions at American Top Team Murrieta and the Glendale Fight Club. I'd even taken my daughter to witness me get my butt kicked at Millennia MMA in Rancho Cucamonga. My body was holding together decently, and my recovery time was improving.

It'd been 3 months since Matt Horwich and the gang at Kings MMA had exposed me. Matt, who was 2 weeks away from a fight in Poland, was already on the mat stretching. Fernando Bettega was there, too, and I assumed he was teaching when he invited me to train. I threw on my gear and noticed UFC heavyweight Fabricio Werdum and veteran Renato "Babalu" Sobral had joined the warm-up, bringing us to an even dozen. After we'd run a few laps around the mat area, Master Rafael Cordeiro, a former fighter and considered one of the best trainers in MMA, walked in. When we broke to stretch, I introduced myself and thanked him for allowing me to train. He smiled and continued around the circle.

Cordeiro took us right into instruction, beginning with the basics. I partnered with Matt, starting off slow, working the jab, cross, and blocks. Every few minutes Cordeiro added a new move to the series, until we built up a solid eight-strike combination.

My punches and low kicks felt okay, but my head kick barely reached Matt's chest. Cordeiro adjusted my stance and everything flowed a little better. Even when I wasn't sure Cordeiro was watching, I found myself trying harder.

Thirty minutes later we grabbed kick shields and started with 10 right low kicks as powerfully as we could. My shin smacking into the pad felt good. We switched and I braced myself, taking 10 from Matt. Cordeiro added another kick, then another, 10 solid reps every time a kick was added to the combination. This went on for a solid 25 minutes before we were told to put away the shields and grab some water.

I could barely walk, but even though I was exhausted, I was also proud I'd made it through the workout. I didn't feel 40 when I was throwing the kicks.

Brian pointed out everyone else was putting on gear. Cordeiro told us to hurry; it was time to spar.

Oh shit. The last time I went against Matt it was a very humbling and miserable 5 minutes. All I had to do was make an excuse, say I had to leave. No one would have cared.

Brian shrugged his shoulders and said I should probably sit out if I was too tired. As much as I wanted to take his advice, the desire to save face was stronger. I slipped on my headgear and told Matt I'd give it a shot. Of course, Matt dominated me again the entire five minutes, but was careful pulling the power off his strikes. Then Cordeiro told me to go with Fabricio, the 6'4", 260-pound Brazilian with 22 fights, the last 2 being huge UFC victories.

I couldn't be disrespectful and say no, so I hoped for the best; maybe it'd be like my round with Matt, some light touches to let me know I was exposed. And maybe Fabricio wasn't that great on his feet. I hadn't watched many of his fights and supposed he was more of a jiu jitsu guy.

Cordeiro stood off to the side, focused on us. I tossed a soft jab because I wasn't about to escalate things. If I kept it light, maybe Fabricio would too.

Bam, bam, BAM! Two rapid jabs jacked back my head, and a brutal body shot dropped me to a knee. It had been 8 years since I'd experienced anything like that. This was real.

I got back to my feet, put my hands up, and bit down on my mouthpiece. I parried a jab, ate one, slipped another, but ducked too low. Fabricio grabbed hold of my neck, pulled me down, launched a knee right into my stomach, and backed away as I fell.

I realized I must have done a decent enough job on the shields because Cordeiro told me to go harder, obviously mistaking me for a fighter. I tried to move my head, to back Fabricio off with my jab, but I couldn't come close. He blinded me with his jab and blasted me with a right. Everything went black and I went down, reacquainted with the feeling of nearly being knocked out. I took a few seconds to shake it off, and then got to my feet and put my hands back up.

It had been a long time since I was in such a lopsided sparring session. Even at the Las Vegas Combat Club when I sparred with Frank Mir, I didn't feel this terrible. Frank always got the better of me, but I would give him a hard time for a minute here or there. Sparring against Fabricio reminded me of being thrown to the wolves when I moved to Vegas, with only a dozen rounds of boxing sparring under my belt before going against undefeated heavyweights with more than a dozen professional boxing matches. But even then I would hit back, land a couple of shots. With Fabricio I didn't dare throw anything hard because he'd kill me.

This went on for 5 minutes. I lost track of how many times I had to stop to get my bearings back, but I'd guess it was close to 10. Everything hurt, including my pride. I glanced over at Brian, whose eyes were wide. He mouthed the words "holy shit." Yep, it had been as bad as it felt.

The next round, I went against Jessica Martinez and recouped a little despite her repeatedly tagging me. When the buzzer sounded I hoped the training session was over, but there was one more. I thought Cordeiro was joking when he told me to get in the cage with Babalu. He wasn't.

Babalu isn't as big as Fabricio and a good 20 pounds lighter than me, but no one in their right mind would want to lock themselves in a cage with him: tattoos running up his neck, eyes that see right through you. The elbow pads were a sign that something bad was about to happen.

I acknowledged that old feeling as I walked across the mat. I was fucking scared. The 37-year-old held black belts in Muay Thai, Luta Livre, and BJJ, and was a three-time Brazilian National Wrestling champion. He'd been fighting since 1999, gone the distance against Fedor Emelianenko, won a decision against Robbie Lawler, and had twice as many fights as Fabricio, with 10 of them in the UFC.

With only a minute between rounds, there wasn't time to question Cordeiro or tell Babalu I had to go light. I reminded myself that the worst thing that could happen would be that I got knocked out. Not something I wanted to happen, but it wouldn't be the first time. I took a deep breath and entered the cage. The door clanged shut, the pin slid in place. Five more minutes. I just had to survive.

The buzzer sounded and Babalu lit me up with a four-strike combo. I snapped my jab, but he went right over it, cracked my head to the side. I didn't even see the inside kick to my thigh that took me off my feet.

I got up wanting to spit out my mouthpiece and explain why I shouldn't be in there, but a jab was already coming at me. I jabbed back, threw a tentative right hand he easily slipped. Babalu got both hands behind my neck, jerked me off balance and kneed my head. I fell to all fours.

I shook it off and looked up, hoped that Cordeiro, Babalu, Brian, anyone would say, "that's enough," and throw in the towel. Babalu motioned me to get up, his face showing frustration. I flashed to the fight that got him released from the UFC when he refused to release a choke because his opponent had earlier disrespected him. Was my playing fighter and wasting his round a sign of disrespect?

The round wasn't even halfway over. I forced myself up and tried to use the cage to keep distance. Babalu blasted my legs, inside and out. He hit

me with quick combos, dropped me at least 3 more times. I knew he wasn't
going 100%, but some of those shots felt pretty damn close.

The buzzer rang and I wobbled out of the cage. Even if Cordeiro
didn't end the practice, I was done. I felt nauseous and needed a second, but
pulled it together enough to stand and pretend to listen to his speech.

My head hurt and there was no way I could conduct an interview. I
barely knew what day it was, so Brian drove us back to my house. Getting
the crap kicked out of me wasn't something I ever wanted to experience
again. I was finally going to get back in shape as I had promised myself so
many times before. I told Brian I would run that night. Ten minutes later, I
told him to scratch that, I wasn't going to be walking, let alone running.

* * *

Two weeks later, I was driving 5 hours to Fresno, the start of the 11-
day trip. Originally, I'd planned to fly to the Bay Area, but Dan Bruce, a
college teammate of mine, told me I should stop in Fresno at Dethrone
MMA, co-owned by UFC fighter Josh Koscheck. I told Dan that Josh didn't
seem like the kind of guy I'd want to spend any time with. Dan said that
wasn't the case.

I arrived at Dethrone at the end of the Thursday afternoon workout
and met the bleached-blond curly-haired middleweight. Since that night's
class wasn't until seven o'clock and I had no plans, Josh invited me to his
house to hang out. I followed him to the gated community where his
beautiful five-bedroom house sits on a lake. Unlike many fighters that
reached his level, the 34-year-old Koscheck had been smart with his money.

Josh had spent nearly his entire career in the UFC, making a name
for himself as a contestant in the first season of The Ultimate Fighter. Over
the last 8 years he had won 15 of 21 matches, dropping 2 decisions against
Georges St-Pierre and most recently one against Johnny Hendricks.

I sat at the kitchen counter while Josh put together a healthy but
delicious lunch. We talked a bit, and I could barely detect the brashness that

rubbed a lot of people the wrong way. After lunch, Josh recovered from his workout with a short nap while I wrote in the living room.

It was late afternoon when I set up to record the interview, Josh relaxed and kicking back on his couch, a lit Christmas tree behind him. He talked about the grandparents who raised him, and how growing up biracial in an all-white area of Pennsylvania affected him. Wrestling from the age of 5 had kept him on a focused path and earned him a scholarship to Edinboro University of Pennsylvania, where he was a four-time All-American, something only a couple hundred people have accomplished. As Josh revealed himself, and explained why he had adopted the fighting persona that many despised, I came to a new level of respect for him. We decided we wouldn't release the footage, that the talk had already served its purpose. It was the perfect reminder that I should never judge.

The interview had taken longer than we had planned, and we rushed to the gym for the stand-up class. Josh, who had already changed, told me I'd better hurry as Jasper Tayaba, their Muay Thai instructor, didn't play around. I wrapped my hands as fast as I could and slipped on my gloves. There were 6 guys already shadowboxing in the ring, while the short Thai, on the outside ledge, pointed out bad habits. I pulled myself up and was ducking through the ropes when Jasper stopped me with a hand on my shoulder. He shook his head and said, "Only fighters allowed."

Jasper was 4'11", but his no-nonsense upturned face was ready for a challenge. He reminded me of my old instructor, Vut, whose powerful legs could chop down trees. I apologized and climbed down.

Josh laughed and told Jasper it was okay, that I was a writer. Jasper wasn't happy about it, and told me to stay out of the way. I climbed in and assured him that was my plan.

With the added pressure of Jasper just waiting to throw me out of the ring, I concentrated on my form, tried to emulate the movement around me. Thanks to the drilling at Kings, I held my own on the pads and didn't feel that far off ability-wise from a few of the amateur fighters. At the end of practice, Jasper said I did okay and should come back for sparring.

The next day I arrived at the gym early to interview Chris Honeycutt, who'd been wrestling since he was 4 and had recently graduated from Josh's alma mater as a two-time All-American. It was in the 11th grade that Chris first thought he might want to eventually fight, but he waited until sophomore year in college to make the decision. Having devoted most of his life to wrestling, Chris continued to give it his full attention and focus, figuring he'd have plenty of time to transition into MMA. He had already set his goal to become a champion, confident that wrestling gave him the determination and drive to achieve it.

After the interview, Chris and I got on our gear. Jasper eased us into sparring, Chris going with Josh and the experienced fighters while I went with the amateurs. I felt I had a decent workout and Jasper even made some positive comments. I used my size advantage when we sparred and hung in there. I felt good going into the last round, and appreciated it when Josh came over and said it was his turn.

It didn't take long to realize I'd made a mistake. Josh turned the intensity up a few notches, his technical skill precise and his strength surprisingly overwhelming. I tried to move around and keep away from his power, but he put it on me, not going hard with head shots, but letting me feel his pressure. My eyes tracked the clock, and I was relieved when it got down to 10 seconds. But then Josh jumped up and delivered the hardest kick across my thigh, a powerful thud that made me question if it could be broken.

I left the gym with a limp, my thigh already purple, and could barely walk the next day. Part of me wanted to call Josh a dick, but he'd given me a wake-up call. If I was going to be dumb enough to get in there with guys like him, Babalu, Fabricio Werdum, or any other fighter, I had to be prepared to face the consequences. If any of those guys wanted to, they could annihilate me at any moment. Josh just gave me a reminder to not be so reckless; a painful reminder that went off every time I took a step.

* * *

I rolled into Oakland, CA, late Sunday night, taking my time so I didn't accidentally turn down one of the streets Tim "The Bohemian" Lajcik had warned me about. Tim had offered to let me stay with him at his house, even though we'd only met once. That had been nearly 14 years ago, and we'd been locked in a cage for an underground fight in Los Angeles.

Tim dominated the match and I tapped at 7 minutes. We shook hands and went our separate ways, Tim fighting in the UFC and Pancrase events in Japan, while I moved to Vegas for a failed attempt at boxing.

And now there I was standing on the front porch of a guy I'd only exchanged a few emails with and a couple of sentences on the phone. Tim opened the door, just as massive as I remembered, boulders for shoulders, thick forearms, and a neck the size of my thigh. Absolutely nothing like the average 47-year-old.

Tim noticed my limp as he showed me around. He chuckled when I shared the story of the souvenir Josh had given me. We talked for a few hours, but rarely about fighting. If someone listened in for a few minutes, they'd never assume Tim was a fighter.

Not being stereotyped as a fighter, or anything else for that matter, was exactly what Tim wanted. As someone striving to realize his whole potential and not wanting to limit his experiences, Tim loathed labels. His speech was calm and deliberate, much softer than I'd heard from most men his size. He was aware that he shrinks down around people. "I don't want people to be afraid of me," Tim said. "I don't want people to listen to me because I'm imposing."

The gentle giant knew himself well, not surprising for a world traveler who lived most his life wandering in solitary, an introvert who spent a great deal of time in his own head. He said he was a curious mixture of good and bad, his interests varied and constantly evolving. Tim was a lover of words and was working to become a better writer. He'd challenged his shyness by working as an actor and a stunt man, which seemed appropriate since he'd been flinging himself at things for 4 decades.

The next day, Tim took me to lunch at one of his favorite spots, an Ethiopian restaurant near Berkeley. I was amazed Tim was a vegetarian, and had been for most of his life. At 6'1" and a solid 240 pounds, Tim was not the image that came to mind when I thought of vegetarians.

Waiting for our food, Tim took me back to when he was a cute little blond boy growing up with an older brother and sister in Thousand Oaks, CA. His father, a huge man, parented largely through intimidation and his mom, a nurse, worked long hours. Positive reinforcement was in scarce supply at home and the already-shy boy with a stuttering problem withdrew deeper, becoming a regular target for bullies. When people teased, pushed, or punched Tim, he would just stand there and take it, trying to hide the pain.

Tim would come home and escape in his comic books, studying them for clues on how to become a real man. On his wall next to the Superman poster, he had photos of Marvin Hagler and other great boxers of the era, guys he was drawn to for their toughness. He dreamed that one day he would be like them. One day he wouldn't be scared.

Very pragmatic, even in elementary school, Tim figured the best way to get better at fighting was to actually fight. He and another boy would meet every day after school and fight each other behind the gas station. They didn't have any kind of beef with each other, it was just something they did. This went on for an entire year, the gas station workers always watching and placing bets.

Although Tim was getting tougher physically, he was still bullied. In junior high, a bigger kid held a knife to his throat, and Tim was so scared he pissed his pants. The primal fear of being hurt by a predator flipped a switch for him. Tim said, "That whole notion of being afraid of people, of the physical violence, I lost that."

Being afraid wasn't the answer; he had to do something else. The next time Tim was bullied, he came unglued and beat up his attacker. It reinforced for him not to be prey and proved that when he faced his fears, the outcome was much better. "I'd been afraid in my life, and I sure didn't like it," Tim said. "I tried to always find ways not to be afraid. That's the defining characteristic for me."

Tim had been a decent athlete growing up, playing both soccer and basketball, but not doing that well in either. Wanting to be a man, but stuck in a small, 135-pound frame, Tim went out for football and wrestling in his freshman year in high school. He was awful at both, riding the bench and losing every match that first year.

That very first wrestling match was humiliating for Tim, wearing the polyester monkey suit, splayed on his back nearly the entire match, and trying desperately to survive. After the match his coach said, "You tried really hard out there, and if you keep that up, you'll be okay." The coach had probably said the same thing hundreds of other times, but because Tim was so desperate for positive feedback, especially in the face of failure, he held on to his coach's advice.

Tim said, "I desperately wanted to be good at something." The coach's words had given him hope. Even though he didn't know what to do to get better, Tim knew effort was required, something he was not afraid of, a noble inheritance he had acquired from his mom. He did things like walking to school carrying 60-pound buckets of tar, going a little farther every day without setting the buckets down. After he had gone the whole distance, he would add a strip of tape around the handle to make the grip a little bigger. The unorthodox training made him very strong for a kid his age, and when he saw improvement, it just fed that fire even more.

Wrestling was the best teacher in Tim's life, and it helped him understand that he hadn't been giving himself the best chance to win. He said he thought of himself as "a valiant loser." Because of his low self-esteem, Tim never really believed he would win, although he would try his best not to lose. Thanks to the ridiculous volume and intensity of his training, and the new positive outlook towards competition, Tim became a formidable athlete his senior year, an impact player on the football field and in the wrestling room.

Tim went on to play football and wrestle at the University of California, Davis. During his first year, he was mediocre, but over time he turned that around and became an All-American twice in wrestling and once in football. Even with this success, though, Tim didn't really appreciate it. It had been instilled in him early on that he could always do better. Disappointment at placing fifth in the country in wrestling his senior year made him not want to compete for a year, he was so afraid of losing.

Our food arrived, a massive plate of vegetables served on a giant sheet of injera. In between bites, I told Tim that although our childhoods were remarkably different, we shared many personality traits. I had always been painfully shy, terrible my first few years of football, the small kid obsessed with becoming tougher and stronger, and unable to be pleased with any performance.

I told Tim how it took a trip to a psychologist to point out that I was a perfectionist, a term I hadn't heard before. I'd learned that by setting unrealistic goals for ourselves, by demanding perfection, we ensured we could never be satisfied. I used to think it was a good trait, and chalked it up to being humble. Tim rationalized it by saying it helped him avoid being complacent, never settling for less than he could achieve. Both of us still needed to work on it.

On the way back to his house, Tim talked about being a Golden Gloves champion, coaching wrestling at Davis, and wrestling for the national team a number of years until 1992. When he missed the competition, he got talked into entering an MMA tournament, even though he thought the UFC was a spectacle, like 2 guys fighting in a liquor store parking lot.

"My intentions every time I got into a cage or ring was to end that thing as quickly as I could. I never felt angry or anything like that," Tim said. He told me that what he had to say next was embarrassing and something he would only admit around certain company. "I like to fight. I like testing myself against another man," he said. "I like the physicality of it. I like socking a guy. I try not to like it too much, but when I get hit, it gets my blood up. You're alive and you're in it. I relish that sensation."

He loved fighting because it stripped away everything and left him with the essential. In the hours immediately before or after a fight, Tim would have crystalline images or thoughts and write them down in poetry, a different type of art capturing something he loved.

I imagined it must be difficult to no longer fight since he had spent so much of his life around it, training fighters at local gyms, and presenting seminars around the world.

Tim said it was a hard thing to shake. He still sparred and hoped he could do it for a handful more years. He was haunted by the fact that he never made it to the top, and it bothered him that he didn't realize his potential as a fighter. Even at 47, Tim would get offers to fight, and had tried to make comebacks, but every time his body failed him. He would remind himself that he'd been a fighter his entire life, but it was time to do something else.

Springtime in Osaka

Spring rain falls on Osaka,
Wet concrete and cherry blossoms.
I lay naked on the hotel bed
     and wait…
     anxious sweat.

Tonight's fight approaches
Like my father's heavy footsteps
     outside my bedroom door
On one of those old angry nights.

Only this time
     I'll fight back.

Tim Lajcik

-Written March 31, 2001 in the late morning before fighting a Japanese fighter named Kengo Watanabe that night (won by first round knockout).

CHAPTER THIRTEEN

December 12, 2012

I arrived at American Kickboxing Academy (AKA) in San Jose an hour before fight team training. Javier Mendez, the founder and primary coach, greeted me at the front desk. In Fresno I had hung out with "Crazy" Bob Cook, who also managed some of the fighters and helped coach the team. Bob had already let Javier know I wanted to train and do interviews. Javier sized me up, asked me how hard I wanted to go.

Tim Lajcik and a couple others had warned me that the sparring at AKA was no joke. My right forearm was sore and the bruise across my right thigh was a subtle reminder that I could really get hurt if I continued being reckless. I told Javier I could only go light.

Javier's sly smile said I was smarter than I looked. We talked a bit about his life, how he'd gone from picking strawberries in the fields with his immigrant parents, to professional kickboxing, and then on to coaching one of the top MMA teams in the country. He shared his opinions on fighters, stating that most are very intellectual, especially the ones who are successful. He pointed to all the top-level wrestlers that transitioned beautifully into the sport, like AKA's Cain Velasquez, who was 2 weeks out from trying to reclaim his UFC heavyweight title from Junior Dos Santos, and Daniel Cormier, the current Strikeforce heavyweight champ.

"It (MMA) used to be more of a freak show, but now we have high-level athletes coming in from all disciplines and sports," Javier said. "Kids coming in young at 10, aspiring to be MMA fighters, not football or basketball players. Most kids used to become boxers out of poverty, not of a desire to fight."

I thanked Javier and thought about what he'd said as I explored the massive gym. Everything was clean and shiny, top-of-the-line, from the lounge to the giant pro shop to the photos of the team's successes covering the walls. This was a 27,000-square-foot, state-of-the-art health club that focused on producing better martial artists, not a ratty boxing gym with crummy equipment. Even if the fighters were making much more money, the percentage from their purses wouldn't support the gym. Like nearly every gym I visited, it was the everyday members that paid the bills and kept the doors open, with the kids' programs often being the life blood. I wondered how many of the kids that took classes at AKA idolized the fighters and already aspired to be just as tough, brave, and famous. How many of those kids' parents had those same goals for their children, and were paying for classes as an investment in the hope their kid could make millions?

I'd been to more than 5 dozen gyms, and none of them compared to AKA. Upstairs was the jiu jitsu room, weight training and cardio equipment, and a therapy room. The downstairs contained numerous matted rooms behind glass, racquetball courts that had been converted for contact. There was a cage in one, heavy bags in another, and one empty for wrestling. The hallway, lined with huge fight posters, led around to the back where other rooms held weights, a trampoline, a boxing ring, and various training gear for all aspects of the sport. In the middle of the facility was the colossal main training room, its upper walls ringed with larger–than-life posters of the individuals that helped form and cement AKA as one of the best gyms in the world.

It was a sparring day, so not a whole lot of talking was going on among the fighters. I warmed up with the team, about half of whom I recognized from TV. These guys were going hard from the very first round, not trying to knock each other out, but still something I had no business being a part of. Instead, I alternated between hitting the bag and shadowboxing, stopping every few minutes to snap photos.

I didn't notice Daniel Cormier until he walked up and asked if I'd like to go a round. I flashed back to Fabricio Werdum and told him I'd better not, that I wouldn't be any use to him. I was a writer, not a fighter. Daniel said not to sweat it, that he'd just finished some hard rounds in the other room with Cain and could use a little break.

Daniel kept it playful, sticking with stand-up, popping in and out and taking angles so I couldn't touch him. At the buzzer, he gave some pointers and then pushed me a little harder for a second round, again taking the time to help me when it was over.

Before I could get back to my camera, Josh Thomson offered a round. I'd seen more than half of his 25 fights and jumped at the chance. Cool like Cormier, Josh put just enough on his punches to make me want to stop eating so many.

All my retreating during the round had winded me, but Nate James, a middleweight fighter, wanted to work. Just like his teammates, Nate took it easy, landing shots, but not hurting me, his jab slipping through my gloves again and again.

At the end of the round, Nate showed me a few of the things I'd been doing wrong and how he'd been landing that jab. During the next round, Nate continued with the instruction, slowing down his jab so I could practice a parry. I thanked him and said he could help me even more by doing an interview. The 34-year-old Oklahoman liked the idea and met me in the weight room after showering.

Nate, whose stubble was the same length as his shaved head, had been an athlete all his life, competing in track and football, but focusing on wrestling. In high school, Nate was ranked fifth in the country, but back surgery in college ended dreams of being an All-American. He went on to earn his bachelor's degree in marketing, and began chasing money in sales before he stumbled upon MMA.

"Ever since I chose fighting as a career, my life has been so much happier," Nate said. "I feel at ease in any situation. I feel very happy, very fortunate, in a very good place." He'd been at AKA nearly 5 years and felt at home. "These guys only judge you on how hard you work."

Over the last 6 years, Nate had put together a respectable record of 13-8-1 fighting in Strikeforce and Bellator. It'd been more than a year since he'd been in the cage, and he knew he would have to reassess his situation fight by fight. Although Nate was confident in his skillset, he knew he might not realize his dream of becoming a world champion.

Nate, who was working towards his MBA in finances, talked about how much it took to be a professional fighter. "It's a lifestyle; it's your diet, financial position, relationship." Speaking to younger fighters, he stressed the importance of having a strong support system. "Have good friends and family around you, because it gets really hard. You're going to question what you're doing and why you're doing it. You're going to have a lot of conversations with God."

With all the superstars in the gym, Nate knew what it was like to be treated mainly as a sparring partner. He wasn't complaining, but he said that could've been avoided if he'd been smart early on and had the right trainers and training partners. He warned other fighters not to be like him and think they were tough enough to fight without paying for quality instructors.

After Nate's interview, I walked back out and saw Phil Baroni, a muscular welterweight, who had just sparred 15 minutes with Josh Thomson. Phil had a reputation for being difficult to deal with at times and could be very intimidating with his bodybuilder physique and dark scowl. The last thing Phil wanted to do after the brutal workout was to do an interview, but I mentioned a mutual friend and he agreed to it, plopping down against the wall, shirt off, veins popping on his biceps.

Whether it was how he identified himself or just part of being a performer, when I asked him his name and age, he said, "I'm the New York Bad Ass, Phil Baroni." The 36-year-old Long Island native played football and wrestled in high school, and did some amateur boxing and kickboxing, winning all 17 of his fights by KO. Phil wrestled all 5 years in college and earned his bachelor's degree. Frustrated that he hadn't accomplished his goal of becoming an Olympic hopeful, coupled with his desire to be a professional athlete and not wanting a 9-5 job, Phil saw the UFC and knew immediately that's what he wanted to do. As a wrestler, he'd often thought that he would be able to defeat his opponents if they could punch. MMA seemed perfect.

Phil had been fighting 12 years, 10 of those while living in Vegas. He'd been through his share of battles and was 15-15. Ten of his fights were in the UFC, but it'd been nearly 2 years since he was released by the organization. His last fight had been a big knockout win in the Philippines. The next was a few weeks away, New Year's Eve in Jordan.

When asked who he was outside the cage, Phil thought about it for a few seconds. "I don't know, dude. What you see is what you get. I've transformed into this guy that's always in the cage. Maybe back in the day I was different, but I've been doing this so long there's not much of a difference." He said maybe other guys flip a switch when they go home to their kids, but he doesn't have any children. With a slight smile, Phil said, "I have a bad temper and I'm a fighter in every sense."

Phil's longtime trainer in Vegas used to tell people he dealt with Phil by keeping him tired. "When I'm exhausted I don't have an itch to be in trouble or be a pain in the ass," Phil admitted. "I always find trouble when I'm not fighting. That's why I moved up here."

Phil compared his relationship with fighting to that of an addict and his drug. "Addicts can either have a really good high or a really bad low, but they're still crazy enough to take that drug. It's almost like that every time I sign up for a fight or go into the ring. I'm going to bust my ass for two months, sacrifice, miss out on a lot of things, starve myself, get my face punched in." All that effort to prepare for a 15-minute fight and a modest salary. And, like an addict, he still took that pill.

"Why I like to fight is because I've been doing it for so long. I don't know anything else really." Phil expressed a desire to be involved in some aspect of the sport when his fight career was over, maybe coaching or commentating, but he acknowledged he wasn't the most technical guy. "And I've taken so many shots over the years my speech and stuff isn't what it once was. It's not like it was when I was 26, 27. I've paid the price in a lot of ways."

I had noticed some slipups in Phil's speech and a tiny bit of stuttering, but he'd just finished sparring. He wasn't punchy and had carried on an intelligent conversation, but I understood what it felt like to no longer have the same control over speech and thoughts as I did in college. It was kind of sad seeing where he was in his life; hoping he'd have some big breaks, but afraid it'd be more of a slide in the wrong direction.

Just as with wrestling, Phil hadn't achieved the goals he had set for himself in MMA and wasn't ready to stop, even if that was financially possible. He talked about fighting for smaller organizations around the world and how it would be bittersweet if he could win at least one small championship. "Even though it wouldn't be the UFC, it'd be a little feather in the cap," Phil said. "At least I could say I accomplished something in my career."

* * *

My right forearm was next to useless the next morning, a sharp pain ripping through it if I tried to make a fist. Fortunately, Thursday was grappling and I would be able to get by. I got dressed to roll, but suddenly wasn't so sure it was a good idea to train when I realized all 20 guys had on their MMA gloves.

I stayed to the side and took photos while the team warmed up. The mood was much different from Wednesday's sparring, with Daniel Cormier cracking jokes and keeping things fun as they jogged around the room. I recognized most of the guys from the day before: Jon Fitch, Todd Duffee, and a handful of others who fought in the UFC, a good number of midlevel fighters, and quite a few who were at the start of their careers.

Denis Roberts, a tall Australian shrimping down the mat, was 1-0 as a pro and had given up a lot to pursue his passion. The 31-year-old, who had taught himself Japanese in 3 months so he could go to school in Japan on a wrestling scholarship, said things would have been much different if he'd stayed at his old job. "I could have had a house. I could have a very cushy life doing something a lot easier than what I am doing. And here I am scraping by. I love what I do, but every so often you have a thought, you're lying in bed, you're aching, you just got beat up in training. You ask yourself, 'What am I even doing here? Why did I choose this life?' I had this easy life that I could have coasted through, but I threw that away and now I'm going the hard route, and there's not a lot of payoff." He explained that those thoughts are few and far between and he really does enjoy MMA. He said it comes down to something he truly believes: "You got to do what you love."

Denis was smiling and seemed happy on the mat. Most of the guys appeared to be the same. Jiu jitsu was fun. They would train hard, but this was time to learn and perfect a craft that had pulled quite a few of them into the fight game.

One of the injured fighters watching practice agreed to take photos, so I no longer had an excuse not to train. We started with a half guard drill I hadn't done before, but I picked it up as my partner performed it on me. We rotated and Cain grabbed me as his partner for a quarter guard sweep. I didn't understand the movement, but Cain said it was no big deal and walked me through it.

Class got easier as I became more confident and stopped worrying about how little I knew. When it came time to roll, I got mopped up by a 5'4" amateur middleweight. For the second round, I went with Christian Wellisch, a heavyweight that I'd almost been matched up against 10 years before in Monterrey, Mexico, as the promoters of Octongono Extremo scrambled to finalize fights the day before the event. The Hungarian Nightmare had been out of MMA for 3 years since he'd been released after his fifth fight for the UFC. He now only trained occasionally, keeping it to rolling because of the risk of head trauma. Still strong and very technical, he played around with me, letting me attempt moves so he could work on defenses and sweeps.

By the end of the round, my forearm was throbbing as hard as my heart. I sat out the rest of class and took over camera duty as the fighters added punches to the grappling. After class Christian joined me in the lobby and shared his story. Both he and his brother had been physical kids in Hungary, learning boxing from their father, a little bit of Tae Kwon Do at an academy, and plenty of roughhousing emulating the WWF. The family moved to Austria when Christian was 12, and then 2 years later to the U.S. Christian made the transition fairly easily, his imposing size a deterrent against being bullied.

His parents encouraged him to play basketball because he was tall, but Christian never liked it. He also didn't like wrestling, the next sport they put him in. But Christian turned out to be a natural and did very well through high school, acquiring a love for the sport he dedicated so much of his life to. His only motivation for going to college was wrestling, and Christian dropped out when a shoulder dislocation kept him from competing. After a few years of unfulfilling work in the high-tech industry, Christian went to AKA and took jiu jitsu. It wasn't long before he was approached to fight. That first MMA match was the biggest high of his life. He was hooked.

Christian fought 13 times between 2001 and 2009 while also pursuing a newfound interest in academics, specifically in the field of justice. While fighting once or twice a year, Christian earned his master's degree in philosophy, and then attended law school while in the UFC. He now had his own law practice and taught philosophy and ethics at San Jose State. He pointed out the correlation between fairness in MMA and in the court room. The idea of a fair fight was something many fighters had claimed was a major draw. With weight divisions, judges, referees, and rules, MMA certainly does seem fair.

I asked Christian if he saw any of my Mexico fight in which I took the idea of fairness too far. Even though our records were incredibly lopsided—mine was 2-3 and Travis Wiuff was 23-4—that wasn't an issue. I'd agreed to it and was feeling confident from the sparring I'd been getting in with Frank Mir. The fight had gone all 3 rounds, but the crowd wanted more and the referee asked if we would fight another round. I'd been getting the crap kicked out of me, but said I would. Travis said he wouldn't, it was only a scheduled three-round fight. The ref raised my hand and awarded me the trophy. Travis was furious. Both of us were aware I hadn't really won the fight. It'd been the first time I'd ever been picked up on someone's shoulders and slammed down, and he'd done it a couple times, landing tons of elbows from inside my guard as I made weak submission attempts. I told the promoter I didn't win the fight, and we walked back into the cage and gave the trophy and win to Travis. It might have been a very stupid move, but it was only fair, the right thing to do.

I usually hated telling the story because it seemed very foolish, but Christian understood. I didn't reverse the decision because I felt I hadn't won. I reversed it because the decision was based on rules neither fighter had agreed to.

Fairness in fighting had several meanings to Christian. He had even created his own label that he wore on his fight shorts—Certified Organic Fighter—to declare he never used any performance enhancing drugs. He also started a nonprofit to recognize athletes who are willing to live by those standards and promote the idea that you can achieve success without drugs.

Christian said the biggest problem in the industry is that promoters have an incredibly unfair advantage in bargaining, even though the fighters are the producers and the promoters should work for them. When discussing how little fairness there is between the two parties, he said, "This isn't child's play. It's a rough sport. It's a tough way to make a living. Every time you go out there you risk injury, you risk ending your career, and you're making money for somebody else."

Christian knew firsthand just how unfair the promoter-fighter relationships were. In 2008, he, Josh Koscheck, Cain Velasquez, and Jon Fitch tried standing their ground against the UFC, refusing to sign over an exclusive lifetime contract for their video game likenesses. They were immediately cut from the UFC's roster, a bold move intended as a statement to any other fighter that got the crazy idea that they owned themselves.

Within 24 hours, the dispute was resolved and all the fighters were signed back into the organization, tails between their legs.

As an advocate for fair competition, fair contracts, and fair pay, Christian had played a big part in Assembly Bill 2100, a bill proposed by California Assemblyman Luis Alejo (D. Salinas). The bill hoped to expand the Mohammed Ali Boxing Reform Act—which had been passed by Congress in 2000 to protect boxers from exploitation, coercive contracts, and corruption—to include MMA fighters. Christian believed the bill would have been passed into law if money hadn't poured in from the opposition. Take a wild guess who opposed it.

Although disappointed in the results, Christian was not about to stop fighting. He brought up a subject few people discussed openly: the need for fighters to have a collective voice. "To a kid who has never made a significant amount of money, to make 10K is a lot of money," Christian said. "You can't retire on a million dollars. Your career won't last longer than five years with few exceptions. You're risking injuries and you're making money for other people. I believe that's wrong, and with a little solidarity that could be changed."

Here are the 10 fundamental rights that Christian states every fighter possesses. Visit his website, *fighterfairness.org*, for more information on how to get involved.

Fighter's Bill of Rights

1.   Free Negotiation: You have the right to consider all offers and to maximize the compensation you receive as a fighter. No contract shall restrict you in bargaining for the full market value of your services.
2.   Right to Work: You have the right to fight whenever you are physically ready to compete. No contract shall prevent you from earning a living in the profession of your choice.
3.   Right to Profits: You have the right to full disclosure of the profits that you and your fellow fighters generate. You have the right to a predetermined minimum pro rata share of the profits based on your rank, and other objective criteria.

4.   Representation: You have the right to hire qualified professionals to represent you and negotiate on your behalf, the right to associate with your fellow fighters, and to appoint representatives for collective bargaining.

5.   Fair Competition: You have the right to fair competition, unbiased officiating, and judging based on objective criteria.

6.   Objective Ranking System: You have the right to ascend an objective ranking system based on wins and losses.

7.   Mandatory Title Shots: You have the right to a mandatory title shot based on your rank, and other objective criteria.

8.   Right to Name and Likeness: You have the absolute right to own and control your name and likeness.

9.   Adequate Health Care: You have the right to be insured against the short-term risks of the sport while you compete, and to be provided with adequate health care for the long-term effects thereafter.

10.   Retirement Benefits: You have the right, upon retirement, to receive benefits from a pension plan supported by the industry that relies on your services while you compete.

* * *

It was Friday morning and I was exhausted, parked in front of AKA, trying to decide whether I should lug in my gear. Although Thursday's roll hadn't been too intense, the rehab session I'd had afterward with Jose Garcia, the sports recovery coach, had wrecked me.

The hour session was intense and ranked in the top 5 most painful moments of my life, just below having the flesh stitched back to my toe after a motorcycle crash. It was also unbelievably effective, well worth the $60 and the discomfort. Because Jose got paid out of the fighters' pockets, several of the lower level fighters simply couldn't afford to see him. The ones Jose did work on said they couldn't afford not to.

Jose had recommended I give my arm the day off, an option fighters didn't always have. I took his advice and headed inside the gym without my training gear, and found Jon Fitch finishing some light cardio and about to start his strength training. I turned on my handheld camera and followed him around the room, asking questions between sets.

The 34-year-old from Fort Wayne, IN, answered each question a little out of breath, his hair messed up, an AK-47 adorning the front of his shirt. He wasn't worried about appearances or watching what he said. I liked him already.

Jon was super competitive from the very start, a trait he inherited from his grandfather. Wanting to be the best at whatever he did, Jon had his sights set on becoming a professional football player, but at 6' and 190 pounds, he lacked the size and speed that colleges were looking for and couldn't land a scholarship. Although Jon knew he might not be good enough, he walked on to the Purdue University wrestling team. His first 2 years were rough, but he kept grinding and consistently improved until he became team captain his senior year. He came close to becoming an All-American that season, his disappointment only made worse knowing he was still improving but no longer had an arena to compete.

Jon was unsure what he wanted to do after graduation, but thanks to winning an award that paid for a year of grad school, he had extra time to decide. One idea was to try out for the Olympic wrestling team, the other to compete in MMA. Jon's assistant coach, Tom Erikson, had been fighting in Japan and brought Jon into training sessions with MMA standouts Gary Goodridge and Mark Coleman. This was in 2002, several years before the UFC popularity boom, but Jon understood that the top-level guys were making a decent living doing something they enjoyed.

Jon admitted that a big part of his decision to fight was the realization that he no longer wanted to become a teacher. His stint as a student teacher left a terrible taste in his mouth. Disillusioned by a broken school system, Jon jumped into MMA, figuring he could always go back and teach if fighting didn't work out.

Jon began fighting in July of 2002 and moved to AKA after going 5-2 that first year. Eight wins in a row over the next 2 years got Jon into the

UFC, and he'd been fighting for them since. He put together an amazing eight-fight win streak before losing a welterweight title shot against Georges St. Pierre. He won the next 5, had a draw with the legend B.J. Penn, and then suffered a quick knockout against Johnny Hendricks.

The loss to Hendricks had a lot of people questioning whether Jon was starting to slide. He'd just hit the 9.5-year mark, the number that some statisticians have calculated as the average point of decline. The number was by no means an absolute, and a lot of factors affect longevity. Some of the factors, like Jon's grinding style, meant he'd probably taken less damage and could physically last for a while; but hard sparring, which AKA was known for, could be a huge negative.

Just 2 months earlier, Jon had come in as the underdog against Erick Silva at UFC 153. He had an excellent performance and silenced his critics with a unanimous decision and *Fight of the Night* bonus. At 24-4-1, he wasn't done competing by any means.

After Jon's workout, we headed downstairs to the main training room so Jon could stretch out and wrap his hands. Now it was time for the real work.

Jon got on his gear and talked about what an honest sport MMA is. Like Christian and so many others, Jon said it is a pure sport: you can't fake it once you are in the cage. All lies are stripped away, the competitors naked and exposed. He said maybe if more people would train, or at least understand that idea, and begin to live that way, perhaps the world would be a better place.

A couple of fighters were already getting warmed up with shadowboxing. Jon put in his mouthpiece and joined them on the mats. It wasn't long before they were sparring, striking, executing takedowns and jumping back to their feet.

I'd only watched 3 of the training sessions, but I'd noticed that Jon was constantly moving forward, pushing the pace, not relenting. He'd talked about how much of that he'd gotten from wrestling, how the sport prepares you for life. He said most people only come across hardships occasionally, but in wrestling you push through hard times every day, surviving minute by minute.

Jon believed hard work is its own reward, but what he was going through right then had a bigger purpose. He was 6 weeks out from his next fight, putting himself in the best possible position to earn money for his family.

Across the room, the pairs of twos were punching each other, individuals cracking the heavy bags, the larger-than-life posters poised above them. Each guy had his reasons for being there, but for those who trained full time, the financial reward and shot at fame were at the top of that list.

Thursday night I had done some research into salaries, trying to get an idea of who was making what. Because of undisclosed bonuses, sponsorship deals, and organizations that weren't required to release salaries, it was difficult to get solid figures. Guys that had yet to break into the UFC or Strikeforce would be lucky to make a few thousand per fight, and have 4 or 5 fights a year if they stayed healthy and had a good manager. If they were fortunate, they would have a partner to support them and perhaps a part-time job to pay their bills.

Of the 220 fighters I'd talked with, only an eighth of them had made it to the UFC, and only a few of those could support themselves strictly through fighting. Even here at AKA, salaries were not what one would expect. The men up on that wall had put in blood, sweat, and tears, but how many had reaped true financial reward?

Josh Koscheck had made a good amount in the cage, but he'd also been very smart about managing his money, which allowed him to own the fancy cars and plane. Cain Velasquez made $100,000 when he lost his title but got $200,000 for winning the following fight, a significant amount of money for the year. Daniel Cormier, who was working with lightweight phenom Khabib Nurmagomedov, had earned a disclosed $100,000 for each of his last 2 Strikeforce matches. Khabib, who was 18-0, netted $20,000 for each of his last 2 fights in the UFC.

The intensity of the sparring session assured me I'd made the right decision to sit out. Another round ended and Jon found a new partner, coming forward, attacking, and putting on pressure. Jon knew all about pressure and had been under a ton before his October fight against Erick Silva. Not having fought in a year, coupled with other factors, had caused him tremendous financial difficulties. Securing the win and *Fight of the Night* bonuses had earned him $190,000 (plus any undisclosed bonus and sponsor pay). Once again he had breathing room.

In Jon's 17 fights in the UFC, he'd made a little over $1.2 million. It sounds like a lot, but that was over 7 years, with 20% going to the gym and management and a huge chunk going to the government. I'd guess his portion was roughly about $90,000 a year. More than he'd be making as a teacher, but not by a lot, especially considering the UFC didn't offer a retirement plan.

Another round started, Khabib matching up against Phil Baroni, both battling for takedowns. Phil's last fight in the UFC had been 2 years prior, earning him $25,000. The 4 fights he'd had since probably didn't add up to much more than that. And that was before taxes, training fees, and all the other expenses. But there he was still taking the pill, not knowing what else he could do. Fighting because he'd been doing it so long he didn't know anything else. Doing it because he needed that championship, a chance to say that at least he'd accomplished something.

CHAPTER FOURTEEN

January 8, 2013

It was the second Tuesday of the year, a few minutes before four o'clock, when we pulled up to The Arena MMA in San Diego. Brian grabbed the camera bag and asked if I was going to train. He'd watched me get my ass kicked at Alliance Training Center in Chula Vista that morning. If it hadn't been for my New Year's resolution to get in better shape, I would have left my gear in the car.

Jeff Clark, the head coach, greeted us when we walked in. We'd emailed back and forth, so he knew what I was looking to do. When Jeff mentioned the night's session would focus on striking, I told him I'd gotten in a little over my head that morning and taken some shots I probably shouldn't have. Jeff assured me that that wouldn't be a problem with any of his guys and encouraged me to join them.

After a quick introduction to the team, Jeff paired me with Jake Mapes, a 33-year-old from Hawaii who played pro baseball before injuries led to his release. I outweighed him by about 30 pounds; otherwise, we were about the same size. He was 6-0 as a pro, as well as a BJJ black belt who was very much a teacher as he helped me through the workout.

When it was time to spar, Jake put just enough pressure to make me work without worrying I might be knocked out at any moment. That round made me feel safer and more relaxed going into the next rounds with his teammates. I was getting hit a lot, but not by anything with bad intentions behind it. I'd guess they were probably only going about 70% with me, which was all I could handle.

After the workout, I interviewed Jake and a few other fighters. Most shared the same vibe: very laid-back and mellow. Their coach, Jeff, who'd been involved in the martial arts for more than 30 years, had a similar attitude: friendly, calm, and confident.

There was something else that set The Arena apart from other places. The gym served as a haven of sorts. In addition to Jake, there were several other fighters from Hawaii. Joe Duarte, UFC fighter Jon Tuck, and striking coach Vince Salvador all hailed from Guam. With friends and family so far away, the gym was a second home to many of them.

The gym also had many members who were active military, not surprising with Marine and Navy bases nearby. And several fighters had been in the military. Pat Speight, the other head coach and BJJ black belt, was a former U.S. Army paratrooper, having served with the 82nd Airborne before finding MMA to fill what was missing in his life. Joe Duarte, a 29-year-old Strikeforce fighter, enlisted in the Army and served two tours of duty in Iraq. Shane Kruchten enlisted in the Marines when he turned 17 and was fighting in Iraq a few months later.

I interviewed Joe in a crowded room, music pumping and buzzers ringing. We had a good talk but didn't dig very deep into his military past. For Shane's interview, we had an empty room to ourselves and plenty of time to talk. He raised his shirt to show me the tattoo across his back, a memorial with the names of 19 of his fellow Marines that never made it home. He talked about how the war affected him, how post-traumatic stress took over his life. The PTSD led to drugs, drinking, and fast food, a self-destructive path that surely would have killed him had he not found MMA. It was hard to imagine the 6'1" rail-thin featherweight weighed 250 when he took his first fight with no training, just a drunk lured into the cage by the $500 bar tab prize. Later, as a professional, Shane lost his first 2 fights, but was on a 10-fight win-streak and making a difference in the lives of other military veterans who are too ashamed to discuss the struggles they face.

I can't see how anyone could go into battle and not come back a different person. Civilians like me can never fully understand what it is like to be in war, knowing you might die at any moment, seeing friends lose their lives, taking lives yourself. Going through that and returning to the 'real world' is one of the biggest shocks for vets, and many have a difficult time adjusting. The range of feelings they experience varies, but one common emotion is they feel they no longer fit in.

The fight team and gym offered a brotherhood for these men, less intense than the bonds they built in war, but still powerful. The Arena was a place where they could release their aggression, drive out their demons, push themselves, trust their partners, and only be judged by how hard they worked.

But it wasn't just veterans that needed to train for overall health and well-being. Toby Imada didn't have any military experience but had racked up 47 fights over the last 14 years, more than the other 6 interviewees combined. He'd been a 20-year-old college student when he began fighting and said he had zero idea where he would be if it weren't for martial arts. He just knew it wouldn't be good.

Toby's childhood was a place of pain. He said, "Kids are some of the meanest people in the world." When he was 2, Toby's Mexican mother and Japanese father split. He went to live with his mother in Mexico, where the kids teased and bullied him because he didn't look Mexican. He fought all the time. When he was later sent to live with his dad in the U.S., the Asian kids didn't accept him because he didn't look like them, and even though he spoke Spanish, Toby still didn't look Mexican. Again he fought, this time with both groups.

That's how his life went until he began learning judo at 13 and built the confidence and skills he needed to stand up for himself and not be a target. His life became focused and he began wrestling when he entered high school. After high school, Toby turned to grappling, and his early success got him invited to compete at the first Abu Dhabi tournament. It was there that he met many of the top No Holds Barred fighters, who convinced him the cage should be his next step.

Now here he was nine days out from a bout with James Krause, whom I'd interviewed at Grindhouse MMA in Kansas City. Toby had taken the rematch on short notice, something he'd done throughout his career. He acknowledged his reputation and said, "Some people might call it stupid or foolish, but here's the thing, I fight not because I want to be tough or for recognition." Toby said, "I've done this my whole life as a hobbyist, as a martial artist. It's kind of like a test of myself." He tried to think of other reasons and shook his head. "That's the only reason I do it. Fortunately, now there's a payout, which is great. It's a perk. It makes it all more worth it."

Toby looked to be in great shape and didn't display any signs of having suffered too much damage, but it was on his mind. The 33-year-old BJJ and judo black belt said, "I also gotta remember I don't want to be that dude that's pushing 40 and still fighting guys that are half his age and getting hurt every fight. It's a hobby, not a career." He made it clear, however, that the daily training is a lifestyle and not a hobby. "It's who I am. It's been life changing for me."

The man who didn't fit in as a child blended back in with the group of fighters by the benches. They were different sizes and ethnicities and had various skill levels. Some had been in real battle, others only in the cage. But none of that mattered. The gym gave them a place to belong. A place to fit in, to prove that they were good, that they had skills, that they weren't crazy. It was a place where they could give and earn respect.

* * *

It was Thursday morning, just before 10. I drank a little water and wrapped my hands while stretching. Even though I'd already trained at Alliance Training Center the last 2 days, I was still surprised by the number of high-level fighters who were present. I hadn't considered San Diego as having much in the way of MMA, but I was mistaken. There were two dozen fighters warming up around me, several of whom had been in the UFC.

The double sessions the last 2 days had beaten my body to hell, but all I had to do was get through the next hour and a half. I blocked that negative voice in my head telling me I was foolish for being on the floor with the fighters. Head coach Eric Del Fierro put us through a thorough warm-up and started us on striking techniques.

Learning new combinations from top-level coaches was a great opportunity, and I was finally retaining some of the knowledge. The only problem was that sparring was next, and I'd already taken my share of the standard bumps and bruises, including a nice kick upside the head and a toe across my eye in a rough round with a retired heavyweight.

Even though I was now telling everyone that I couldn't spar very hard, I could never become upset when someone turned up the volume. That was the risk I took by being out there. If I wanted to play pretend, I had to accept responsibility. These guys were training to get better, not to babysit.

Now that I'd been with the team a bit, I had a better understanding of who I should partner with. For the first round I went straight to Casey Ryan, a jiu jitsu black belt and instructor at Alliance whom I'd already had the pleasure of working with the past two days. Casey reminded me a lot of Jake from The Arena, both black belts, tall, and very mellow. The 4-0 middleweight made me work, but pulled his punches and kicks. Instead of power, Casey worked on movement, pushing himself to get better even if I offered no match. He wasn't there to cruise through practice.

Casey's martial arts journey began as a teenager when he convinced his mother to rent the second UFC on video cassette. As a skinny kid who was always getting beat up by his older brother, Casey was fascinated by Royce Gracie, the little guy defeating all those giants. Wanting to learn those same skills to use on his bigger brother, Casey started training BJJ and fell in love with it. From there, he followed the same path as so many others, what felt like a natural progression: BJJ tournaments, sparring in stand-up classes, kickboxing smokers, then on to the cage.

It took a lot of hard work and self-realization over 12 years to earn his BJJ black belt, and Casey admitted that jiu jitsu was his main love. Originally he thought receiving his black belt would mean he'd be done and know everything, but now he understands it was just a beginning. Although earning that belt was his biggest accomplishment, Casey said the rush, the fame, and the benefits that came with fighting were awesome too.

"I think of martial arts and fighting as a way to better yourself. Jiu jitsu especially gives you the discipline and pillars in your life to make the world a better place, not just yourself." Casey smiled as he talked about all the changes he sees in his students. "That's what martial arts should be, to improve not just your life, but other people's lives." If forced to choose between MMA and BJJ, Casey would be content developing his Spider Monkey Jiu Jitsu, and spreading his knowledge to fighters, adults, and children.

The next round I went with one of the heavier guys for a much slower round. The third round was also uneventful. I sat out the fourth round and grabbed some water, watched Dominick Cruz, who was recovering from a torn ACL, lace up another fighter's gloves. Up in the ring were 27-year-old Danny "The Gremlin" Martinez and 22-year-old Justin "The American Kid" Lawrence. Danny was 16-4 and hoping to make it to the UFC, and Justin was 1-1 in the organization, in need of another win. Both had been wrestling their entire life, but Justin had also been involved in other martial arts since he was 6 and a national champion kickboxer since he was 10. The two worked well together, displaying tremendous speed and ability.

I'd thought about trying to get in one last round, but I'd had enough. I peeled off my gear and watched 2 guys going hard in the cage, 11 years of professional experience between them: Paul "The Gentleman" Bradley, an 18-5 welterweight trying to get back into the UFC, and A.J. "The Mercenary" Matthews, a 6-2 middleweight who was fighting for Bellator, both with their college degrees. I watched them shoot and sprawl, punch and kick, and thought about what A.J. said about being at the separation point between the good and the best where guys had to decide how much they wanted it. Either they were going to train every day and make it their lifestyle to progress to the next step, or they'd never get past the local stage.

I took a quick shower and headed back to see if I could catch anyone for an interview. Several people stood around the cage watching a fighter hitting mitts. It was Michael Chandler Jr., the undefeated Bellator lightweight champion. He had on sweatpants, a sweatshirt, and a beanie, all part of his weight cut for his title defense against Rick Hawn just a week away.

Michael's striking was impressive, as was his silence. He did as he was instructed without hesitation or complaint. He didn't show any sign of distress, only determination.

Of the 250 interviews I'd conducted, some were amateurs, but most were pros. An overwhelming majority of the fighters had winning records (they tend to be the ones that stick with the sport) and a fair amount were undefeated, but none were champions outside the lower levels. I was grateful that after his workout, Michael gave me an hour of his time.

Michael grew up in a small Missouri town, a wild kid who played every sport he could to get out all his extra energy. He was raised in a supportive, loving home, and his parents let him pursue anything he wanted. By the time he hit high school, the honor roll student had narrowed his athletic pursuits to wrestling and football, with the emphasis on wrestling since he was only 102 pounds and excelled at that sport.

Although Michael was good in high school, his late start held him back a bit, and he didn't land a scholarship. Instead of being depressed, Michael walked on to the wrestling team at the University of Missouri, where he went on to become an All-American and earned a BA in personal finance. Not ready to quit competing after graduating, Michael transitioned straight into MMA, which he was familiar with because he had been teammates with respected fighters Tyrone Woodley and Ben Askren.

Having set his goal to become a champion in the sport, Michael moved to Vegas and began training at Xtreme Couture MMA. After training a few months, Michael began fighting, forgoing amateur bouts and winning the Bellator championship his second year. Michael had only positive things to say about Xtreme Couture—the huge gains there, the great boxing, the grappling coaches he'd had, and how it had led him to the title. But he'd been at Alliance the last 8 months, and the move felt right to him.

Mental toughness was the most important thing in fighting for Michael, but a strong team was right behind that. "Having a team that supports you and works as hard as you gives you a mental edge," he said. Just as in wrestling, the top fighters always come from strong teams. You need hardworking teammates to better each other every day, and you're only as good as your coaches and teammates allow you to be. In high school he had 2 awesome coaches who were great motivators and mentors: loving and kind, and who made him into a better man. Those were the type of people Michael insisted on surrounding himself with.

In the early days of the sport, many top fighters got by running their own camps, but that was no longer the case. Michael said a fighter should not be deciding what to do day-to-day, and needed an intelligent plan designed specifically for them and implemented by coaches. To get a big leg-up on competition, a fighter must trust his coaches and use them to fine-tune nutrition, sleep, diet, and all the things that go into making a complete martial artist.

Michael believed he had that at Alliance. He loved the strong team atmosphere, impressive competitors and coaches. I pictured him hitting the mitts and running through his workout when he said, "Everybody here has the mentality of 'I'm going to show up, shut up, and do what coach tells me to.' To me that's the best recipe for success in this sport."

I asked if he felt any extra pressure as a champion, but he shook his head and explained that although he's not okay with losing, he knows it will happen one day. Because he was okay with the uncertainties in a fight, he didn't have insecurities. Michael echoed Joe Lauzon's statement about being prepared when he said, "If you do everything you need to, there should be no nervousness. Just accept that anything could happen and go and compete at a high level. My God and my family still love me if I lose. There is nothing to be nervous about."

Michael's approach was to do exactly what he needed to do to be a champion, but not to take MMA too seriously. Fighting was just a step in his journey, nothing more and nothing less. What mattered to him was integrity and trying to be the best man he could be. His take on fighting and life was one of the best I'd heard, and I appreciated how his goal was to use fighting to create a platform for a higher purpose where he could help others. With his dedication, work ethic, and motivation, I couldn't see how anything would stop him from achieving his goals.

* * *

It was Saturday morning and Brian and I were back at Alliance for the fifth day in a row. The day before, I'd had a great strength and conditioning workout with coach Doug Balzarini, but the focus this day was enjoying the gym's 5-year anniversary party and getting in a couple of interviews with the coaching staff and some fighters.

One of the guys I interviewed could no longer fight but was still part of the family. Diego Garijo, a muscular 34-year-old middleweight, had gone 7-1 as a pro before a detached retina prevented him from pursuing his passion. Although he missed the sport, he was content applying himself towards another challenge; professional arm wrestling.

Diego had brought in his arm wrestling table for demonstrations and gave me a quick lesson, repeatedly slamming down my arm despite my bigger size. Diego, who didn't have a father figure in his life growing up, said he had never gotten into sports and didn't have the right mentality to do well when he was young. It wasn't until he was in his twenties and saw the documentary *The Smashing Machine* that he considered MMA. Not one to waste time, Diego found a gym the next day, quit college 3 months later to train full time, did many BJJ tournaments, and began fighting in the cage.

Although Diego believed the retina problem was genetic and not the result of fighting, he still talked about the dangers of MMA. "People should be realistic about what they're doing to their bodies. I'm not complaining just because I had to leave the sport. I'm realistic. I did what I did; I did some damage to my body for sure. The year before I quit, I had some concussions that were really bad." Diego shrugged his shoulders and said, "And I would do it again. It's risk versus reward. It's a very exciting life. If you want to accomplish something great, you have to take risks and pay a different price. I accept that."

Diego said he wouldn't encourage his kids to be fighters. "If you're a tough fighter and you had tough fights, when you're older you'll have some issues." At the same time, he wouldn't discourage them. Diego said it would be pointless to try to talk anyone out of it. "If you have the desire to fight, no one is going to stop you."

The festivities were under way, people filling the gym to watch demonstrations, get autographs, and talk with their favorite fighters. The parking lot was packed with members eating and playing games as a DJ provided music. When there was a lull in the action, I managed to sneak away with the UFC, and former WEC, bantamweight champion, Dominick "The Dominator" Cruz.

Dominick took me back to his childhood, growing up poor in Tucson, AZ, and feeling very responsible for his family. He said, "My dad, when I was five years old, he gave me this speech: 'You're the man of the house. I'm sorry, but me and your mom have to separate.'" Dominick thought about it for a second and said, "You know, just the normal speech that you get. I felt in control, I felt like it was my family."

I told Dominick I didn't know how normal I'd consider that speech. My parents were still married, and I never had that kind of responsibility dumped on me, especially at such a young age. Dominick said that although he didn't know it at the time, it served him well. It gave him the drive to succeed.

While Dominick's dad was abandoning him, Michael Chandler's dad was enrolling his son in wrestling, being supportive of anything he wanted to pursue. The difference in the backgrounds of the two champions illustrated what I'd been seeing across the country. Fighters came from all walks of life and various situations. There wasn't one factor, including the presence of a positive male role model, which guaranteed someone would fight or indicated whether they would be successful at it. I hadn't analyzed the overall numbers yet, but I guessed the San Diego interviews were like interviews everywhere else. Several fighters said their dads were pieces of shit, 2 using those exact words, 3 more expressing the same sentiment. But just as many guys praised their dads and were very grateful for their relationships. Everyone was different, and it wasn't the situations they faced that determined who they became, but instead their reactions to those situations.

Thanks to Dominick's father leaving, money was even tighter than it had already been. Sports were the only thing that made Dominick feel like he belonged, but he was limited to playing soccer, baseball, and basketball because they were inexpensive and generally considered safe. Those sports taught him a lot, mainly how much he loved to compete and that winning was everything.

In junior high, Dominick went looking for soccer tryouts and stumbled upon the wrestling tryouts. When Dominick explained that he was in the wrong room, the coach shook his head and said, "You're not a soccer player, you're a wrestler." Dominick stayed for the tryout and discovered that he was a natural. Dominick said, "I just needed a place to belong and wrestling gave that to me."

Not belonging was something I'd struggled with until I found football, a place where I could interact, try to prove my worth, have something in common with other kids. A sport was also a place to escape, to become someone else, to show the true you, and to chase dreams so big they're hard to verbalize.

Always searching for similarities, I wondered if Dominick had been as shy as I had been. He was very charismatic, friendly, and high-energy right there talking one-on-one. But who had he been as a teenager?

Dominick said that anyone who knew him from high school would say they don't know who he is now. "I've always been that guy that sat in the background," he said. "I'll sit in the corner, I'll analyze the situation and see how I need to go about it and then handle what I need to handle as quietly as possible until I make it through. My goal in life was squeezing through the cracks to the top, just staying out of people's way, the path of least resistance. I didn't know how much it was holding me back until I got older."

Wrestling became Dominick's new path, but he tore ankle ligaments his senior year and colleges lost interest. With wrestling gone and hopes of college out the window, Dominick needed to get a job. Actually, he needed 3 because he'd left home over differences with his family. His new goal was to prove to them that he was a man and could make it on his own.

A year into his independence, Dominick experienced what he described as a rock-bottom point in his life. Understanding he was depressed because he missed wrestling, Dominick replaced one of his jobs with a position as a wrestling coach, not because he wanted to coach, but to wrestle with the guys on the team.

During his third year as a coach, one of the students suggested Dominick try the MMA class he attended. "I told him I'm not a fighter at all," Dominick said. But the student told Dominick if he could wrestle, then he could fight. Dominick agreed to try out the class, and it turned out the same as that first wrestling tryout: one class and he never stopped.

Dominick wasn't allowed to spar for 6 months and used that time to apply his wrestling mentality towards learning boxing. When he began sparring, he found himself dropping 35-year-olds, a powerful feeling for any teenager. Three months later he had his first MMA fight, barely winning the decision but loving the experience. He decided that fighting was what he really wanted to do it, and he went on to win his next 5 fights in Tucson where he did most his training on his own, really working on cardio so he could gas everyone else out. From there he moved to San Diego and worked his way to a 19-1 record, his loss to Urijah Faber avenged when Dominick defeated him 4 years later in his first fight in the UFC.

When asked who he was as a person, Dominick said he is often misunderstood, but there was a good reason for that. "Outside of the cage I'm like everyone else. I'm just a normal person. I'll talk to anybody. I'm not too cool for anyone," Dominick said. "You see me that week of the fight, which is when I would say ninety-five percent of the audience sees me, is when I'm getting ready for a fight. You don't want to be around me. I'm not a happy camper. I'm cutting weight, I'm about twenty-five pounds lighter than what I'm supposed to weigh." Dominick said, "My brain goes to a different place. I separate myself from everything. I literally move my life the last two weeks. I move out of my house, I put myself in different scenarios. I make myself solitary. I put myself in the mentality that I'm ready to go to war. It's a real war, that's how I build my mind up for the fight. By the time I get to fight day, I'm a completely different person." Some fighters liked to talk about flipping a switch and turning into someone else once they stepped into the cage, but for fighters like Dominick, this personality shift was a process.

We talked about the gym and the number of high-level fighters, many of whom were competing in the same divisions. Dominick said, "Every fighter at Alliance has their own path and their own drive for why they're here and what they're doing. I'm here to keep doing what I've been doing, and that's winning and being the best fighter on the planet. Everybody here shares that." Dominick said, "I think that carries over between all of us as teammates, is that we help each other. It's not a one-dimensional sport." Dominick went on to describe the old-school mentality that MMA is a solitary sport where fighters trained themselves. "That style is gone and played out," he said. "The team gets you to the top. That's the mentality we have here at Alliance." He appreciated everyone that trained there, and said everybody was there for a reason and they built each other up.

When asked what he was most proud of, Dominick answered it was winning his world title because that had been his focus and everything that he'd worked toward. But then he thought about it and said, "I could have all the titles in the world, but if I don't do something good with it then it really doesn't feel good. For me it's about sharing the experience with other people. So I got my brother, my mom, my family, friends that I've been able to bring out from back home to help them accomplish goals and things that they want to do." He had to smile about it. "Just getting out of that dump that I was in growing up. To help my family out. That's been my biggest accomplishment."

I thanked Dominick for his time and returned to the party. Parents and children were swarming the place. There was laughter and smiles, everyone hugging and happy. This was what Dominick was proud of, why Michael loved the team, what Casey described as the main goal of martial arts. Gyms weren't just places to build fighters. The good ones were creating better people and a better community, giving individuals a place to belong and improve themselves.

CHAPTER FIFTEEN

July 2, 2013

It was Tuesday morning, the Vegas sun beating down on us. Brian and I had just finished the four-hour drive from Los Angeles, plenty of time to catch up on what we'd been doing during the 6 months since Alliance. I hadn't trained since February and I'd done no physical activity after my son, Jake, was born in May.

Having a new baby in my life was incredible, and I felt blessed to have my son, but there were challenges I wasn't handling well. Besides the lack of sleep, dirty diapers, and screaming, I had a much different mindset then when I'd been the stay-at-home-dad for my daughter. With her, I had been grateful to stop working a real job, but now I was trying to put the finishing touches on my second novel and frustrated I couldn't work on Unlocking.

I felt guilty about abandoning the family now, but put that on hold when we pulled into the business park where Syndicate MMA was located. The building was one massive 16,000-sq-ft room, most of it matted, with a cage and weight lifting area tucked into the back. John Wood, the head coach and co-owner of Syndicate greeted us. I'd been friends with John when we both fought out of the Las Vegas Combat Club back in 2003.

John had stayed in great shape, never taking a break from MMA even though his focus had switched from fighting to coaching. He was 37 but looked just as strong and dangerous as he had 10 years before. I, on the other hand, was about to embarrass myself by jumping into the fighter session.

Training certainly was not part of my lifestyle, and I was about to pay the price.

When I got out of the locker room, I recognized Jacob Noe, who was finishing the no-gi grappling class. I'd first run into the light heavyweight a year before on a hot Sunday afternoon at Memphis Judo & Jiu-Jitsu. I had taken note when he mentioned that his friend and training partner, Quinton "Rampage" Jackson, and some other fighters had left the area to pursue their dream out west. Back then, relocating to pursue fighting had been a scary thought for Jacob, but now, with his recent success in Bellator, it looked like he'd made the jump.

Practice was about to start. There were nearly 2 dozen fighters on the mat, quite a few signed with the UFC. We started slow with shadowboxing, then put on big gloves and went over technique. Everything was much harder than it had been 5 months before, but that's what I had to expect. When it came time to spar, I sat on the sidelines, but Robert Navone, a coach from Philly who had only been there a few weeks, asked me to work with one of his guys. I gave him the "I'm not a fighter" speech, and he assured me the smaller fighter would take it easy. The featherweight was lightning fast, in and out, and I couldn't touch him. For the next round, Navone stuck me with an even smaller guy who peppered me with shots. I ate punch after punch, my punishment for being so lazy.

There was one round left, and I wanted to quit, but Navone had me go with Maurice Jackson, the 6'9" kickboxer out of New Jersey. Five seconds into the round, I realized I should've worn headgear. Things just got very serious. I couldn't get past Maurice's jab or kicks, and only landed a handful of my own. Even though Maurice was not going hard, he had enough on his shots that they hurt if I didn't avoid them.

Relief was all I felt at the final buzzer. I cleared the cobwebs and wiped off the sweat, then sat down with Maurice for a short interview. His good friend, and fellow fighter, Joey Angelo, went right after. It had been a long time since I'd done an interview and I was inspired by both of their stories, ready to get back into the project.

Although my body was hurting from Tuesday's double session at Syndicate, we were back an hour early the next morning to talk with Heather Clark, a slender, but muscular 33-year-old strawweight coming off a split decision loss in Bellator. Female fighters were hard to find, and I was very interested in seeing how, or if, women fighters differed from the men.

From the little bit I'd talked to Heather the day before, I could tell she was a positive and happy person. Unlike Maurice, Joey, and Jacob, who all had fairly rough childhoods, Heather had come from a happy home. Having a physician as a father, she had access to a broader range of opportunities and played every sport she could, including ice hockey.

I hadn't met any females who played hockey, and I had no idea that coed hockey even existed, but Heather explained she played on teams with males in high school and college before going on to play professionally in Canada and Switzerland. Playing against males forced Heather to become much tougher and a better skater so she could avoid the boys who had no qualms about laying out a girl half their size.

When asked about the aggressiveness of the sport, Heather got a huge smile. "I loved it. I loved hockey, and I still do, but MMA is so much more, mentally and spiritually. I've never been in such great shape as I am now."

I believed her. There was no question Heather was an athlete.

When asked about her earliest influences, Heather said her dad raised her on the movie *Rocky*, and nearly every day he'd play its theme song, "Eye of the Tiger." Even their pet cockatoo could whistle the song that Heather now walked out to for each of her fights.

Hockey wasn't the only rough sport Heather tried. She did some boxing and kickboxing, training during the off season in college, but it wasn't until she was 28 that she took up kickboxing at an MMA gym to get back in shape. One of the coaches convinced Heather that with her athleticism and hockey experience she could become a formidable professional MMA fighter. She started training immediately with her intention set and never looked back.

After 4 months of training, Heather realized to be the best you should train with the best. For her that was Jackson-Winkeljohn's in New Mexico. After the move, she had one kickboxing smoker, one BJJ tournament, and then went straight to a pro MMA fight, excited to show off her skills. Heather lost that first decision but wasn't dissuaded, and went on to win her next 4 fights.

Heather acknowledged that being in the cage was addicting, but it was so much more than that. "I do love fighting. I love training. I love waking up and being exhausted and getting through that and getting here. I get so excited when I know I'm coming to the gym." She said, "I've never felt passion for anything like I feel for MMA. Like jiu jitsu, which I want to do until I'm one hundred. I want to be that old lady whooping on the kids. My motivation is my love for this sport."

A bonus that came with fighting was being an inspiration for females too scared to chase their dreams. With the rise of women's MMA, Heather saw an added responsibility and opportunity. Dana White had said females wouldn't fight in the Octagon, but now that Ronda Rousey had headlined UFC 157 back in February, and the soon-to-be-aired season of *TUF* had both male and female fighters, there was this huge shiny carrot dangling in front of her, a new dream to chase. Although it wasn't yet a fact, Heather's optimism rang true when she said, "The fact that I'm going to be in the UFC one day is really awesome."

Heather was passionate, as both a person and a fighter, and only did things she loved to do. With a B.A. in photography and her own studio in Vegas, Heather was not fighting for the money. "I'm an artist," she said. "I live my life to be happy, not to have money to buy things I don't need or to show people."

Although her 5-4 record was not what she hoped it would be, Heather was proud of what she had accomplished. She put it all out there every fight and overcame a lot of adversity. In her last fight, she had broken her arm in the second round but fought through to the finish. "It's so empowering," Heather said. "It's like a meditative state. It's so real. There's nothing more real than two people trying to kill each other. It's an honor to have the chance to do it and I love it."

Heather said, "If I can do this, I can do anything." Then it was time to wrap her hands so she could try to punch her friend Colleen in the face.

* * *

Thursday was the 4th of July, the gym packed with fighters from all over the country who were in town for UFC 162: Silva vs. Weidman and the UFC Fan Expo. We still had about 10 minutes before practice started, so I sat down with Colleen Schneider and interviewed the 31-year-old bantamweight while she wrapped her hands.

Ten minutes isn't much time to try and understand someone, so we jumped right into it, a fun, engaging conversation, just like Heather's. Colleen, a 5'9" brunette who was raised in Syracuse, NY, with her 2 brothers, described herself as both a nerd and a jock. She grew up playing many sports, including soccer, track, and skiing, but her introduction to the martial arts came when she'd tag along to her brother's karate class. Their mother had specifically chosen karate as a sport that her brother could do without her, but Colleen loved watching and begged to train until her mother finally caved.

"It was never about doing something boys did or my brothers did," she said. "If I liked something, I wanted to do it. It didn't matter if it was what I was 'supposed' to do, what I 'wasn't supposed' to do, and I'm kind of still like that. I don't fight because girls aren't supposed to fight and I'm trying to break some stereotype. I don't give a fuck. I like fighting, so I fight."

Colleen laughed when I asked how competitive she was. "There are times where it's good and it drives you and you get to the next level because of it, but sometimes you just need to relax and let things go." She said, "I think I have a better balance of that now than when I was younger but I'm definitely competitive by nature."

The competitiveness is one of the things that drove her through 4 years of karate and then Tae Kwon Do in college at Berkeley, where she fought for Nationals and later coached. She was seriously into TKD, but when she saw MMA, she immediately recognized she possessed a select subset of skills. "I could kick like crazy, amazing kicks, right, but I couldn't box for shit. I didn't know how to wrestle. It made me realize how little I knew." Colleen said, "As soon as I looked at it, I knew I wanted to do it. I could train forever, and I'd never master it."

Searching for similarities between us, I asked about risk-taking behavior. "I think anyone who fights is an adrenaline junkie to some extent. I am," Colleen said, "but I've never been in a fight outside of MMA. I've never even gotten in trouble in my life. Perfect student, very good kid, very well behaved. I like to do things that push me. I like to do things that scare me."

Although Colleen had brushed over Berkeley and being a nerd, I asked her to expand. She earned a B.A. in physics and did some postgraduate astrophysics research, not because she intended on ever using that knowledge for a job, but simply because she loved learning about the world and how it works. Like Heather and the overwhelming majority of the fighters I spoke with, Colleen was not an unintelligent brute fighting due to a lack of options.

Colleen wished people unfamiliar with MMA would approach it with an open mind. "There's so much to it," she said. "The reason I love this is it's as challenging mentally as it is physically because there's so much going on in there. I've done sports my whole life, and nothing has challenged me the way mixed martial arts has."

Colleen and I got on the mat with over 2 dozen fighters, many of whom fought in the UFC. During warm-ups, I thought about what Colleen had said about an open mind.

Even though my attitude towards MMA had become much more positive, the sport was still something I didn't want my daughter doing. As we ran around the mat, I realized my fear that Olivia might turn into a fighter was ridiculous. While I wouldn't ever want her taking physical damage, why wouldn't I want her turning out like these women I'd interviewed?

Colleen described herself as intense, loyal, honest, and confident. Heather was giving, thoughtful, outspoken, and determined. Both were chasing dreams and choosing the most difficult challenge they could. Both were energetic and fun to talk with, and, even more impressive, they were happy because they were pursuing their passion and challenging themselves.

* * *

Thursday was sparring, no time for technique. I partnered with Joey Angelo, a 24-year-old father of 3 from Brooklyn, NY. Joey said he'd grown up as a fat redhead with freckles, buck teeth, and Tourette's—an easy target for bullies until his dad put him in boxing at 12. All his years of amateur boxing, kickboxing, and MMA, had had a huge, positive impact on Joey's life. It was also making a huge impact on my body, as Joey's punches and kicks knocked me about the entire round.

Coach Navone had me go a few more mild rounds before I finally sat out to recoup. Brian pointed out Evan Dunham, a 14-4 lightweight sitting in the stands and suggested I interview him before the practice ended. I'd put my body through quite a lot in the last few days and didn't want to miss out on Dunham, who'd just lost what I thought was a bad decision to Rafael Dos Anjos in Brazil.

A few minutes into our talk, I was thinking how the 32-year-old, rather unimposing at 5'10" and 155 pounds, came across as gentle enough to be a preschool teacher, not someone who made a living as a full-time fighter. This image conflicted with the clips I'd seen of a grinning and bloodied Evan in the cage. Although Evan said he was never one of the better athletes, his competitive nature carried him through. In sixth grade, Evan saw the movie *The Mighty Ducks* and told his dad he wanted to play hockey. I'd heard that before, but I was surprised when Evan said he liked the sport because of all the fighting.

When they went to the hockey rink, Evan's dad discovered the sport was too expensive and signed him up to wrestle instead. The move changed Evan, instilling in him a strong work ethic, teaching him what it meant to commit fully.

In college, Evan replaced wrestling with jiu jitsu, the art taking over much of his life. Although he received his B.A. in sociology, he majored in BJJ, using class time to write notes on what techniques he'd learned the night before. After college, Evan felt lost and didn't know what he wanted to do. He took a fight and loved it. "It's the most real feeling you could have," he said. "You go in, you react, you don't think about anything. It's a very primal feeling and I love it." Fighting was the most natural thing Evan knew.

Practice ended as we finished the interview. Brian brought over another UFC fighter, Mike Pyle, a 38-year-old from Tennessee who'd been fighting for more than a dozen years. The 6'1" welterweight was in his second week of camp, exhausted from a tough practice, and anxious to get home to spend the holiday with his family, but was cool enough to sit down for a quick talk.

Mike said he had always been slow, long and lanky, and never into sports. He did have a strong passion for martial arts, but he grew up in a small one-horse town, and was limited to pretending in his backyard that he was Bruce Lee. When he moved to Alabama at 18, Mike went to a TKD academy and loved it. This was right around UFC 1. Mike became infatuated with Royce choking people and catching them in armlocks. He sought grappling through video tapes and magazines and when he moved back home with no access to training, Mike turned a shed into his dojo and taught himself using his sister, cousin, or a friend as opponents in exchange for a six-pack. He was infatuated with using his body and mind as a weapon and MMA gave him the arena to do just that.

When asked why he decided to fight, Mike pointed out there was no money in it when he started in 1999. "MMA wasn't a sport. It was shunned upon," Mike said. "It was competition plain and simple, my skills against yours, let's try this, let's see who's better."

Mike fought 23 times over 7 years before finally making it to the UFC, probably earning much less per year than he would have if he had worked a regular job. After 10 fights with the UFC, he was making a good living, around $40,000 to fight, another $40,000 if he won. But even with that kind of money, Mike said the attraction was still just competition.

We'd only talked for 5 minutes, but I was a fan. When Mike left to be with his family, Brad Tavares, a 25-year-old from Hawaii, took his seat. The muscular middleweight won his first 7 MMA fights and had earned himself a place in the UFC by making it to the semifinals of *The Ultimate Fighter Season 11* and going 3-1 since. Unlike Mike and Evan, Brad was one of the better athletes in most of the sports he played. As a big, strong kid, his focus was on football, his goal to play in the NFL.

Fighting, however, had always been in the picture. In Hawaii, fighting was part of the culture and Brad often got into scuffles on the street. Boxing was watched at home, and when Brad was a teenager, he and his friends bought gloves and boxed every day after school. When Brad watched the UFC with his dad, both became instant fans of the sport.

Brad was surprised his first MMA fight was the only one he was nervous about. "And it was weird to me because I'd gotten into so many fights just on the street or whatever. And I've even had times where I had to fight more than one guy." But there he was worried about fighting a guy who he had prepared for. "Once I got in there and we started going at it, it felt comfortable. I loved it," he said. "I love just going at it with another guy and punching each other in the face."

Brad said he probably would have gotten into a lot of trouble with partying when he moved to Vegas at 21 if it weren't for MMA. The sport helped keep him focused and matured him. He realized how much work he put in and did not want to throw it all away by being irresponsible. He achieved his dream of becoming a professional athlete and was on a mission to become the best.

Brad wrapped it up by bringing up the expo. "It's always the most gratifying to meet these little kids that actually know who you are and watch you." Brad said, "They look up to you and you don't want to let them down."

* * *

Friday and Saturday had been devoted to the expo, Sunday and Monday for recovery and writing. Tuesday morning it was time to get back to work. We arrived at Syndicate early, plenty of time for me to stretch and take in the entire facility. John Wood was holding mitts in the cage, looking slick. I tried remembering how much I really knew about him back when we were training. We both were into loud, angry music. We both came from a weightlifting background. He'd driven 8 hours to help corner me for a tiny show. I didn't remember much more about him, probably due in part to our hard sparring sessions.

There was one thing I clearly remembered. January 2004, driving down to Gilbert, AZ, to fight in Rage in the Cage, figuring we'd corner each other and hope there was some space between our fights. They couldn't find a match for me, but John's guy was a definite.

The guy they matched John against already had 16 documented fights. This was John's first, and with only me as his corner. He still had weight to drop. I told him I didn't think it was a good idea, but he was determined to fight.

The lightest I'd fought at was 225. I'd never cut weight in my life. I don't think John had either, but he got through it. I don't remember any of the fight, but I remember the feeling, the nerves I had just watching him step in there. I didn't want to watch a friend fight, let alone feel like I had nothing to offer as his corner.

John lost in the third round, but I only know that because I checked. What I do remember is that he was brave enough to take that fight without hesitation. Now, I wanted to know how he got to that point. What other similarities did we share?

John had lived in Vegas since he was 6 years old, his parents divorced. He loved watching boxing and kickboxing with his dad, and was a huge WWF fan. At school he got in a lot of fights and liked it. He wasn't a model student and was suspended a lot of the time.

None of those things were part of my childhood. However, we did both start working as bouncers at 18. I'd never considered my bouncing experience as fighting, but John's talk of the nightclubs in Arizona pulled me back to all the brawls I'd broken up. The surge of adrenaline knowing you could get hit by anyone, with anything, no telling who had a weapon. John said that real life application was where he learned close-quarter combat.

John was a big fan of the UFC from the start, watching each VHS tape over and over. He wanted to test himself in a fair fight without the worry of being arrested and make a few bucks while he was at it. He loved MMA and knew he needed it in his life. He wanted to bring it to others and opened a 1,500 sq. ft. gym in Summerlin, outside Las Vegas.

"I was coaching half my time and running a gym," John said. He took fights he wasn't prepared for and felt he was only into it 50%. "I was just hoping I was better than the other guy." Not the best approach in today's highly competitive field.

John hadn't fought in a few years, and, although he missed it at times, coaching and Syndicate was all he needed. He provided a friendly environment where entire families trained. The way he lit up when talking about Syndicate's kids' programs and the change it was producing reminded me of why we'd been friends.

Besides being a great place for fighters from around the world to train, Syndicate also enabled fighters to supplement their income through coaching. Over the last week I'd talked to several of the instructors, each of them having only great things to say about John and Syndicate.

One of these instructors was Fredson Paixao, a short but dangerous BJJ black belt with 15 fights under his belt. He couldn't stop talking about how incredible it was to see mothers, fathers, and their children all training together, sometimes on the same mat. He held his phone so we could both see videos of his kids on the mat. They were so happy rolling around with their father.

Casey Millikin, a 25-year-old from Maine with seven pro fights, had opted for the much safer and consistent job of teaching, stating that three hundred bucks and a broken jaw wouldn't bring him closer to reaching his goals. Jiu jitsu had changed Casey's life and he loved being able to bring that to others and help them grow. He said he owed that and so much more to John, an opportunity he was very grateful for.

Practice was tough, mainly stand-up drilling. When it got time to spar, I pushed myself a little harder. After taking some of Jacob Noe's punches, I backed off a bit and went with the smaller guys. I was exhausted, but there was just one last round to go. Coach Navone told me to go with Maurice Jackson, the 6'9" giant who was 31-0 as a kickboxer.

We touched gloves, then his glove touched my head. Again and again. I couldn't run away, but I couldn't get close, Maurice's long arms and legs were picking me apart. Where was that happy-go-lucky guy I'd interviewed last week?

Maurice threw a spinning back kick right in my ribs and suddenly nothing else mattered. There were no worries about books, deadlines, or if we needed more diapers. Punches were flying at me. They were connecting. They hurt.

My head was throbbing, my heart ready to burst. I wanted to quit, but had too much pride. There was only a minute left. I was going to make it.

Bam! Everything snapped black. There was still sound, but it was all fuzzy.

I was on one knee, both hands on the ground. It'd been a while since I'd been cracked like that. I'd forgotten how much it sucked. The 4-hour ride back to Los Angeles guaranteed I'd remember it.

CHAPTER SIXTEEN

July 29, 2013

I arrived in Albuquerque Monday morning and headed straight to Wink's Gym, the place quiet and cool, a nice break from the blazing sun. Professional fighter Clint Roberts paused the MMA class to welcome me. I took photos as the 6'2" heavily tattooed Texan demonstrated the Anaconda choke to the class of 10 people, some older than me and only a few other guys who looked like they were there to fight. The 29-year-old wore a heavy-duty knee brace and guarded the knee when he rolled, still recovering from surgery.

After class, Clint told me how competitive he'd been in baseball from the age of 10. He also played football and did rodeo like lots of his friends, but baseball was his passion and he was playing around the nation at 16. In college, Clint got moved from catcher to pitcher and lost the love for the sport, felt it was becoming a job. His dream of becoming a professional baseball player died and he dropped out his junior year, quickly discovering that working a real job wasn't what he wanted either. Clint partied too much and was making bad decisions until he walked into the Grappler's Lair MMA in Belton, TX.

I expected him to say he'd gone to the gym simply for physical activity, but Clint said that wasn't the case at all. His dad was a huge Mike Tyson fan and appreciated all forms of fighting. From the moment they'd watched an early UFC together, Clint knew he wanted to compete in MMA.

I wondered how a kid with the desire to fight but no training would turn out. How had he handled confrontations prior to his training?

181

Clint shook his head when he told me that he'd always been the tough guy and had more than a few street fights. He knew he was a good athlete and figured he could fight without any training. His cockiness at the gym earned him time in the cage with TJ Waldburger, 3 years younger than 22-year-old Clint. TJ beat the hell out of Clint, who clearly remembered his broken nose, how he couldn't stand and just lay there trying to hide the tears. Clint thought he had been beat up before but nothing ever like this. It was humiliating.

But he was back the next day.

Why? Why return when it would happen again?

It came down to Clint not being able to accept that some little kid was better than him. He knew he could be as good as TJ and he'd made up his mind he wanted to fight. The beatdown had only made him more determined.

The guys at the gym accepted Clint and put him on an intense training regimen of 6 hours a day for the first 3 months leading to his first fight. A fight where he almost pissed himself after seeing the jacked 35-year-old he was about to battle.

Clint went on to win that fight and the rest of his amateur bouts, finding success fighting with emotion, feeding off his anger and aggressiveness. In his first professional fight, he discovered that approach won't always work and he needed to switch styles. Working with renowned master striker Mike Winkeljohn helped Clint change his mentality from emotional to technical. It wasn't wise being the brawler and he had to learn how to play the game. Clint pointed to Jon Jones and other top fighters and said you could see how focused they were, face calm, no excess breathing. That's where he was trying to be.

The mental game is the hard part. Learning not to be nervous, not relying on emotion. Clint talked about all the guys in the gym that never make it as professionals even though they might be the better fighter in the gym. Some guys just can't perform under pressure, a fact that had been very true for me.

Although Clint's mindset was much improved, his body kept giving him problems. Throughout his career, Clint has been plagued with injuries, part of the reason he had a 4-year break. In one fight, he beat a guy in 15 seconds, something he would have been thrilled about had he not broken his hand, requiring 2 surgeries and 9 months off. He talked of his latest knee surgery, tearing his groin off his pelvis, and the injuries that could have ended his career. Clint's not ready to stop; he's at a point where he doesn't care about the pain and just works around the injuries.

For very little money. For seemingly small reward. Why continue to fight?

"When I first started, I wanted to do it to tell the girls," Clint said. "That's what I used to tell her, I'm a cage fighter."

I was glad to hear I hadn't been the only one.

"I've always wanted to be a pro athlete. A good pro athlete," Clint said. "It's not about the money, it's not about the fame, or any of that stuff, it's all just me getting myself to the top and going as far as I can go in that sport."

He motioned at the room he'd just taught in. "This is what I love, this is what I live for. Even coaching these guys, you see them, I got them from sixty to eighteen. Some have never done anything before in their life, and how great it is to see both adults and children walking with their heads held high."

Clint talked about how much he's learned from so many different people, both on and off the mat. He credited Mike Winkeljohn as being the most influential, and, he said, all he wants to do is give back and pass on that knowledge, just like Coach Wink.

* * *

That night I headed north to Rio Rancho to snap photos of the Mean1 MMA team training. At 6', 145 pounds, 22-year-old Andres Quintana stood out because of his ability and composure. Although quiet and polite, Andres seemingly had a rougher side. He'd grown up in Roswell, NM, raised mainly by his mother and stepdad. He'd been in a lot of fights as a kid but brushed it off by saying the fights were normal.

At 12, Andres began boxing, reaching a rank of No. 4 in the world. After getting robbed in a decision at 18, Andres decided the sport was too political and devoted himself to MMA, which he'd already been training for 2 years. Andres lost his first 2 fights, but then went on an 8-fight streak. He learned to believe in himself.

Andres, who was 6-1 as a pro, said that when he steps into the cage he goes to a different place. "I'm just real focused on what I have to do. This is how I make my living, so losing isn't much of an option. I really need that win bonus to continue my career, so I'm always thinking I'm the best in there, that no one is going to beat me."

This wasn't cockiness. This was belief in himself and a powerful psychological tool. When asked about his future, he said, "I've been fighting for ten years now and I'm barely reaping the benefits. It's been a struggle, but now I'm making some decent money." Andres had just been signed to Bellator and he said in 5 years he wants to be at the top of his sport.

There was another tall, lean fighter at the gym, but he was unable to train. Steve Garcia was fresh from knee surgery, a move he'd tried to avoid because it had cost him his spot on the Bellator card I'd be attending Wednesday night. The clean-cut 21-year-old, although disappointed with his current situation, was a pleasure to talk with, well-spoken and thoughtful. He identified himself as a Christian and credited God with his victories in his 1 pro and 13 amateur fights. As Jason Manly and others had explained, Steve was fighting to show the talent God gave him.

Steve said he'd never been an aggressive person and only started training because he was getting into fights at school and wanted to defend himself. He was very competitive and always wanted to win, whether it was baseball or football, so it was only natural for the competitiveness to play out in martial arts, first in jiu jitsu, then kickboxing, and finally MMA.

Like Andres, Steve seemed much older than his age. Martial arts helped them mature and learn self-control. While most guys their age were out partying, Steve was spending time with his family or in the gym bettering himself. "MMA changes you. You fear less. You don't worry about stuff," he said. "It's not just a fighting mentality. It's a mentality that always gives you confidence."

When asked how he developed such a strong mindset, Steve said, "You put in that work to have the confidence in the cage. It's a switch." He said, "I'm a nice guy, but when we're in the cage, it's either me or you. I'm not going to be on the losing side of it. You always have to have that confidence in yourself that you'll perform, do well, and get the W."

I asked him about his future and without hesitation, he said, "I'm going be a top contender. And eventually a champion."

It was easy for Steve to be confident because he trains with some of the top fighters at Jackson Wink and Mean1. He said that even if he's not as good as those guys, he's at least able to hang with them. With his work ethic and determination to train harder than any opponent, Steve knows it's just a matter of time before he reaches that level.

"If you step into a cage or a ring, and you have a doubt in your head then you've already beat yourself. There's no point in going in," Steve said. "Running and all this stuff sucks when you're doing it. It's never fun. But that's how you become confident."

Tuesday I was back at Mike Winkeljohn's gym, taking photos as he coached the children's MMA class. When the kids finished, I joined the dozen adult students for kickboxing. Like Clint's class, the group was mixed, some older than me, others half my age, only a couple committed to competing. I hoped I was going to make it through the entire class, but I let Wink know ahead of time what kind of shape I was in. He kept an eye on me, made sure to partner me with the right people, and didn't make me feel like a coward when I would bow out a round to recoup and take photos.

The training was great, and I was excited to be spending the next few days picking Wink's brain and interviewing fighters at the main gym, Jackson Wink MMA Academy, which Greg Jackson and Wink had developed into what is often considered the top MMA gym in the world.

I arrived early Wednesday morning and Wink began feeding me fighters, making the interview part of their training. Everyone I'd interviewed had great things to say about Wink, and I was gaining an appreciation for both striking as an art and coaching by watching him in the cage.

Wink pointed out several young fighters that would most likely be successful in the sport. One of them who really left an impression on me was a 21-year-old, Landon Vannata, who had moved to Albuquerque to pursue MMA 3 years before. Landon raced BMX bikes as a toddler and became a 2-time national champ and was ranked No. 1 in the world by the time he was 6. Despite his success, he stopped racing and didn't play any sports until high school.

"By the time I was in fifth grade I had probably been in like thirty street fights," Landon said, not seeming to think much of it. "But not once since sixth grade," he said, the same year he tried aikido. That experience hadn't been a positive one, but it did teach him he wanted more. Landon needed more of a challenge. High school wrestling gave him that and so much more, but it was still not enough.

Landon clearly remembered the first time he saw MMA, the UFC 30 videotape, a gift from his aunt. As a fan of action movies, and someone who'd had his share of confrontations, Landon watched the tape every day after school and would practice moves on his own. MMA was his biggest passion and he said he wanted to fight from the first time he saw that tape.

Unlike a lot of guys who said they wanted to fight at a young age but didn't begin training until adulthood, Landon started grappling at 13 with the intention to fight. Just as it had for anyone who stuck with the sport long enough, the training changed him. "I used to be very self-conscious. I didn't have a lot of confidence," he said. "I didn't speak my mind. When I started training I became much more relaxed and comfortable with myself. Overall I became a more confident person."

The motorcycle-riding adrenaline junkie said that confidence shows in the cage. Because he has incredible coaches, the toughest teammates, and the desire to be the best, he's completely relaxed when he walks out to compete. He was 2-0 as both a pro and amateur and already in good control of the mental game. He fought in a calm, but focused, state and saw each fight as an opportunity to showcase his art.

Landon's biggest accomplishment was not letting fear stop him from moving across the country at 18. He had the confidence to go for his dreams, knowing he could always change direction if it didn't work out or he no longer enjoyed what he was doing. Of course, there are no guarantees in life, and especially in fighting, but if I was a betting man, I'd say that, just like Steve and Andres, Landon was going to make an impact on the sport.

* * *

There were a lot of fighters floating around Jackson-Wink's who had their left their mark on the sport. One of them was 6'3" 250-pound Frank Mir.

Before I could introduce myself, Frank asked my name and where he knew me from. I was surprised he even recognized me, but I had been one of his sparring partners at the Las Vegas Combat Club in 2003 and 2004, right before he became the UFC heavyweight champion by snapping Tim Sylvia's forearm. Frank was one of the few guys whose fights I'd followed, and I'd enjoyed seeing his success, especially his color commentary. He is a great example of a big, strong, intelligent man who also enjoys competing in mixed martial arts.

I thought back to our sparring sessions and wondered what I must have been thinking. At the time, Frank, 7 years younger than me, was already a black belt in American Kenpo, a dangerous BJJ brown belt, taller, stronger, in better shape, and beating guys like Tank Abbot and Wes Sims in the UFC.

As much as I wanted to, and as hard as I tried, I wasn't going to get the best of him.

I didn't know Frank very well then, but I do remember that he was confident. Some people took it the wrong way and thought he was cocky, but it wasn't that at all. Through wrestling, jiu jitsu, and then MMA, he had proven to himself that he could learn techniques and apply them in competition. He had proven he was one of the best fighters in the world.

Of the 300 fighters I'd interviewed, how many could I point to as being either successful or unsuccessful largely because of their confidence? Probably a lot, especially if I was given an honest assessment of the person. Even if they never spoke of their confidence, fighters' demeanor and posture were telling when asked about their goals and dreams.

I felt I had a decent handle on the huge number of factors that play a part in but don't predetermine why someone would compete in mixed martial arts. But I hadn't closely looked at the differences in fighters to determine why some are successful while others, like me, aren't. Wink, a fifth-degree black belt in Kenpo Karate who'd earned 3 world titles in kickboxing, had spent 3 decades working with every level of fighter, and more than his share of champions. He could surely tell me what makes a champion, but first I wanted to hear what he thought motivated someone to fight.

"It probably can be deep as to why they fight," Wink said. "Maybe they were abused as a kid. Maybe their dad beat them up. Maybe they were bullied. There's something and I don't know what it is. But I think there is something that motivates these people to challenge themselves. Some people just like the competition, they like the challenge."

Wink said MMA had changed a lot since the early days and now that the sport is getting bigger and people can watch it on TV, the motivations were changing as well. Kids are now looking up to fighters as they do other athletes. "They want to be like them," Wink said. "They want the fame, they want the money, they want to be great at something."

What traits contributed to the success of a fighter?

Mental traits came first. Wink mentioned toughness and willingness to stand up for themselves but insisted the most important thing is the fighter's self-confidence. "That's huge," Wink said. "They could be the most skilled, knowledgeable person out there, but at the moment, under fire, if they panic, if they don't believe, if they overthink it, it all falls apart. It's the ones that believe in themselves." He sees it all the time with guys who are shown a new move and then try it out in the cage 5 minutes later because they believe they can do it. "I believe that's the biggest thing, that they believe in themselves."

I was surprised to hear Wink's last trait and how much emphasis he placed on the willingness to help others. "A kid that comes in that's willing to give to others," Wink said, "other fighters in the gym start helping him out." That's one of the main reasons the team of fighters Wink and Greg Jackson had formed is so good. The fighters help each other learn and almost don't need coaches because they have so much knowledge and openly share it with each other.

When asked what kind of people Wink came across in the sport, he said, "Most MMA fighters that I know are just great guys," Wink said. "They're the kind of guys that are going to hold the door open for the ladies. They're the kind of guys who are going to take care of the weak. They're the kind of guys who are respectful and courteous and want to shake your hands. They don't need to prove themselves. They're not usually the guys who are going to posture and act tough. Because they're tough, they don't need to act that way." Wink said they're also very smart. "It's a chess game. The guys that fight at the highest level understand what's going on." With a huge smile, he said, "I love the MMA guys. The guys that are successful usually are very, very nice guys and intelligent."

Was the training largely responsible for these positive traits or something inherent in the people that choose to fight?

"The guys that stick around, through time, I think they learn a lot about helping others, about becoming good people. Understanding that being the tough guy is not the most important thing. Being tough is important, but not being the tough guy; those are two different things."

The change happens because MMA is bigger than just another sport: it's mixed martial arts, and the traditional values inherent in martial arts have found their way into it. "Honesty, courtesy, respect, discipline." He said, "I think they become better people the more they do it. They see the value in it, it gets engrained in them. I honestly believe society is a lot better off for it."

We wrapped up the interview by talking about how they'd created a family-oriented gym. "It's about having fun in a controlled situation," Wink said. "We have guys that are going to the highest level. I have two instructors on their way to the UFC and I train them. But at the same time, I have people who want to come in and have a good time, learn to defend themselves, feel better about themselves."

I mentioned how much I'd enjoyed Tuesday's class, how getting battered around in sparring had made me feel more alive. Wink said, "There's no doubt about it. The feeling's real, when you're actually in there and you're actually wrestling, you're actually getting hit. You do feel alive. You feel like, wow this is what it's like. Oh, I was able to take that punch, I was able to slip that punch. You feel stronger, you feel that you're living the moment. You're not watching it on TV like most people."

It's why some people get hooked on combat sports, one of the reasons I was beginning to enjoy it. Maybe it wasn't too late for me to learn a few skills. Maybe I could get in the cage one more time.

CHAPTER SEVENTEEN

August 1, 2013

It was Thursday morning, six o'clock, way too early for the alarm to be blaring. I hadn't returned to my hotel until after midnight and had trouble sleeping, my emotions running high from covering the Bellator fight outside of Albuquerque. The fights had been intense, over a dozen solid matchups, and I'd been sitting at the press table unable to cheer for the 2 competitors I cared about. It was tough watching Jacob Noe get knocked out by King Mo Lawal, but Michael Chandler's brilliant second defense of his lightweight belt helped ease the blow.

As much as I wanted to get a few more hours of sleep, I wasn't going to miss out on the interviews I'd already planned, the day's focus on females. On the drive to Jackson Wink I was thinking about the general public's perception of female fighters and how different it was from when I was a kid. Back then, one of the biggest insults was having your physical skills compared to a girl's. Whether it was throwing, kicking, or punching, if someone said you did it like a girl, it was on. Everyone knew that after junior high, girls couldn't physically do what boys could. Sure they could cheerlead, play softball, or bring the boys water, but real sports were out of the question.

When I began training in the late '90s there weren't many women in the fight gyms. Occasionally you'd come across some who'd grown bored with the kickboxing classes and wanted to train the ground game, but there weren't a whole lot. I'm sure this had a lot to do with the overall lack of respect from the guys who assumed the women would get hurt and be in the way. Fighting was for men.

The first time I saw women fight MMA was back in '98 in El Paso, TX, for SuperBrawl 9. Several of us male fighters came out of the dressing room to witness the fight, a lopsided 24-second victory. I remember being surprised, not at the fighters' abilities, but their desire. I'd always considered women the softer, kinder version of men. Why would women want to fight?

Even though it was still harder for me to understand why women would want to compete in mixed martial arts, I had the same level of respect for them as I had for males, if not more. I hadn't always been like that, largely because female fights were few and far between and the ability level in MMA had been relatively poor. But things had changed.

In Orange County, I'd trained alongside Ashlee Evans-Smith and Jessica Martinez. At Combat Sports Authority, I watched Alexis Davis, Sarah D'Alelio, and Elaina Maxwell push through their workout. At El Niño Training Center, Leslie Smith ground through a wrestling clinic, the only female on the mat. I was ringside when Alexis DuFresne, a young fighter out of ATT Temecula, overwhelmed her opponent in the first round, and Saturday, just before I got on the plane for Albuquerque, my wife and I went to watch Heather Clark box.

After Heather's match, we threw on the UFC and watched Julie Kedzie, the fighter I was on my way to interview, fight a 3-round battle with Germaine de Randamie, a very talented kickboxer. Although Julie took a good deal of punishment, she hadn't stopped pressing the entire match. It was a close fight and she lost the split decision.

Now if I'm ever accused of fighting like a girl, I'll assume they're talking about these ladies and I'll thank them for the compliment. I can no longer listen to how women can't fight, that they lack the skills, the strength, the determination, whatever it is that makes men feel superior. These women would beat the average untrained man. Match them up pound for pound and I'd bet on the women every time.

Unfortunately, being a fan doesn't help one bit with my research. My sample of female fighters was still too small to make any worthwhile comparisons. Even with the rise in popularity and great events like the all-female Invicta, there are not nearly enough female fighters out there and they only accounted for 8% of my interviews. What were their reasons for fighting? Were they the same as the men's? How similar were the statistics and patterns?

But even if my sample was going to end up too small for the study, I still wanted to learn all that I could. I pulled up in front of Jackson Wink, excited to hear Julie's story.

The 32-year-old bantamweight met me at the front desk with a smile. Julie said she had always been competitive and martial arts had been part of her life since she was 5. She recognized martial arts had given her a sense of self that she didn't get in regular school and her Tae Kwon Do academy became her community. Although she competed in TKD and sport karate through her early teens and college, Julie eventually grew bored with point fighting. When she saw a HOOKnSHOOT video of all female fights, she was immediately intrigued and thought she could do it. Julie began competing in jiu jitsu and Muay Thai, explaining that, "I wasn't into theory. I was into practice. I wanted to fight. I wanted to be competitive."

Julie took her first MMA fight at 23 and won by armbar, falling in love with the sport. Over the next 9 years, she fought another 28 times, going 16-12, which she thought was a terrible record. What she was most proud of was not quitting despite those losses, some of them to the best fighters in the world, such as Gina Carano, Alexis Davis, and Meisha Tate. Julie said, "The addictive side of MMA is that if you don't achieve what you set out to achieve, you either quit, or you go right back into it."

When Julie first fought in 2004 she swore she would be a UFC fighter, but just getting into the organization wasn't enough for her. "I want to be a good UFC fighter," Julie said, upset she hadn't performed to the best of her ability. All she wanted was another chance to prove she was better than what she'd shown the world. If she could have, she would have fought a rematch that moment.

She became more intense and said, "I've got to get better. I've got to be the best. Whether it's in a small stage in New Mexico in front of friends and family, or on a big stage in front of millions of people, I need to be the best."

Julie said she had to be the best so many times that I asked if she was that way in the rest of her life. Was she a perfectionist like me who had a hard time being happy?

At first Julie shook it off, but then she recalled how much she enjoyed writing and drawing but never pursued those arts because she thought she wasn't good enough. Often she would throw work away because of that self-doubt.

When asked who she was in the cage, Julie shared her frustration. "I don't know who I am in the cage. I'd like to give you some definite answer, but I don't know that," she said. "I know who I was this last Saturday when I lost, and it wasn't who I was supposed to be. I wasn't pulling the trigger."

Some nights were great and Julie would live up to her potential, but other nights she felt as if she were off mentally. She explained that in Saturday's fight she had made all the mistakes she makes in her worst days of sparring. "MMA is a sport where you can't be half-assed," Julie said. "You have to be present. And I've learned that lesson over and over and over. That you can't be overtrained or undertrained, that you have to be exactly right."

Despite being upset about this last fight, Julie was still very friendly and personable. With her English degree, a passion for writing, and a love for commentary, Julie had other options in life, but chose to fight, a martial artist wanting to prove her art. "It's a crazy thing to keep doing what I love to do," she said with a huge smile. "There are so many paths I could have taken, and I just stuck on the one that was so hard and I'm glad."

Looking on the bright side, Julie said, "I'm pissed about my last fight, so pissed, but at the same time it helped me let a lot of things go." UFC president Dana White and others had commented that the fight was boring, but Julie understood that those 15 minutes in the cage were not a true reflection of her ability or who she was as a person. "That was one instant, one night that I had off in the history of a 32-year-old woman. Sorry it sucked but that wasn't indicative of who I am as a human being."

When asked about the way women were viewed in the MMA world, Julie brought up some of the popular magazine spreads that female fighters had recently been appearing in. Although Julie isn't a fan of the racier Maxim-type spreads, she admired how Ronda Rousey's ESPN magazine shoot displayed a powerful image and Gina Carano looked gorgeous in her photos. Julie had tried doing photo shoots early on in her career and realized right away it wasn't for her. Now she hoped females could look at her and see they could be clumsy, not have six-pack abs, and still have a rewarding career. Julie felt the choice to capitalize on one's sexuality, whether male or female, was something each fighter needed to decide for themselves.

Julie hadn't always been happy with herself. "No, I was never there, and I still struggle with body dysmorphia at times. Aging helps," she said. "When you grow into your own mind and your own body, it helps a lot."

Another thing that's made her happier is embracing being selfish. "When you're a fighter, it's kind of a solipsistic pursuit; you can't do it thinking about other people. You have to put yourself first." Julie said, "I want children and I want a family, but those things have not presented themselves to me in a way in where they were more attractive to me than in the way that I'm living."

Fighting also helped Julie develop the strength to stand up for her beliefs. Even when she knows she will take heat from other fighters and coaches with opposing viewpoints, she stands her ground. Julie said fighting has helped her to not get worked up by other people or their comments. Opinions couldn't hurt like the elbows, fists, knees, and shins flying at her.

Julie had given so much of her life to MMA and it had paid off in a multitude of ways, but it was more than the training and competing that affected her life. "Greg Jackson has a great deal to do with me changing and turning into who I am at this point. He really is my best friend." She said, "It's such a lame thing to say, but there's that Samurai code, where you devote yourself to your masters. And to me that's Greg and Wink, my instructors."

* * *

The tiny 27-year-old smiling behind the desk seemed more like a ring girl than a fighter. Michelle Waterson, the Invicta atomweight champion, told me that's what led her into MMA. While working on a double major in college, Michelle was a ring girl at an event and thought it would be way more exciting to be fighting than holding up a sign.

The Karate Hottie had always been intrigued by martial arts. She said she and her older brother were movie buffs and comic book nerds who watched *Power Rangers*, *Mortal Kombat*, and *Teenage Mutant Ninja Turtles*. Michelle adored her brother and always wanted to do whatever he did, especially when he began training American Freestyle Karate. Michelle started karate at 10 and was thrilled to discover they could do the same awesome moves as the people on TV.

Michelle said, "I wouldn't be the person I am today, if it wasn't for martial arts." As a child, she struggled with low self-esteem, largely because she was missing her four front teeth until she was 8 and needed a lot of dental work after they grew in. The shame turned her into a people pleaser and a pushover. "Doing martial arts gave me the confidence and the ability to stand up for myself, and grounded me as a person," she said. The confidence manifested in many ways, including beginning a modeling career after high school.

Martial arts was a huge part of Michelle's formative years, and she never dreamed of leaving it despite working at different jobs and attending college. Early on she realized she'd like to be an instructor, but to do that she felt she needed to be proficient in both the artistic and combative sides of the art. Michelle took naturally to the artistic side, flowing gracefully through katas, but sparring had always been a challenge. Instead of taking the easy way out and changing paths, Michelle decided she'd go to Thailand to learn Muay Thai. She came back to the United States an improved striker, anxious to test herself in the kickboxing circuit until she realized there was no money in kickboxing. Not compared to MMA.

The thought of fighting became reality soon after Michelle turned 21. The rush was addictive, and Michelle decided she'd found her calling. Although she was close to finishing a double major in theater and physical therapy, she left college because that wasn't where her heart was.

"I don't think you'll ever feel anything like the adrenaline that you do when you go into a fight," she said. "You know the person across from you has trained just as hard as you have. And then they close the cage behind you. You can't crawl out; you can't say no. It's kind of like being in labor: you can't turn back. It's an adrenaline rush."

Michelle knew about labor, proud to have delivered her daughter naturally. She had known that just like fighting, childbirth was going to hurt, but the reward outweighed the risk.

I asked if being a mother affected her ability to compete. Jessica Philippus has said motherhood had made her softer, more compassionate. She'd cried when she recounted punching a mounted opponent until the woman's eyes rolled back in her head.

Michelle had a different take. She said motherhood could increase a female's ferocity. She went back to the cavewomen who'd watch over the young while men were off hunting. A mother's role was to protect her young, to fight tooth and nail, make every sacrifice for them.

The other reason Michele cited for why it shouldn't be surprising that women would enter combat sports is that females have a certain passion and drive to perform. The problem is that people outside of MMA don't see it as a sport in which 2 individuals are competing against each other. They see it simply as a fight in which people will get hurt.

Michelle had some concerns in the back of her mind about injuries. Having been in more than a dozen fights and countless sparring sessions, she understood what she was doing guaranteed she would suffer pain. But that wasn't what truly scared her. Her greatest fear was the one Julie was dealing with: not being able to show the world her capabilities.

Being a top-ranked mixed martial artist and a mother of a 2-year-old wasn't easy and didn't allow for the admittedly selfish lifestyle Julie enjoyed, but Michelle said it was no different than anything else in life. If you want something bad enough, you'll make the time for it. Fortunately, everyone was very supportive at the gym, and Michelle said it was a great setting for her daughter.

When asked what kind of people fighters are, Michelle said they are some of the nicest people she's ever met; definitely not the stereotypical brute meatheads who want to smash their opponents. But she had a theory that many of the fighters, especially male, were in MMA to keep their rage under control.

Quite a few fighters had told me how much they needed MMA, that they had trouble self-regulating without it. Michelle believed that a great many people don't know how to control themselves and some of them find their way into MMA, the sport becoming a great source for self-discipline and improvement.

I'd seen this with a good number of fighters, especially younger guys, and I thought back to how true it had been for me and lots of my teammates. I was a very angry and negative person during those years, and having a fight scheduled was the best form of self-discipline I'd ever had. When some other guy was training his ass off so he could kick mine, I eased off on the partying and self-destructive behavior.

Michelle wrapped up the interview by saying she wished people would see martial arts as more than the 15 minutes of fighting seen on TV. The martial arts could give someone a good moral foundation in life, a chance to challenge and fulfill themselves. MMA was just a small part of that.

* * *

It was three o'clock and miserable outside so I hurried into the gym. FIT NHB was an older building without frills, and had a similar feel to Tri-Force MMA in Rhode Island. People were coming here to work hard, not look pretty.

The 24-year-old atomweight I was there to interview probably didn't feel pretty at the moment, her face a little banged up from her Pancrase fight in Tokyo the previous weekend. Amber Brown was wiped out from the weight cut, her third-round victory, and all the hours on an airplane, but she was happy to share who she was and why she was fighting.

Amber showed me into the quiet back office and filled me in on her fight while I set up my gear. The experience had been so powerful that she had a hard time believing she'd only been training in the martial arts for less than 4 years. She was eager to spend many more going after her goals.

Like Michelle Waterson, Amber was a mother, but she didn't begin training until her daughter was 1 year old and only because she wanted to get back in shape. She chose FIT NHB simply because her boyfriend was already training there.

It didn't take long for the boxing classes to turn into sparring sessions, and Amber realized she had a passion and talent for the sport. She had 4 amateur boxing matches and loved the adrenaline rush, but it was difficult to find opponents and when Amber lost her pro debut, she knew she needed a change. The switch to MMA seemed like the most natural thing to do, so she jumped straight into the pros and went 3-1 in the last 9 months.

Besides the better pay and activity level, Amber loved how much more challenging MMA was than boxing. She said there was so much more to worry about, so much more to perfect. She could train the rest of her life and never learn it all, but she wanted to try, dreams of owning a gym starting to seem attainable.

Amber said that although the fans were cool, she wasn't fighting for money or fame. "It's a self-test," she said. "It's about how good I can be and how much better I can be every day."

I thanked Amber for her time and thought about her story while taking photos of her teammates training. As with all the males I'd encountered, there was obviously no one answer as to why a female would compete in MMA. No list of factors that guaranteed they'd become a fighter. I had been having a harder time understanding why females would want to fight because I'd been viewing both them and the sport from the wrong perspective.

Julie, Amber, Michelle, and most fighters see MMA as a way of life. It's part of who they are. They've acquired a wealth of knowledge, want to prove that knowledge in the fairest test possible, and eventually pass down that knowledge.

Although I couldn't imagine ever encouraging my daughter to compete in MMA, I would encourage her to train in the martial arts. I'd constantly remind her that she can do absolutely anything she wants in life, that she's never inferior to a man. I was also going to sit down with her one day to watch these interviews and clips of their fights because most of these ladies were great role models that I'd love my daughter to look up to.

CHAPTER EIGHTEEN

August 3, 2013

It was Saturday morning, my last day in Albuquerque, and I was at Jackson Wink's, splitting my time between grappling, taking photos, and conducting interviews. A lot of my focus was on Donald "Cowboy" Cerrone, a UFC fighter I admired for his talent, toughness, and willingness to fight anytime, anywhere.

During a break, I approached Cowboy to ask if he'd be up for an interview, and he agreed to sit down with me as soon as he was done training. I went back to snapping photos of guys I'd interviewed over the week. At the buzzer, a smaller fighter with short hair and a bushy beard walked over and introduced himself as Nico Lozada, asked if I'd care to interview him. The 25-year-old was from Northern California and at Jackson's to prepare for his third amateur fight.

Cowboy was gathering his gear. I considered brushing Nico off in favor of interviewing the famous fighter, but I couldn't do that to someone who wanted to share his story. I'd caught glimpses of Nico grappling and knew he was committed to the sport since he was doing camps here to prepare for an amateur bout. I also knew that if I really wanted to know who Cowboy was and why he fought, I could turn to the internet and take my pick from several interviews.

Nico, who was in college and worked full time with kids from kindergarten through sixth grade, was open from the moment we started the interview. When asked about his childhood, Nico shook his head. There had been some good moments, but he had been through hell, mostly at the hands of bullies.

Now 5'7" and 135 pounds, Nico had never been one of the bigger kids. He also had large teeth and had been hyperactive, leaving little chance he wouldn't be a target. In first grade, Nico was diagnosed with ADHD and prescribed drugs; the amounts and types constantly changing as doctors played a guessing game trying to find the magic pill combination that would fix him.

"One day I'm taking something that causes me to put on twenty pounds eating McDonald's because I was hungry all the time," Nico said. "The next one I'm convulsing. The other ones I wasn't sleeping. The other ones I was sleeping everywhere and getting in trouble for sleeping at school."

Besides being made fun of for fidgeting, for sleeping, for fighting back because he became so angry, Nico also had to deal with being ridiculed for going to the nurse's office before lunch to take his "crazy pills." He said, "You have enough people call you a sheep, you'll begin to think you're a sheep. You have enough people tell you you're crazy, you might start believing it. That really tormented me as a kid. I'd walk into my doctor's office like I was some kid in a straightjacket."

By the time he was 12, Nico was sent to a wilderness program in Idaho. After that it was a boarding school for 3 years, medicated the entire time. He knows his parents were following doctors' orders because they believed it was best for him, but that approach was not working.

Nico lived in a state of depression and felt worthless. "I couldn't sleep. I'd cry at night. I felt like I wasn't good enough for people." In the past year, Nico's best friend had committed suicide because he was going through similar issues. Nico's voice cracked when he said, "That's what it really makes you feel like. When you're bullied by people you feel like life is meaningless and the world would be better off without you. I feel like it truly affected me for many years."

I turned off the camera and said we should take a little break. I appreciated how open Nico was being even though it was painful for him, so

I shared that one of my closest friends had also committed suicide at 23 and that I'd struggled with self-destructive thoughts most of my life. I was glad both of us no longer had that mindset.

Nico said he was ready and we talked about his transformation, how he got off his medication and found martial arts. He started out with Muay Thai, jiu jitsu, then finally MMA, a sport he had always enjoyed watching but never thought he would do. Training in the martial arts gave Nico a place to expend his extra energy, build confidence, and be himself because teammates only judged him by how hard he worked.

The martial arts training and Muay Thai bouts had probably brought about most of the changes in Nico, but there was something about fighting in a cage that excited him. "When you're in a ring it makes it feel like more of a competition," Nico said. "Yes, you want to win that fight no matter what, but when you're in a cage and that fight-or-flight moment comes in, there's only so far you can move and it feeds that animal instinct. It not only drives my competitive side, but it drives my inner beast that's been in our DNA since the cavemen."

Nico said, "I love the aspect of forcing my will on someone else and breaking them physically, mentally, to the point where they don't want to be there. I love the competitiveness of it and I love the fact that it feeds my fear, too."

When the cage door closes, Nico's anxiety goes through the roof. He embraces that feeling and feels it's necessary, that everyone should test themselves. "If you're never overcoming your fears and pushing through it to that uncomfortable point and finding the solution, then you're never going to find a solution through life."

Nico's experiences made him appreciate what he now had and he wanted to share what he had learned with others. "When you find something that you truly love, like I found martial arts, when you focus on it and make that the point of your life, everything around you will become better. You'll find more meaning to life, more of a sense of living."

I thanked Nico for being so honest with me. At the end of the emotional interview, he said he was telling me all of this, not because he hoped it would make people like him or follow his career. "I want to be looked upon as the person who found something he loved and he did it. I just want everyone to look at my life and be like, 'I want to do that. I want to find something I truly love, even though I'm depressed and feel like I want to end it. I want to find something I truly love and do it.' That's what I want to show."

* * *

Back at the hotel, I took out my list of fighters to see how many admitted to being bullied. Out of 300 fighters, I would have guessed there'd be a decent percentage that'd experienced bullying. Mike Winkeljohn had also speculated the number of bullied or abused males who became fighters might be high. However, I wasn't finding a great deal.

A couple of fighters had talked about getting into fights when they were older, but very few claimed to have been bullied. The few who did stuck out in my mind. Alex White, a 6-0 pro out of Destruction MMA in Missouri, was the youngest of 4 and grew up poor. He clearly remembered watching his older brother being bullied and the helplessness they both felt. Alex, who as a neglected young boy had ingested gasoline and damaged his vocal cords, was an obvious target and was bullied until he finally started fighting back.

Toby Imada, the journeyman with 50 fights that I'd interviewed at The Arena MMA, said that kids were some of the meanest people ever. He'd been bullied everywhere he went, just as John Hahn, the retired Marine and FBI agent who worked at Xtreme Couture. John had attended 20 different schools, and was always the poor little new kid, a target who had to learn to fight back so people wouldn't pick on him or his 2 younger brothers.

Around a dozen fighters had used the term bullying, but something Wink had asked made me realize that number was much higher. Wink asked if John Dodson had told me about being hog-tied. He hadn't. Bullying just didn't come up when I interviewed him.

In addition to not directly asking every fighter if they'd been bullied, I hadn't considered that many might not care to tell that story. Maybe they were tired of retelling the same thing over and over, or perhaps they just wanted to forget it and not bring up painful memories from the past.

Nearly all the bullying stories followed a familiar storyline: Kid is bullied, kid goes into shell and remains an easy target, kid continues to be bullied until he begins training and refuses to be a victim.

But one of the lessons I'd learned was that not everyone reacts the same way to the same set of circumstances. Two of the fighters I'd interviewed at Jackson Wink's on Wednesday had been affected by bullying, but the topic almost hadn't come up with either of them.

When I first sat down with Tommy Truex, I didn't know what to expect. If I hadn't already seen the chilling tattoo that covered his back, or the ones snaking down his arms, I might have imagined this clean-cut lightweight as a cute little Dennis the Menace who grew up to be a salesman. But Tommy wasn't a regular 9 to 5 kind of guy. Aside from the occasional MMA fight, the 29-year-old was also an active duty lieutenant in the Army, an actor, and co-owner of Desert Forge CrossFit. He was 5-1 and 2 weeks out from a fight in Guatemala, but there were other things he wanted to talk about.

As an Iraq War vet and active duty recruiter, Tommy cared deeply about fellow vets. When I asked him about the staggering rate of veteran suicides, he said frankly, "My friends are killing themselves all the time." We talked about PTSD and why it is so difficult for military members to ask for help. He made a plea to other vets to reach out to him if they were feeling suicidal. He insisted life could still be good after the experiences on the battlefield; that anything could be overcome and life was good.

Tommy's other passion surprised me, just as it would his own parents had they been sitting with us. Tommy had struggled with anorexia/bulimia since he was 11 years old, battling in silence for most of his life because male eating disorders are not something that are talked about. Even his wife, who had been his best friend for a dozen years, only recently found out. Like Nico, Tommy wanted to share his story with others dealing with the same issue. He wanted to prevent suffering, to encourage people, whether boys or girls, men or women, to get help, to talk to someone.

I liked the advice he offered both veterans and people with eating disorders. "Go deal with your problems," he said. "Facing things is what takes courage. Running away from things and pretending they don't matter, that's being a wuss."

Tommy was committed to the upcoming fight and he looked impressive hitting mitts with Wink, yet he didn't have unrealistic expectations of what he would do in MMA. It was an obvious joke when he said he wanted to become a UFC champion. "There are a lot of fucking dudes out there who are better than me. I just want to compete at the highest level I can and have a blast."

For Tommy, the training was what mattered. That's what helped him manage his emotions. As he dealt with PTSD, his eating disorder, or just the stress of everyday life, MMA grounded him. Although he hid it incredibly well, he appeared to be the type of guy Michelle Waterson said needed the sport to help them contain their rage.

I learned there was a point where Tommy had been that happy-go-lucky little kid. That changed when he became the victim of bullies, and when stood he by helplessly while his sisters were picked on. The constant teasing and pushing only grew worse, the anger eating away at Tommy until he snapped. The smiling straight-A student wanted payback, grabbed a baseball bat and retaliated.

His military experience may have amplified Tommy's anger, but the Army also gave Tommy exactly what he needed: a place to embrace and expend that emotion, to channel that energy. Training in mixed martial arts served a similar purpose. It was one of the main reasons Tommy was back to being a smiling, charismatic young man who people wanted to be around.

The other fighter who'd talked about being bullied was the muscular middleweight, Bubba McDaniel Jr., a 30-year-old with tattoos adorning his shoulders and arms, and an accent so strong there was no question he was from Texas. Although I hadn't watched Bubba on *TUF Season 17*, 4 months earlier, he assured me he wasn't the asshole the show made him out to be, he was just there to fight. Bubba had been nothing but friendly and likable with me so I told him not to worry. My time with Josh Koscheck had convinced me not to hold onto preconceived notions, especially ones shaped by a "reality" show.

Bubba came from a large family, having 4 sisters and 3 brothers, but not one of them a full-blood sibling. Growing up he'd been the tall, skinny kid who always got injured and was never good at football, the only sport that really mattered in his town. "I always got hurt, and I still get hurt. For some reason, I picked a sport where you get hurt all the time." With a smile, he said, "I don't know why, but I love it."

I started to jump ahead with him to MMA but decided to backtrack to his early years. Was he social, a class clown?

There was a noticeable shift as Bubba decided how much he'd share with me. The smile was still there, but it wasn't a very happy one. "Okay, here's a crazy story for you. In middle school I was the picked-on kid. In high school I was the picked-on kid. I was the guy that literally got shoved in lockers." He said, "People took me as awkward."

When Bubba was finally big enough to stand up for himself, he began to get in a lot of trouble. "My retaliation was over the top," he said, going on to describe how he got kicked out of 3 schools in 2 districts. By the time he was 16, he had been court ordered to take the GED test.

"It cost me a lot of time, a lot of friends," he said. "My life was kind of turmoil. I thought people were my friends and then they're not. And that bugged me a lot. So once I found MMA, that was the point where I found someone who could accept me for anything. I went in and worked hard. Everybody could understand that."

It was obvious that Bubba would rather be done dredging up painful memories, but I asked if he'd share what bullying can do to a young person.

"A lot of people take it a lot of ways. Some kids kill themselves." He said others go into a depression and have a difficult time through all their life. "That's the way I felt," he said. "I'm the weird kid. That's my role."

He was called awkward so he became awkward. "It pushes you into it," he said. "They make you believe something that you're not. Like I'm a good dude, I love to hang around, I love to smile, but you wouldn't fucking know it."

Bubba spoke about the fear he has of his own children being bullied. "I turned mine into a bad thing. I was in juvenile hall a lot. I didn't do any long stays but I spent a lot of time in there. It was regular I was getting picked up as a young adult. I remember having my first trial at eighteen years old."

It's hard for Bubba to believe he'd ever been that boy, but he reiterated, "I believed what they made me believe. And it really pisses me off now, and I'll be damned if my kids are gonna have that happen."

Bubba said, "I still have grudges from middle school. I really do." He stressed he would never act on those feelings and do anything detrimental to his life, but speaking to his bully, he said, "Man, I still think of you at times. I'm thirty years old; this happened when I'm twelve, thirteen, maybe even before that. It's horrible, it's over half my life ago, and it's still in the back of my head."

All that anger steered Bubba towards working as a bouncer and participating in Toughman contests, ways to challenge himself and prove he was a man while still a teenager. He also started watching the UFC. "I thought it was cool. I thought it was the thing to do and I wanted to see if I could do it. I went to my first gym and got completely wrecked by everybody." Bubba said, "They tried to force me out. It was brutal. They didn't like me, the guy I was around town. I wasn't the likeable guy." He said he didn't blame them. "Looking at that punk kid nowadays, I would have said, 'You got to leave my gym.' I swear to God I would've kicked my own self out."

But Bubba stuck it out, dealt with the punishment 5 days a week, and before long the fighters began teaching him skills. He took his first MMA fight after training for a single month and learned a lesson in patience the hard way.

Bubba said that, without a doubt, MMA changed him. "It gives you discipline. It kept me levelheaded everywhere else. I didn't have that rage still built up."

Bubba had gone 21-6 over the last 8 years, and was 4 weeks away from his UFC fight against Brad Tavares, the biggest payday of his career. Money had always been tight for Bubba, but what he did make, he wanted to spend on family. The bullying had caused Bubba to isolate himself from his family, but now his family was his priority.

Countless people had helped turn Bubba into the person he now was and he was grateful for everyone who saw a little bit of good in him and encouraged him to pursue his dream. Whether they offered kind words, new gear, or a couch to sleep on, Bubba said he loved those people and wouldn't ever forget what they'd done for him.

I wrapped things up by asking Bubba what his reasons for fighting were. Was he in this to become a champion? Was it the fame? To showcase his skills?

He said, "The bullied kid, the picked-on kid part, it's still in my head. And I still have fears." Even with all his fights, he said, "I fear every fight. Win or lose, if I put on a good performance, it's me overcoming that shadow." Bubba said that shadow still lingers and it's a bad one. "I fear being that kid again." Speaking of MMA, Bubba said, "It's honestly about me trying not to be that scared, timid kid."

* * *

Back at the hotel I gathered my stuff and headed for the airport. On the way, I thought about what I had just learned. How many fighters had been bullied as children? How many had been transformed by training in the martial arts? How many of them still had a rage burning inside that the training kept a lid on? What would happen to them when they stopped fighting?

I got on the plane back to Los Angeles, thinking about Nico, Bubba, and Tommy, wondering how different their lives might have been if they hadn't been bullied. How would things have turned out if they'd been exposed to the martial arts much earlier? Would they still have found their way into fighting?

In my talks with other fighters, the subject hadn't been that important to me, probably because I never personally experienced it. But that wasn't entirely true, because only now did I remember my freshman year in high school when I had to get my older brother to demand my stolen books back from a bigger kid. And I'm sure there were other times, more than I wanted to remember.

But if anyone asked if I'd bullied, I'd still answer no. Not like these guys. Not like the kids who take their lives or spend them in jail thanks to their self-destructive reasoning.

Fighters sharing their fears, insecurities, and pain caused by being picked on gave me new respect for the men and women I'd met that were striving to prevent bullying. They were saving lives.

In San Diego, UFC flyweight Danny Martinez devoted much of his time to Gremlin's Kids, his program for low-income and single-parent children. He gave anti-bullying talks at elementary schools, motivated by years of watching his twin brother being constantly bullied. Danny understood how bullying could shut kids down, and he was making a difference in his community by helping those kids establish their confidence.

In the Northeast, UFC veteran Tom Murphy dedicated much of his life to the nonprofit anti-bullying organization Sweethearts and Heroes, which he started with his college roommate and wrestling teammate. Even though Tom hadn't been bullied, he cared immensely about the subject and became obsessed with recording people's stories about bullying. Tom said everyone has a bully story, and many times that story might stick with them forever. "It helps create who we are. It helps shape the way we treat other people and the way we feel about other people."

Tom pointed out that 100,000 kids drop out of school each year and will never go back due to bullying. He said, "And that's in a zero-tolerance climate. But remember, ninety-six percent of bullies get away with it." He spoke about the sharp drop in empathy among kids, especially in last 10 years. "Kids just don't care about kids anymore. It's in such a rapid decline."

Like Nico and Bubba, Tom said, "The child that goes home and makes the worst destructive decision and takes their own life—they believe that they're the problem." Bullying is habitual and the repetition causes kids to accept what they are told over and over. The way to combat it is for other kids to intervene. He said, "We all have the power to become someone's hero."

One of my favorite fighters, and my first coach, Bas Rutten, has also taken a stand against bullies. Bas, who had been bullied as a sickly kid, was now using his celebrity filming anti-bullying commercials. It's powerful to see how many MMA athletes are making a difference in their communities. These men and women understand how detrimental bullying can be and what a difference training in the martial arts can make.

Martial arts may not be the only answer to reducing the instances of bullying, but I'd say it's the best. Through martial arts, bullies are humbled while the bullied are built up. The playing field is leveled as confidence and self-respect rise. If bullying is an issue, martial arts is an excellent avenue to explore as a solution to stop it in its tracks.

CHAPTER NINETEEN

October 14, 2013

The rounds at 10th Planet Jiu Jitsu Headquarters in Los Angeles were 8 minutes long, and there were still 2 left on the timer. I took a deep breath, figured I'd get tapped at least 5 more times before the round ended. I was right, and my buddy, Brian, was there to witness it all—round after round of me getting smashed by guys every size and every belt, submissions coming from every angle.

I thanked my partner for the lesson and headed straight for my water bottle, glad class was over. A lot of people kept rolling, but three or four rounds were all I could muster. This was only my sixth training session and I had zero endurance, many of my taps due simply to exhaustion.

Brian came over and said something sarcastic about it looking like fun. He asked if I'd happened to set up any interviews.

Interviewing fighters was why I had originally checked out the gym, but was no longer my focus. This was the first gym I'd paid to train at in nine years. Besides making a yearlong financial commitment, I was also committing time. The 45-minute drive downtown was often twice as long on the way back thanks to traffic, but it was tolerable twice a week. I saw something different in 10th Planet. It was well-suited for MMA because that's what its creator, Eddie Bravo, had developed it for. I'd felt it the first time I'd trained at 10th Planet Burbank, and I was reassured of it every time I made it to class at HQ. The entertaining talks Eddie gave before class were an added bonus.

I told Brian I hadn't talked to anyone, but maybe we could grab Alan Jouban after he finished training. I sat and gulped down some more water, glanced over at the MMA team. One of the coaches waved me over.

He nodded at the 6 fighters shadowboxing by the heavy bags. "You ready?"

I laughed, the sweat dripping off me. "I think I'm done for the day."

"Come on. You said you wanted to train with the team."

I had said that. Interviews were usually better when I trained with a team once or twice, and ever since my visit to Albuquerque I'd been seriously considering trying to fight again. Instead of saying I had to pick up my daughter from school, I said, "I don't think I can give you much."

"Alright, we got a big guy. Get your gear on."

Two of the fighters slipped into the ring. I knew Matthew Spencer, former college football player, and father of 3. He was one of the guys who always partnered with me because we were closest in size. I didn't know the other guy, but I was concerned he had on headgear. Spencer bit down on his mouthpiece as the round started. The other fighters gathered around the ring. Fuck, I'd just signed up for sparring.

I finished wrapping my hands, asked Brian if he was ready for some fun photos. He saw what was going to happen and told me I didn't need to do it, especially if I was tired. In the nicest way possible, Brian said I looked like hell.

It'd been over a month since I'd done any stand-up, but I felt like the few private sessions with striking coach Tyler Wombles had corrected some of my problems. This would be a good opportunity to see if there'd been any improvement. Most of these guys were in their early 20s and fighting amateur. If I was going to test myself, this was perfect.

The round ended and I warmed up, patting the heavy bag so I didn't waste any energy. Spencer stayed in since he had a fight coming up. I was glad to see another fighter selected for him.

Fourth round the coach called me Big Man and told me to get in there. The way he said it made me think he was referring to what I was already aware of: just because you're big doesn't mean shit. He wanted his guys to see that.

Spencer, a strong middleweight with knockout ability, had been warmed up with the 3 rounds and could have destroyed me. Just as he did with jiu jitsu, he took it easy and I was thrilled to make it through the round, figuring I could do 1 or 2 more of those if I had 3 rounds to recover in between.

I ducked down to step through the ropes. With a big grin, the coach said, "No. Big Man stays in."

Fuck. I could have said no. I could have done the smart thing and bitched out, but that didn't seem like an option at the time. I returned to the far corner, tried to control my breathing. Brian was snapping away, getting the right light on my scared face.

I made it through the round, took a few rounds off, and then went back in for 2 more, my arms so heavy, my hands by my side. But I survived. I even stayed for the conditioning, but only after the coach made fun of Big Man not having what it takes.

Brian and I left the gym and headed to our cars. Besides everything hurting, I felt good, proud I'd pushed through. I asked Brian if he got any decent photos. He assured me he did, then took a second before he asked, "Hey man, have you ever thought about writing an article on brain damage?"

I shook my head. "No. Why?"

"It's all over the news right now. You could write a good article on it."

I wasn't interested. Sounded like too much work.

Brian asked, "Have you seen any of the latest research?"

"Nope. But I'm guessing I know what it says. Getting hit in the head isn't a great idea."

Brian nodded. "You might want to look at it." He took a second to figure out the best way to say, "I'm not trying to be a dick, but you just spent four rounds getting hit by athletes half your age."

"Was it really that bad?"

"It wasn't Werdum or Babalu bad, but you were getting hit."

"I appreciate it, I really do, but the sparring doesn't seem to bother me. I feel fine, they weren't throwing too hard at me."

Brian shrugged his shoulders. "I just think you should check it out."

I thanked Brian for telling me and swore I'd check out some studies. That night I went to bed with a bad headache, but the next day I followed through on my promise. I discovered that knowing getting hit in the head isn't good for you, and understanding why it's not, are 2 very different things.

The more I read, the more I feared I had really screwed up. I was a reckless kid, experiencing my first serious concussion when I was 6. It's impossible to count how many I'd had since, but there had been plenty. In 7 years of football, I lost consciousness at least 6 times. On top of that I'd had daily trauma playing defensive line like a ram, always striking helmet to helmet. While attempting a fight career, I was knocked out twice. On another 2 occasions, my brain was rattled so badly that I completely lost 15 minutes of time, and there were a ridiculous number of times where I left the gym with a moderate concussion. While boxing I constantly slurred my words and reversed their order. Add a few motorcycle accidents to the mix, and it is amazing I can write my own name, let alone a novel.

The cumulative brain trauma made me a prime candidate for dementia and might be responsible for my spotty memory. And that damage was a good 8 years before I began this project, out of shape and unskilled, taking unnecessary blows to the head. How ironic that now I'd found my passion for writing, wanting to do it until the day I die, it looked like there was a good chance I'd spend some of those years drooling and crapping in a diaper.

I talked things over with my wife who was relieved to hear my decision. Not only would I throw away the dream of fighting again, I wasn't going to take any more strikes to the head. My health and family meant too much to me and I could no longer rationalize the risk. Had I been younger, without the previous damage, and with something to gain by fighting, it might not have been so easy to make that decision. Having a love for jiu jitsu helped, something to feed my competitive side. But I'd hang up the gloves.

A few days later I was back at 10th Planet. After class ended, I grabbed my bag and headed for the locker room. The coach stopped me and asked where I was going. "Come on, Big Man, come join us."

All the fighters I'd worked out with were standing around, everyone listening. I nearly caved, but said, "I'm afraid I won't be able to anymore. I'm done taking blows to the head. Gonna stick with jiu jitsu."

I told myself that same thing every night as I prepared for my next trip around the Northeast. I added more jiu jitsu based schools to my trip, and tried to set things up so I could join no-gi classes instead of striking. Looking for even more accountability, I wrote the commitment to my health on social media. I wasn't going to spar again.

I put off packing until the last minute. The suitcase was 2 pounds over the limit. I took out a pair of shoes and jeans. I left the gloves and shin guards right where they were, even though I'd promised everyone I had no more use for them.

* * *

Monday morning, I stopped by Rosky Combat Sports in Rahway, NJ. Dave Rosky, who was close to my age and fought around the same time, had transitioned from fighting to coaching and making combat gear. I'd tried his snapback mitts when I'd stopped by Endgame MMA the year before and was so impressed I picked up a pair. J.A. Dudley, a fighter who had helped me with my camera at Endgame and introduced me to the mitts, was at Rosky's and was just as interesting as Dave. I enjoyed listening to J.A.'s positive and unique perspective on things and could have talked to him for another hour, but my schedule didn't permit it. I had to be at Brown University in Rhode Island by six o'clock.

I felt silly hurrying across Connecticut to watch Brown's Grappling and Mixed Martial Arts club instead of a normal gym with professional fighters. Athletes were looked down on when I was at Brown, especially football players and wrestlers. Other students and a couple of professors had made it quite clear that we didn't belong at the school and if it hadn't been for our physical ability we'd never have been accepted. If traditional athletes were treated this way, I wondered how the Grappling and Mixed Martial Arts club could take off.

Instead of the 4 or 5 guys I expected to see rolling around in a cramped room, I was blown away by the 3 dozen young men and women training in the brightly lit multipurpose room. About a third of the participants were females, and just as at any MMA school, they were training with their male teammates.

The club, which had grown to 60 members in its 3 years, was impressive. Students listened carefully as Tri-Force MMA's head coach, Pete Jeffrey, demonstrated techniques, and worked well with each other when it was time to practice. Several of the students took the time after training to tell me how the club had changed them. Although only one of the interviewees had any MMA fighting experience, there were a few that were toying with the idea. For many of them, it was the first time stepping out of their comfort zone, the first time they wouldn't be top of their class. Whether or not they wanted to compete, without a doubt, practicing the martial arts had improved their lives.

There hadn't been time to talk at length with Pete, so the next morning, my buddy Karl and I hit Tri-Force in Pawtucket, RI. Pete co-owned the gym with his brother, Keith, whom I'd interviewed on my first trip a year and a half before. Although I'd interviewed a handful of fighters who had siblings that also fought, this would be the first time talking to both individuals.

Keith, who is 5 years younger than Pete, had described what it was like as the youngest of 3 brothers who roughhoused all the time. Keith was now one weight class above his brother, but growing up he had always been the little kid on the losing side of things. The desire to be just as tough and strong as his brothers pushed Keith to become very competitive, and at a very young age, he vowed he'd be a champion one day.

Now it was Pete's turn to talk, the middle child's memories of those formative years. "My brothers and I always wrestled around and we wrestled our friends. My dad watched a lot of boxing," Pete said. "So it was like boxing and hockey, football, contact sports. You know with three boys in the house, we were basically just wrecking the place, but we had a lot of outlets so it was good."

One of those outlets was sports, his favorite being hockey, but when he turned 11, Pete discovered a love for music, a nice balance to his athletic side. He even went on to earn degrees in music and began teaching.

Meanwhile, Keith had started jiu jitsu training under Mat Santos. One Friday night, Pete watched the Fight Night where Mat split his students into 2 teams and had them grapple against each other. Pete wanted in and began taking private lessons with Mat, eventually training under him at the Mat Santos Academy, one of the few schools in Rhode Island that had MMA fighters at the time.

The idea of MMA didn't appeal to Pete; he was afraid he might damage his hands and ruin his music career. "But I loved to grapple;" he said, "so one thing led to another. I actually took my first fight on a bet." Tired of Mat and his teammates always asking when he was going to fight like Keith, Pete said he'd do it if Mat could get a fight for him immediately. Mat made a phone call and locked in the fight that Pete went on to win in under 2 minutes.

Pete enjoyed the experience and decided to pursue fighting part time, having 10 fights over a 6-year period. He talked about how much the sport had evolved in that time and said he hadn't had the opportunity to train smart like the guys today. "We were killing each other. And trying to make it as close to the fight as possible. Lots of times we didn't make it to the fight." During that 6-year stretch he'd had 3 broken hands, knee surgeries, and a torn shoulder.

Was it worth it? Had it changed him at all? Pete said absolutely, 100%. "I'm glad I have something like MMA in my life. It's really like the yin and yang, that push and pull."

Always one to push people to compete, to confront their fears, Pete said, "If you never do anything hard in your life, you're never going to do anything."

I thanked Pete for his time and hurried back to Brown, exhausted from the strenuous workout but excited about my appointment with Professor Michael Kennedy. The professor, who taught a course called Martial Arts, Culture, and Society, had offered to help with my project. It was a beautiful afternoon, the sky blue, clouds puffy and pure white, but being on campus brought back that old feeling of dread, always waiting for someone to point at me and shout, "You don't belong here."

I took a deep breath and entered the Sociology department. I couldn't help but feel that I was about to be graded. All my worries went out the window when Professor Kennedy welcomed me. He is a pleasant and friendly man, a martial artist who had been training his entire life and had dedicated much of his career to understanding and spreading the arts. He said he was excited about my research and thought it was important, words I hadn't expected to hear. We went over my findings, similarities I was discovering, questions that remained. With 300 interviews, I felt as if I'd heard every type of story I was going to, and it was probably about time I closed the project.

Professor Kennedy pointed out the importance of including a comparison group from another sport, the closer to fighting the better. He suggested wrestling, but I told him about my new fascination with no-gi jiu jitsu. A tough jiu jitsu battle could be considered one of the closest things to an MMA fight without striking, and I often heard fighters say they first got bit by the fighting bug while training jits. Plus, I was finally appreciating jiu jitsu as an art instead of a tool, and I wanted to seriously train for the first time in my life. I'd thrown away the blue belt I no longer deserved and had started back at white, ready to learn. And at 10th Planet HQ where people came from around the world, I'd have no shortage of people to question.

Professor Kennedy liked my enthusiasm and plan of attack. In passing, I mentioned that I was using jiu jitsu to suppress the urge to spar and possibly fight again. Professor Kennedy asked if I was serious. He hadn't been aware that I was participating in training and taking a substantial amount of damage. He applauded my valor but hoped I'd continue to see reason. Taking blows to the head was not a good idea for me, for the book, for anyone, he argued. Who knew if I might take 1 shot too many? All my research would be useless if I couldn't write about it.

I left Brown, inspired, motivated, and in a rush. This was the only night I'd be able to hit Lauzon's MMA, and I wanted to see their new location in South Easton, MA. The new building was beautiful with a huge parking lot all its own. Although I'd only trained at Lauzon's former gym a few times, I'd interviewed a dozen fighters and always felt welcome. We had 15 minutes before class, so I sat down with head coach Joe Pomfret for a quick interview. When we wrapped it up, I asked if I could join the team in training. I could only go light, but I'd stay out of the way. He agreed and told me to meet them on the mat. I put my camera and tripod in the locker, peeked out to see what the fighters were wearing. Maybe I'd get lucky and it'd be all ground.

It wasn't. Everyone had on gloves and shin guards. Pomfret told them to start moving. I geared up quickly so I wouldn't have time to really think about it, and joined the shadowboxers. Pomfret said to partner up. Light, he told everyone. Technique, not power.

I teamed up with a big guy, and we were both nice and slow, a mutual conservation of energy. Next round, new partner. Still technique, but add a little speed. Again, no power on the punches. This was fine. I'd been premature with my promise. I could dodge and block and move around, especially if I got in better shape.

My next partner was shorter than me but solid. He seemed nice enough when I told him I wasn't a fighter, but he had this look that told me to keep my hands up.

I thought I had been, but a solid hook connected with the side of my head. I didn't go down, but it rattled me, made me scream inside, "What the fuck am I doing?"

I finished the rest of the practice, exhausted, but disappointed at my failure to keep my promise to others, as well as to myself. Instead of being happy about the interviews I conducted after the workout, I was bashing myself, wondering what drives us to make such irrational decisions.

The next day I stuck around Providence and sat through a fascinating guest lecture in Professor Kennedy's class, only cutting it short because I had to be in New London, CT, in 2 hours. I hadn't accounted for traffic and realized there was no way I was going to make Strike Zone MMA's practice.

When I pulled into the quiet coastal town, nearly every store was closed but lights were still on in the gym. Training was winding down, a couple of the guys working technique, staying late to knock out the interviews.

I appreciated talking with the 2 pro fighters, Will Kerr and John Naples, but I was most interested in Darryl MarcAurele Jr. The 28-year-old was 2-1 as an amateur and wasn't considering MMA as a career, but I'd interviewed his father, Darryl Sr., on my first trip, and wanted to see what I could learn from them.

Thanks to his father, a collegiate wrestler who went on to compete in MMA, Darryl Jr. had been around the martial arts his entire life. He wrestled from the ages of 4 to 14, giving it up to begin training in BJJ, the classes taught by his father in their garage. Darryl was already familiar with submissions because his dad had been trying to duplicate moves on him that he'd watched in the UFC.

Darryl Jr. left the martial arts for three years. He said, "I came back when I was 21. I was laid off, no job, a baby on the way. And fighting looked good to me." He had a fight and loved it, but 70-hour workweeks and a family to take care of kept him away from fighting for another four years. Darryl dropped the first fight back but hit the gym hard and lost 56 pounds in 12 weeks leading up to a first-minute knockout.

He said he had always thought MMA and the participants, including his father, were crazy. But now he understood fighting could make you healthy, make you happy. With work and family, Darryl would be forced to take little breaks from training, but he was adamant he would never leave it.

"If the gym wasn't here, if my dad didn't do it, I would've found my way here eventually," he said. "Fighting is good for you." Darryl talked about being a young punk with anger issues, getting into bar fights. Fighting helped him deal with that anger. He said, "For anybody who comes in here, it helps you grow." He added, "It's just therapy. If you've never done it, you won't understand it."

I'd heard this same sentiment from so many others, many of whom might not ever fight again. They were better for the training, not worse. Maybe I'd been premature with my decision not to spar anymore. Maybe I didn't have to give up MMA.

* * *

It was a cold, wet Friday morning, the dark weather matching my mood. I'd driven through Connecticut and hoped to break up the drive by catching a morning practice, but I couldn't find anything on my route. I'd just about given up when Igor, a friend on Facebook, shot me a message about All Star BJJ in Kenilworth, NJ. I'd stayed clear of gyms with BJJ in the name, especially if it didn't include MMA, but with my new focus this sounded like the perfect place. A few messages later, I had 4 interviews lined up, the last of which was with the owner and head coach, Jamal "The Suit" Patterson.

Jamal was fighting off a cold, but still charismatic; it was easy to see why his fighters appreciated him so much. The 39-year-old had lived in Queens until seventh grade when his dad moved them to a rural area in

Belvedere, NJ. Being the only black kid in town was a culture shock, but it also provided sports opportunities for Jamal, who discovered when he tried out for the football team that he was a natural athlete just like his father.

Although he had a hard time holding onto the ball, Jamal was the fastest kid on the team. He made an impact and played varsity his freshman year. He had no interest in wrestling, but his coaches pushed him to do it. His first year was rough going 7-14, but Jamal finished strong, ranked one of the best in the country his senior year. On top of the wrestling success, Jamal was one of the top rushers in the state. Unfortunately, schoolwork hadn't been very important to him, and he lacked the grades to go to the college he wanted. He also didn't know which sport he wanted to dedicate himself to, so he went to Blair Academy and played both.

The next year saw him transferred to Colgate University and giving up wrestling, which required more work than football and was not nearly as fun. I hadn't met many wrestlers who wanted to quit the sport after accomplishing so much, but wrestling had never been Jamal's passion, just a sport he was told to do.

After earning his BA, Jamal joined the corporate world, pushing himself to make money. Eventually he became burned out and felt like just another number, like he was no longer important as an individual. Lifting weights wasn't enough to satisfy the competitive side he had fed for 9 years. At 27, he began training Muay Thai and then added BJJ. He preferred the striking and said he didn't have much respect for jiu jitsu due to his wrestling mentality.

Jamal's job moved him to Chicago where he had the good fortune of finding Carlson Gracie's school across the street from his apartment. At the time, he was a solid 220-pound athlete who could dunk a basketball and run a 4.5 40-yard dash. "It was the first time in my life I was able to see guys that I was a better athlete than, be able to stop me, be able to do things against me," Jamal said. "And I knew I would be able to get good at it. If they could get good at it, I could get better."

When Jamal transferred back to New York, he began training at the legendary Renzo Gracie's. In 4 years, he earned his black belt, something seldom accomplished, and he did very well at Abu Dhabi, where the top grapplers in the world compete. The entire time, Jamal would go to work in his suit and tie, telling coworkers and himself he was only training for fun. He said, "But in the back of my mind, I really wanted to fight."

Jamal learned from the best in the world and paid attention to detail, felt ready to jump into the sport at 33. Not one to waste time, Jamal's debut fight was for the International Fighting League (IFL) against Matt Horwich, who was 22-4. Jamal won by rear-naked in the first round.

I wondered how Jamal, with so much experience competing in other events, handled the transition to MMA, if it was what he expected. "The first thing I tell my guys is that I was broke in fights," he said. "I feel like the more honest I am, and I don't hide the bad things that happened to me, the better it's going to be when I train my guys. I came from a time where there really weren't fight camps." Jamal prepared himself, but there were times when he went into deep waters, and that little voice in the back of his brain spoke up and told him to quit.

"I guarantee there isn't a person who hasn't been broken." Jamal said, "I've been broken, but I know I've been broken. But the key thing is to work hard enough to not let yourself be broken again."

For Jamal, the walk out to the ring was always one of the worst feelings in the world, but nothing could compare to winning a fight. "It's addicting and I think that's one of the reasons why guys fight too long. Everyone still wants me to fight. I left on a win and I was competitive." Jamal was still competitive and sparred with guys at his gym and Renzo's, but he said, "There comes a time in a fighter's life when he stops competing." He noticed that in the last couple of years he'd stopped being competitive in training and just wanted to get through the workout. "Once that happens, I think it's time for you to end."

The urge to fight came back all the time, but he knew that ship had sailed. He'd continue to focus his energy on his family, his gym, his fighters, and his training.

"I feel like I come in every day and I help somebody. I'm changing guys' lives." He recounted stories of guys with no confidence walking tall after training. Guys that were never athletes that were now part of a team. He joked he should get an honorary degree in psychology for all the counseling he'd done. "I want to spread this art. I want to spread mixed martial arts." He said, "I want people to understand what martial arts can do for your life. It changes a lot of people. It's changed me; it's changed a lot of my students, and for the good. It becomes a lifestyle."

CHAPTER TWENTY

November 7, 2013

I'd originally planned on training at Pure MMA in Denville, NJ, but the rain and terrible driving conditions ruled that out. I arrived at the gym with only half an hour to spare if I was going to make it to my final destination. Although the gym was in a business park, it had a homey, welcoming feel. I was greeted by Andy Main, a 24-year-old BJJ black belt who co-owned the gym and taught with his black belt younger brother, Mike. While Mike taught the gi class, Andy and I set up in the office.

Andy, a tall featherweight, said he'd been very competitive all his life and a bit of a bully, always beating on Mike. "And I was also insecure, to a certain degree, maybe that's partly where it came from. I was getting in fights regularly."

When he reached high school, he changed his name from Andrew to Andy as he became much more relaxed. Although he was social and had friends, Andy's focus was always centered on whatever adventure he was currently on, whether it was snowboarding, skateboarding, or something extreme.

He picked up jiu jitsu at 16, and found it was everything he'd been looking for, especially in terms of people he'd want to be around. This was even truer when Andy discovered the MMA fight team. "It was me finding that group of peers that had that positive attitude, setting goals for themselves." Most of his new friends were adults with responsibilities and families. After only training a few months, Andy become more peaceful and stopped bullying his brother, the values of the martial arts rubbing off on him.

Competing in mixed martial arts became Andy's focus, and he had his first fight in 2007, turning pro 2 years later. With a 4-0 record, he got on *The Ultimate Fighter Season 12* as a 21-year-old. After a loss on the show, Andy went on to fight for other organizations, but came down with mono while training for a fight. His doctor said he might not be able to fight again because the strain of training would shut down what little remained of his immune system. Andy was miserable and tried doing everything to find a cure. He was 7-1 as a pro, his dream of becoming a champion so close. "I don't think people understand. I almost lost what I love." He said, "My family, my girlfriend and my brother—they are the only things I love more than this sport, than martial arts."

Andy battled through the sickness but couldn't fight for two years. Jonathan Brookin, a fellow *TUF* fighter and good friend, suggested Andy simplify his life and cut out all the nonessentials. One month of incredibly clean living and Andy said he knew he was back. Three months later he was back in the cage.

Andy credited fighting for some of the changes in his life, but it was jiu jitsu he wanted to share with the world. "You want to talk about character building, come in here. You'll succeed and you'll fail; you'll get tapped and you'll get a submission, twenty, thirty, forty times in one hour. Most people only get one or two feelings like that in a week."

I had hoped to talk with Mike to see what differences there were between the brothers, but I was already running late for my last stop in Easton, PA. It was still raining and wet on the dark, unfamiliar highway. I accepted I wouldn't make it in time to train, not too upset since I was wiped out. In the last 5 days, I'd hit 10 gyms, driven 1,000 miles, and I was questioning why I was going so far out of the way to hit a relatively small gym.

I pulled into the small strip mall, the parking lot crowded, the windows of Finishers MMA too fogged up to see through. Inside 20 people used up every inch of mat, steam fogging up my camera as 10th Planet Jiu Jitsu purple belts Zach Maslany and Jon Holland took the class through a series of techniques.

Zach pointed out Scott "The Animal" Heckman, a 16-4 professional fighter waiting to be called up by the UFC. Next up was 10-year-old Grace Gundrum, who looked as delicate as a porcelain doll, revealing no emotion as she worked techniques with the adults. Zach said she was going to be a world champion, knew she was going to do big things. I snapped away, amazed at how much this young girl knew and how much I didn't. It provided a much-needed reassurance that I'd made the right decision to throw away my blue belt.

After practice, Scott sat down and shared his journey, the familiar story of a wrestler looking to challenge himself and be competitive in another sport. It was late by the time we wrapped things up, and I still needed to find my hotel and get some sleep.

There were 10 of us in class the next morning, a great way to start a Friday. The workout was the ideal way to unwind and a chance to experience first-hand just how technical Jon and Zach were, picking me apart with submissions even though I had 80 pounds on them.

We cleared out the gym and got to the interviews, Jon going first. Although he was only 24, Jon had a wealth of martial arts training, starting with karate in kindergarten. He took breaks from training, especially during football and wrestling seasons, playing both sports since fourth grade. It wasn't until he got bullied in the eighth grade that Jon became much more disciplined and intent on training.

In addition to testing himself in the occasional karate tournament, Jon began amateur boxing, kickboxing, and MMA with no strikes to the face, only because that's all that was allowed. Jon felt a little lost after high school and fighting gave him something to focus on.

The more Jon trained, the more he wanted to earn the respect of the people he trained with. For him that meant proving yourself in competition.

"You want to be that guy," he said. "I always wanted to be the best guy at my gym."

After training a bit of jiu jitsu, Jon's focus began to change. He understood you couldn't just be a martial artist to fight MMA anymore. You had to be a great athlete, and he didn't have the time or passion to dedicate himself to that. Instead he chose to spend his life learning from masters, passing the art on to others, and teaching them how to learn.

Zach was next, and full of energy. Like Jon, he'd been on the smaller side growing up. We ran through his life. Parents divorced early, Catholic school until sixth grade, wore handed-down clothing, never stuck with any sports, participated in a little bit of martial arts early on. Our circumstances were very different, but, like me, Zach said he'd been a pissed off teenager who punched walls and did crazy stuff.

Like a lot of young men, Zach watched the first UFCs, was blown away by the sport, and decided he wanted to do it. When he picked up training in high school he got to the point that he was beating adults at the academy and thought it was time to test himself, going 2-2 as a pro.

Zach's reasons for giving up the dream of fighting were like Jon's: a love of jiu jitsu combined with the dislikes of grueling camps, weight cuts, injuries, and fight cancellations. But what grabbed me was Zach's reason for fighting in the first place. Now that he was older and in a much more peaceful and positive place, Zach told me that it was the identification of being a fighter that had been such a draw, such a hard thing to let go of. Prior to fighting, he'd just been Zach, some quiet guy no one knew. But then he became Zach the fighter.

Toughness was something that Zach had wanted to prove as well, so I asked him if he had a hard time letting MMA go, especially when he trained others for it. He said, it wasn't that hard because he no longer had anything to prove. He'd rather people judge him by his character, not by whether he could step into a cage.

We talked until it was time for me to check out of the hotel. When I got in the car, I called my wife. She could tell I was excited and asked what happened.

I said, "I'm finally ready to write this book."

* * *

Instead of driving to the airport that night, I headed to Allentown, PA. I had jumped the gun when I told Jen I was ready to start writing. Zach's statement about identity triggered a profound personal revelation. Not only had my identity as a fighter been essential for me during my fight career, it was the reason why I was having such a hard time letting go of sparring. Whether I called it identity or ego, a big part of my hesitancy came from wanting to be cool again, doing something my other friends weren't. Maybe I could be Mark the fighter once more, something to make me interesting. Perhaps not the most positive motivation, but it was there nonetheless.

That was not an acceptable reason to risk serious damage or speed up the possible onset of Alzheimer's or dementia. I wasn't going to possibly jeopardize my future because I wanted to be cool or to prove I was tough. Becoming Mark the jiu jitsu guy would have to be enough.

This clarity was great but if I was ready to write the book, that'd mean playtime was over. No more interviews or training. And I didn't want to be done. I still needed to finalize thoughts on why others were doing it. I also wanted to take a closer look at jiu jitsu and see if I could become any good at it.

I pulled into the parking lot of a large warehouse, the words American Top Team proudly displayed on the side. It was cold and raining, but I'd had such a great time at the 3 other ATT facilities I'd visited that I knew I wouldn't be disappointed. Plus, several fighters I respected had told me I should speak with head coach and professional MMA fighter Carmelo Marrero.

Carmelo was a barrel-chested heavyweight with a shaved head, who looked like he could run through a wall. He greeted me with a kind smile and firm handshake, made me feel right at home. Two weeks before, the 32-year-old had snatched a first-round submission at XFE 28, his 20th professional MMA fight. He wouldn't be training during the evening's pro practice and would only be acting as coach.

Pro practice was still 30 minutes away, so we set up in the lounge for the interview. Understanding Carmelo proved an easy task since he had done quite a bit of self-reflection and had a good command of who he was. The former college wrestler had put together a 15-5 record in 9 years, with 3 of those fights held in the UFC, but said he wasn't chasing a dream. He was staying in the fight game to remain focused and in shape.

"I think of myself as a good person, but I'm a better person when I'm training," Carmelo said. "I'm a person who has anxieties, insecurities. There are things about me that I'm not so proud of how I deal with them mentally." Carmelo spoke with confidence, his hands expressive. "I didn't have that true belief in myself and fighting gave me that. I wanted to be as mentally strong as I was physically strong."

When asked about other motivations, Carmelo talked about people wanting to identify as an athlete or fighter, similar to what Zach had told me earlier that afternoon. "You have to understand that fighters come from all walks of life, and everybody's looking for something a little bit different," he said. "But I'd be lying if I said that fighters are fighting just for fighting. These people are looking for something extra in life. They're looking for their thing, their niche."

I wondered if Carmelo feared he might have suffered brain damage because of all his fights and countless sparring sessions. "It's a serious fear that one day you're going to take that wrong shot," he said. "Something could potentially happen that could cause you not to be that same person that you are. That's a fear all fighters have." Instead of dwelling on the negative though, Carmelo pointed out the importance of fighters taking care of themselves with less sparring, better recovery, and proper nutrition—doing everything to mitigate any damage.

Just as I'd been doing with most fighters I'd interviewed, I searched for signs of damage, symptoms that might indicate fighting had negatively impacted him. Carmelo didn't slur his speech or stumble on any words. He sounded eloquent, intelligent, someone I could learn from. Perhaps he'd accumulated some damage that might show later in life, but even if it did, Carmelo made it clear it was entirely worth the risk.

When we finished, Carmelo invited me to join the workout, a mix of stand-up and ground. I flashed back to the sparring session at ATT Oklahoma City and said I'd better sit out. Ten minutes later, I knew I'd made the right decision. The drills and sparring were controlled, but not something I should mess with. When they transitioned to the ground game, I paid close attention to the demonstrated technique so I could apply it the next time I rolled. I even wrote it down step by step in my notepad. *Get North South. Push shoulder away, turn head, roll hand, sink choke.*

After class, I went back to the hotel and called it a night. The weekend was spent in Philadelphia visiting Renzo Gracie's, Daddis MMA, and Balance Studios. Unfortunately, each of my stops was a bit rushed and I could only do quick interviews with no time for training. Monday morning, I went south and visited Triple Threat Combat Sports in Newark, DE, where I had a fascinating interview with owner and BJJ black belt Kevin Green who was affiliated with the Yamasaki Academy, where I'd be spending time the next 2 days.

I arrived at the Yamasaki Academy in Woodbridge, VA, before the Monday night class and interviewed 2 fighters with fascinating stories. There was Jonathan Escalona, a 10-1 amateur fighter from Mexico whose life was saved by MMA, fighting pulling him from a life of gangs and drugs. The other, Francisco Salguero, the MMA coach, had a positive upbringing, got into wrestling, found MMA, and then suffered a stroke that would not allow him to fight again.

Although head coach Joe Cunningham had never fought MMA, he was a BJJ black belt who had spent the last 15 years surrounding himself with fighters and other martial artists. The first class he'd taken at the Yamasaki Academy in 1998 was brutal, Joe's practice of drinking and smoking 2 packs a day making him puke during warm-ups. But it also taught him something: the martial arts weren't mystical powers he could never master. They were skills that he could learn. "I was never a big tough guy, but I certainly was intrigued by the idea of being the kid, the ninety-eight-pound weakling who could beat up the bully."

As soon as Joe began training, jiu jitsu became an obsession. "The more you train, the more you want to train," he said.

Joe confided in me how jiu jitsu and the Yamasaki family had been there for him during dark periods of his life. He was given a place to work it all out on the mat, to get over the grief, tears mixing with sweat. As I'd heard it described by many others, he said jiu jitsu was therapy.

Jiu jitsu gave Joe the confidence to stand up for himself. "I'm not afraid of confrontation anymore. Not because I'm looking for it, not because I want the fight, but I've learned that the fight is not what's scary anymore," he said. "People who are so afraid of confrontation are scared of the act of the fight and they're not sure they can control themselves. And I get that because I used to be afraid of the same thing." Joe said, "Well, I know how to control myself. People are trying to break my face all day and I've got to control myself doing it."

For Joe, it was never about being competitive. "I knew I would never be a stud jiu jitsu player. I'm not driven by success per se. I have a sense of pride in the things that I do, and I like to know I'm doing things correctly, but I'm not wildly driven by competition whatsoever."

Joe did go on to compete in BJJ matches and did decently, but he never had any aspirations to go to big events. He laughed when I asked what the difference was between the BJJ competitors who don't move on to MMA and those who do. He said jiu jitsu players generally don't want to get hit. "That seems simple," he said, "but a lot of times it's really just that easy."

If it was that simple, I'd have to wrap up my study. Fortunately, Joe wasn't content with his answer and thought about his jiu jitsu career, how he didn't have any intention to enter a cage. "I just didn't think I was good enough," he said. "Not because I didn't necessarily like getting hit, but just because I didn't think I was going to be good enough at it." Joe took a second then pointed out that there are Muay Thai fighters who would never want to do MMA. For them it wasn't about the fear of getting hit either.

"It seems to be more a matter of the higher the belt in jiu jitsu, the less likely they are to try anything else," Joe said. "In jiu jitsu, certain belts carry certain weight. And it allows you to have a certain sense of ego about yourself. And it's hard to have that ego destroyed by walking into some new discipline and being absolutely mauled by someone you know that you could beat if it was in something else." On why people compete in MMA, Joe said, "I don't know if it's the need to compete or it's something more primal, 'cause it's not about hurting the other guy."

This was something I'd heard over and over from the fighters I'd interviewed; the fact that fighting was not about wanting to hurt your opponent, but something more personal.

* * *

Tuesday I circled back north and stopped by the Yamasaki Academy Headquarters in Rockville, MD, owned by Fernando and his younger brother, Mario, who had spent the previous 15 years refereeing in the UFC. The gym was beautiful, the spacious area filled with brilliant white mats to match the walls, and there was something captivating about all the people in gis training on them.

I was there to see Aaron Riley, who was the same age as Carmelo, but about 100 pounds lighter and had more than twice as many fights. I snapped photos in a back room where Aaron coached a small MMA class in the boxing ring.

Aaron had grown up in a small town in Indiana and was fascinated by martial arts. He'd started training karate and Tae Kwon Do at 10. The martial arts became a big part of his life, and he devoured every martial art movie and magazine he could find. When Aaron was 11 he came across the Gracie challenge, an offer for anyone to fight members of the Gracie family in a Vale Tudo (no rules) fight to prove who had the best martial art. Already adopting a humble martial arts philosophy, Aaron was troubled by their arrogance and knew he would love to fight them. The first UFC came out soon after, Royce Gracie becoming the champion. Aaron said that drove him nuts. He decided at that moment that he would fight in the UFC and beat those "Gracie guys."

Some fighters have told me about making the decision to fight at an early age, but not many go after it immediately. As if it was a reality just waiting to happen. Aaron was dead serious and began judo, which he considered his first real martial art because it could be practiced full speed. Aaron found success in the art and won state games twice. He then searched out a kickboxing instructor to learn the next skill he needed to master for his mission.

Wrestling in high school to learn a skill that'd been proven effective in the UFC is something you don't hear often from teenagers, but that was the only reason Aaron dedicated himself to the sport. Wrestling was the toughest thing he'd done up to that point and he said, "You get more tired than you knew it was possible to even get, and you have to push through that adversity if you wanted to win. And I definitely wanted to win." Aaron said, "My goal was standing at the top of the heap of broken bodies with the UFC title. So I was pushing through everything."

Aaron's determination never wavered and he began fighting HOOKnSHOOT shows at 16 years old. Over the next 16 years, he had 44 recorded MMA fights, 9 held in the UFC.

When asked who he was in the cage, Aaron said, "I wasn't a different person, but another side of me came out." Out of the cage he was one of the easiest guys to get along with, but when he was in there he was completely committed. "I never wanted to do any damage to anyone in a fight. I just wanted to win. If a little bit of damage was a by-product of the win," he said, "I would kind of feel bad afterward, but I would definitely do whatever I would have to to win the fight, and I wouldn't have any second thoughts about it."

Other than his ears, there was no obvious signs of damage Aaron had accumulated over the years, and I wouldn't have guessed he'd had his jaw shattered only 4 months earlier. I asked about the damage he'd taken, how he'd rationalized it while fighting, and if he was worried about it now.

Aaron said thinking about potential damage when he was younger would have held him back. Fighters can't dwell on it. It was a concern for him at the end, but not so great that it was what caused him to be finished.

"MMA is an art form. It's the pinnacle of martial arts, of martial arts competition and martial arts expression," he said. "There's the martial side and there's the art side. Yeah there can be some violence and blood. There can be some damage, but the artistic value of it just outweighed that other thing for me.

"I've tried to kind of live by the whole martial arts way of life, that whole martial art ethos," he said. "That encompasses a big range of things. More or less, it is what I said: living with integrity, discipline, and respect for your fellow man, care and a generous heart, a lot of things wrapped up in that. That's how I try to live my life."

Aaron brought up Sam Sheridan's book, *The Fighter's Mind*, and said it was an interesting and awesome read, but it still left the question unanswered: Why do they fight? "After fighting for so long, I can't tell you one hundred percent why I fight either. To me it's the biggest challenge; one of the most physical challenges you could subject yourself to."

I no longer felt so bad that it'd taken me a year and a half of hard research to only somewhat figure out my reasons for fighting.

"It's almost a mystery to me and sometimes confounds me," he said. "But I don't think there is one answer. There are many answers for many different people, and there can be more than one answer."

That was true for myself and so many others: the myriad factors that could influence decisions and lead one to MMA. But no matter what the reasons, it was nearly always a step in the right direction, a positive effect on their life and development as a person.

After Aaron's interview, I sat down with Fernando Yamasaki, quickly understanding why both Aaron and Joe Cunningham spoke so highly of him. The 46-year-old was engaging and friendly, fun to listen to as he told me how his father and uncle were both judokas that had refereed at the 1992 Olympic Games in Barcelona. Fernando and his older brother, Mario, began their martial arts journey very early.

Before I could ask whether he had resented being pushed into martial arts, Fernando told me the story of hiding beneath his father's gi in the back seat of the car and not revealing himself until they'd arrived at the gym 20 miles away. "I have a passion," he said, "and this is my passion. There's always a way to change, a way to modify. There's always something to learn."

I believed I was given a good understanding of the Yamasaki philosophy at Woodbridge, but I wanted to hear it directly.

"My mindset here is to do it for the community," Fernando said. He described how easy it would be to change his teaching methods and place more pressure on students to have them compete harder and win more medals. But he acknowledged that would only be to satisfy his ego. "You can do that, but what about the best part of the martial art: change people's life, self-confidence?"

His smile was genuine. This man had witnessed and been part of so much growth. I asked what it was that caused those changes.

First, he pointed to an expert black belt sharing his knowledge with every person, including the beginner. "Where else do you see that?" he wondered.

Next was how physical jiu jitsu is and that it helps people discover what they are capable of. "That's the gift of Brazilian Jiu Jitsu. Give the person the ability, give the person the knowledge that he or she is going to be able to do something for her own life."

Another giant draw of the martial arts is that anyone can do it. Start at any age and pursue until you die. He told me of his 80-year-old father who still trains and teaches. "Jiu jitsu is ageless," Fernando said.

I shared how much I was enjoying training, but that I wasn't sure whether it would help me get rid of the desire to fight. Fernando understood the feeling and told me of taking students to Vale Tudo fights in Brazil and getting pulled into scuffles. With a smile, he recounted numerous times he'd had to fight when he was disrespectfully challenged in his own dojo. It wasn't surprising to learn that Fernando, like any martial artist who gets to prove their art, enjoyed a fair fight. Since he wasn't opposed to physical combat and well equipped with the necessary skills, I wondered why he didn't go into MMA.

Fernando thought about it a second, searching for the answer. "In 1994, my master was killed. And he was the motivation for me to do things in my life," he said. "He was the person I trusted one hundred percent, and when I lost him, I lost my mentor, part of my confidence, too."

On top of that, Fernando had accomplished all the goals he'd set for himself in his martial arts and was happy with the results. As a family man with a successful business, breaking bones and suffering injuries was not something Fernando chose to do.

I could have talked with Fernando all night, but he needed to get back on the mats, and he said there was one other fighter I needed to speak with. He left the room and came back with a bald guy in a gi, black belt around his waist. Andre Margutti was 34 and had been training martial arts since he was 12; capoeira, a fast and versatile Brazilian martial art, the first 8 years before adding judo and jiu jitsu at 20 when he moved from Brazil to Boston.

"Jiu jitsu, it became a lifestyle for me," Andre said. "It made me challenge myself every day. If I'm in my comfort zone, I know that is not my comfort zone. My comfort zone is outside of my comfort zone."

Like so many other practitioners, Andre fell in love with jiu jitsu. Why wasn't it enough for him? Why did he decide to try MMA?

That was an easy question for Andre. It didn't matter if other students or BJJ competitors thought he was tough. Andre needed to prove it to himself. Like Carmelo Marrero, he wanted to find out how tough he was physically and mentally.

In January 2008, Andre won his debut amateur fight by TKO in the second, the same round he won his pro fight in 8 months later, 2 of the best feelings he'd ever had. Andre enjoyed the challenge and was getting ready for his third fight in 2010, when he started experiencing sciatic nerve pain. He was given painkillers and tried to work through the pain, but it only worsened. Andre didn't have health insurance with his newly founded business, and didn't go back to the doctors until he became so sick that his friend called 911. They discovered Andre had stage 4 non-Hodgkin's lymphoma on his liver and spleen; a huge mass on his back was pushing on his sciatic nerve, causing all the pain.

The odds were not in Andre's favor, about a 1-in-3 chance he'd survive. "In the beginning, I was in shock," Andre said. "I stopped for a moment. I cried. And I knew I had two options: either fight or give up." And from everything he'd learned from the Yamasakis and jiu jitsu, giving up was not an option.

Andre described a jiu jitsu drill where a training partner twice your size would keep side control, pinning you down while Fernando smacked the mat, yelling at you to get out. The partner would continue applying pressure until you escaped, even if it took an hour. There was no choice. You had to escape.

Those drills were amped up even more with MMA, a training partner's knee on your belly as he's raining down shots, forcing you to escape, only so a fresh training partner could jump in and repeat the drill. "You have to escape," Andre said. "You have no other option."

Cancer was driving its knee on Andre's belly, and he had to get away. "You forget about side effects of the treatment. You forget about the bad stuff." He reframed his mind and shifted perspective. He attacked the cancer by overeating, replenishing the calories he'd lose through vomiting. He worked at his business as long as he could and exercised to keep his mind and body strong. Even though he could not train, once a week Andre would put on his gi and walk on the Yamasaki mats to center himself and change his energy.

A big reason Andre could not give up was that he had the jiu jitsu community right beside him, helping him with his fight. With no health insurance, Andre couldn't have received the medical treatment he needed, but the BJJ community put on seminars and events with all the proceeds going to Andre. They raised $40,000 in just the first month. He would have been embarrassed to quit on them and promised he'd fight until the end.

After his 4th chemo and 11th radiation sessions, scans showed that Andre's spleen was clean and his liver was nearly clean. The mass in his back was almost gone. After 2 more chemo sessions, Andre was completely clean.

Andre described how much his life had improved, how much more he appreciated everything. Now in his third year of remission, he had just completed his second triathlon, something he planned to do the rest of his life. "It's amazing. This is what jiu jitsu brought to my life. Cancer was an obstacle, and, once I passed it, everything cleared up," he said. "I don't wish anyone has cancer, but I wish everybody could live like a cancer survivor."

Andre appeared to be in great shape and he admitted he's thought of returning to the cage. But he would only fight again if he was completely prepared. He knew what kind of commitment it took to fight, and he now had more important priorities.

The odds said Andre shouldn't have been alive. The doctors also told him he would never have children. But his daughter had been born 6 days before our interview. Andre showed me her pictures and both of us teared up when he described his love for her, his dedication to be the best father, husband, and man he could be.

I headed back to the hotel, beyond inspired. I'd just completed 2,000 miles, traveling to 8 states, 15 schools, conducting 40 interviews over the last 9 days. Even though I didn't get much of a chance to train, I felt the power of the martial arts and learned from so many incredible martial artists. I was ready to head home.

CHAPTER TWENTY-ONE

December 29, 2013

It was the Sunday night before Christmas, and I was driving to North Hollywood to be a guest on the *Eddie Bravo Radio* show. Over the last 6 weeks I'd been training twice a week at 10th Planet Headquarters, continuing to get smashed by everyone. I'd even matted my kids' playroom and added late-night training sessions with friends, but it wasn't making much of a difference. I was struggling on the mat, using too much strength, falling into submissions, not knowing the warm-ups, most definitely a white belt.

Eddie, on the other hand, was a 3-stripe black belt under Jean Jacques Machado. Eddie had gained notoriety when he competed at the Abu Dhabi Combat Club as a brown belt and defeated Royler Gracie, then went on to develop an entire jiu jitsu system with over 50 affiliates. I hoped we wouldn't be talking jiu jitsu because I barely knew any of the terminology. I knew crackhead control, electric chair, invisible collar and a handful of terms, but after that I got lost in the haze. I was beginning to understand the principles of why the techniques would work in MMA, but it was overwhelming.

The next 3 and a half hours flew by as we discussed the JFK assassination, my dystopian fiction, and my interest in fighting. We talked about badass female fighters, how we'd put money on them over an untrained male, and why the average male would probably disagree with us. Even though only a very small percentage of men trained in the martial arts, it was our belief that the huge majority had an unrealistic understanding of their ability to fight.

When I began the project, I had a false sense of security, believing I could handle myself. Now I knew just how untrue that was. I could probably be awarded Guinness World Record's "Most Submitted Man in America." Most guys who train jiu jitsu probably only train at a couple gyms per year, and there were a limited number of guys that can beat them. Even a white belt that gets beaten by everyone probably doesn't go against more than 30 or 40 people. I, on the other hand, was getting smashed by every pro I went against, as well as most non-fighters taking regular classes, easily over 500 people since I began the project. I was nowhere near the level of toughness I wanted.

Eddie broke down my path and wasn't surprised when he heard I'd decided to fight after playing football in college. "I think everyone's different, but I'm sure a lot of it has to do with fame or aspirations to be a football player or baseball player," he said. "That shit wasn't going to happen, but now there's this shot." He pointed out all the wrestlers who'd gone on to martial arts and said, "MMA created this opportunity. You have a chance to be a celebrity, and it's glorious when you win."

If fame and fortune were key motivators for most, what was the difference between fighters and jiu jitsu competitors who wouldn't fight? There had to be more than a reluctance to being hit.

Eddie said he wasn't so sure about that. He believed every male would like to be that stud in the cage if they could, but most are too afraid or think it's impossible. "If there was a button you could push that would make you famous for knocking people out and being a destroyer, I think everybody would press that button," he said. "Who wouldn't want to be known as a warrior?"

Eleven-year-old Aaron Riley came to mind, the small kid who wanted to stand atop the heap of broken bodies, the belt held high in his hand. I'd always wanted to be the hero, the last guy standing in the kumite; I just didn't think it was possible. Eddie was probably right. No person would want to be on the losing end of a fight.

* * *

The following Sunday morning I drove to 10th Planet Vista down by San Diego, further than I thought I'd ever drive for a jiu jitsu open mat. I'd lined up interviews with the head instructors: Richie "The Boogeyman" Martinez, a brown belt and pro MMA fighter, and his brother, Geovanny "Freakahzoid" Martinez, who had received his black belt in just over 3 years, the fastest time in 10th Planet and 1 of the top 5 in the world.

I hadn't had a chance to roll with either brother, but I'd heard all the stories about how good they were. I arrived early, guys trickling in and stretching. I looked about the sea of brightly colored rash guards and spats, wondered who the killers were. Since many of the guys weren't wearing ranked rash guards, it was hard to tell someone's belt. Also, I no longer judged guys by appearances. The old man could be just as dangerous as the chubby kid with glasses or the lanky guy that could put both feet behind his head.

Part of me said I should just stick with taking photographs and not roll. It kind of sucks knowing that you are going to submit to an entire group of people and demonstrate that your skills aren't comparable. At the same time, I understood my skills would stay the same unless I went through this. I changed into my own flashy clothes, but still got out my camera, using it as an excuse to take breaks between rolls. I got destroyed by everyone I went against, especially Richie, his shin finding a home under my chin, tapping me with gogoplatas, omoplatas, every-kind-of-plata.

After rolling, both brothers sat down for the interview, Richie going first. The 26-year-old was the oldest of 3, and was so grateful for their mother. She had been a movie star in Mexico and won beauty pageants in Los Angeles, but gave up her dreams to raise her children. Her success motivated Richie, and he said he didn't know how he was going to make it big but was positive it would eventually happen. "I haven't been there yet, but that's my struggle," he said. "That's my mission, just to make her proud."

Their mom encouraged them to do whatever they wanted if it was positive, but neither boy had any real interests through elementary school. That all changed when they hit middle school and their neighbor breakdanced for them. Amazed and inspired by the incredible moves, the brothers developed a friendly rivalry with their neighbor, always trying to outdo each other. The neighbor stopped because of an injury, but Richie and Geovanny, who goes by Geo, were obsessed. It wasn't long before their mom was driving them all over to dance competitions.

Although I hadn't been into the scene, breakdancing battles would occasionally pop off at clubs I bounced at. With egos on the line and all eyes watching, it wasn't surprising many escalated into fights. Fighting on the streets wasn't something Richie ever wanted to do, but there were times when it happened on the dance floor.

"Breakdancing gets really close, really personal, really intense, and really emotional," Richie said. "Sometimes people start touching. And I never liked getting bullied." Breakdancing was about making the other person back down, and sometimes it led to pushing. "Once you push or touch somebody, the next thing that comes along is a punch," Richie said. "If you push me or touch me, or someone from my team, which is my family, the Freakshow, I'm swinging."

Richie wasn't into playing sports or lifting weights. The only sport either brother cared about was WWE wrestling, which they'd practice on each other and friends. Richie showed me his Ultimate Warrior tattoo on his shin as proof.

When Geo began training jiu jitsu, Richie didn't pay much attention. But that changed a few months later when he watched his white belt brother submit every one of his opponents in the blue belt division at the Gracie Nationals, a highly respected BJJ tournament.

Richie began training immediately, eager to compete. He went through the typical humbling experience: getting smashed by everyone and wanting to learn to stop it. Just as the brothers had been obsessed with breakdancing, so they became with jiu jitsu, belting up quickly and tearing up the tournament scene. Richie also began watching MMA, paying special attention to jiu jitsu, shocked at all the high-level belts getting beaten by wrestlers and better athletes. Their jiu jitsu wasn't working and Richie believed Eddie Bravo had the answer to this problem. The main reason Richie wanted to fight was to prove 10th Planet jiu jitsu to the world. Convinced it would work, Richie took his first amateur fight as a purple belt with only a year and a half of training, no striking classes, and only a few rounds of sparring. He landed the rear naked choke in under 2 minutes.

He won his next amateur fight and the 2 pro fights after that, fighting out of the San Diego Combat Academy, but I wondered if proving one's art could be sufficient motivation. In the early days of the sport it seemed more common, but most of the current fighters were highly skilled in multiple arts, knowing at least the basics. I asked Richie which of his 3 pursuits was the most important, and if he felt he should let one go so he could excel at the others.

Richie shook his head, proud of the fact he competed in breakdancing, jiu jitsu, and MMA alongside his students and friends. His love for jiu jitsu turned into a love for MMA. "Now I love striking, I love the clench. I love dirty boxing," he said. "It's something that I never thought I could love this much, but I love this just as much as I love dancing."

It was more than just proving 10th Planet jiu jitsu worked. Richie loved the pressure he'd faced breakdancing in front of large crowds around the world, where one little mistake could ruin the whole battle. He loved being in the spotlight, doing something even cooler than his WWE heroes were doing. Plus, there wasn't any money to be made in jiu jitsu, still very much a pay-to-play sport.

Richie said he had no regrets about choosing to fight. With 3 years of training, he dropped from 215 pounds and now fought at 170, the best shape of his life. He had been unfulfilled working in a warehouse, but now he made his living as an instructor. He possessed a wealth of knowledge that people were happy to pay for, and he absolutely loved his job, starting every morning with a six o'clock class. "Now I have to learn more so I can teach more," Richie said. "It definitely changed my life."

Geo, a black belt at 24, shared the same experiences his brother had. The duo were best friends who did everything together. Like Richie, he got hooked on the spotlight, yearning for that WWE type of fame. Geo said the whole family was competitive, but it wasn't until that moment when he and Richie saw their neighbor spin on his head and do other impressive moves that Geo had any focus. "It was challenging. It was cool," Geo said. "And I wanted to learn it."

Learning, inventing, and pushing themselves was fun, but for Geo it was all about competing in battles. "I always liked attention. I always like being that dude," Geo said. "I got hooked to that feeling of being there in the spot and everyone's watching you and all that pressure getting to you. At first I didn't understand what it was, but as I got older I kind of learned how to control it and how to embrace it."

Geo was introduced to jiu jitsu when he was asked if he'd be interested in learning the art in exchange for teaching breakdancing. Geo, who'd been watching *The Ultimate Fighter*, gave it a shot and became obsessed, just as he had with dancing. "Once I start something, I'm not going to stop until I can't do it anymore."

Like other martial artists who had reached high levels in their art, Geo struggled with his ego. He felt he was already at a high-level breakdancing and said, "I thought I was the shit. And jiu jitsu brought me back to zero," Geo said. "That made me feel alive again, made me feel hungry and inspired for a new kind of art."

Geo immersed himself in the art, drilling, studying, inventing. He compared the beauty and fluidity of jiu jitsu to breakdancing. He also loved how both sports were about backing down and dominating your opponent, something he'd been doing in tournaments all over.

I was surprised when he said breakdancing was harder, but it made sense when he explained how his dancing was all self-taught with no coaches. "In jiu jitsu and MMA you can copy others' techniques and patterns that prove effective, and no one would blame you. In breakdancing, if you follow someone's patterns, you're considered a 'biter,'" Geo said, not needing to explain that biters were looked down on in their community. "What's really important in breakdancing is to be original and create your own stuff. So you really have to put your personality and your own style into it."

Geo talked about the rare opportunities for jiu jitsu competitors to make money competing. "Once you hit a certain level, what else is there for you? MMA makes sense. That's the next step of a martial artist. You have to keep going on in your journey."

Although Geo was always in his brother's corner, he wasn't ready to step into the cage just yet. He still hadn't reached his goals in jiu jitsu, and said it was too difficult to try to be the best at both sports. Right now Geo would stay focused on jiu jitsu but said, "I believe my next journey, my next challenge, will be MMA."

I was interested in seeing how this played out, if Richie would continue fighting, if Geo ever would. Either way, I was happy for them, glad they'd made the decisions that had improved their lives.

* * *

It was the end of April and I had 1 week to travel to the Bay Area and get back before my son's first birthday. It'd been 10 years since I'd seen Brian Shepard, an old training partner from Las Vegas. Now he was sitting in the passenger seat of the rental as we drove to a small town just south of San Francisco. Only Brian wasn't exactly sitting, all 6'5", 350 pounds of him sprawled out on the fully reclined seat, constantly adjusting his position, doing anything to alleviate the debilitating pain in his low back. He hadn't been that bad while staying at my house for the last few days, but neither one of us had considered what the previous day's 7-hour drive to Sacramento, followed by sitting through 4 hours at West Coast Fighting Championship 9 would do to him.

The last few years, Brian had been living in Georgia, miserable and unfulfilled, working security at a hotel. I encouraged him to relocate to Hawaii with his family, but first I asked him on this trip. Having someone to help with filming and photos is nice, catching up with an old friend is fun, but I also wanted to see why Brian fought and what insight he could share about who I'd been 10 years ago. From what I remembered we were good friends, but the problem—one that I don't care to talk about—was that what I remembered wasn't very clear. I usually tried to write off the lack of clarity as old age or perhaps the brain's limited capacity to store stuff, but I'd be foolish to think it didn't have a lot to do with the countless concussions from football and fighting.

Brian laughed when asked if we'd been good friends. "Are you crazy?" he said. "We were great friends."

A little embarrassed, I admitted I couldn't remember, most of my memories from that time wiped clean, perhaps intentionally, maybe from all the partying.

He reminded me of our brutal weekly sparring sessions and all the times we hung out outside the gym, something I'd had limited time for since I was holding a full-time job at the juvenile detention center and dealing with a failing marriage. Some of the memories came back vividly. Others not at all.

The one night that was crystal clear was the most surprising because I must have taken at least 40 elbows to the side of my head that evening. My face was a little dinged up, my ear felt like it'd been torn, but Brian had suffered worse in the main event, a nasty elbow splitting open his cheek and shattering his orbital bone. He carried a fistful of napkins around the nightclub so he could dab away the oozing blood while I held a cold beer to my ear. Both of us were disgusted with our losses, but already back to our self-destructive ways.

But the time to reminisce was over. This was a short trip with only 4 days left, the reason we were hitting a gym on Sunday afternoon. Most schools would be closed, but Lana Stefanac, undefeated BJJ black belt and professional fighter, held a regular class at a friend's academy for her faithful.

The 38-year-old heavyweight wore her long dark hair pulled back in a ponytail, her black gi doing little to hide her powerful build. I tried telling myself I'd have a chance to beat Lana in a no-gi match, but I knew that was just wishful thinking. Lana exuded confidence, not cockiness, someone sure of herself and her abilities, definitely not afraid.

Even though my body wasn't in nearly as much pain as Brian's, I was sore and exhausted, and probably wouldn't have trained even if I'd brought a gi. Instead I stretched out while paying close attention to everything Lana was demonstrating. At first I was imagining how the technique played out in the no-gi arena, but the more I watched, the more I appreciated the art and why it appeals to so many.

Over the last few months, I'd been interviewing black belts from several of the 10th Planet affiliates, but I hadn't talked with any that still trained in the gi. I wasn't expecting any real difference, but was unsure where Lana's interview might lead. Sometimes it could take a while for conversations to head in the right direction or reach any depth, but with Lana it occurred with my first question: What was childhood like?

Lana took a moment to respond. With a nervous smile, she asked, "How early?"

There was obviously something there, so I told her to go back as far as she could.

"I had a really, really violent childhood. Not me personally, but there was a lot of violence in my family. My father was an alcoholic, my mother was a little bit for a while." Like me, Lana was a middle child, third out of four; but instead of having a genius older brother, hers had been a destructive whirlwind tearing apart the already-troubled family. "He was a real heavy drug addict, into heroin, cocaine, everything," she said. "Every vice known to man, he partook in and he spent most of his life in prison."

Adding to the unstable family dynamics filled with domestic abuse, Lana lived outside of Cleveland in a rough area rife with fighting between ethnicities. "I grew up in a pretty violent place." And to top it off, she said with a laugh, "I went to Catholic school." She and her younger brother, Mark, were always in fear for their lives.

Despite the violence all around her, Lana excelled; reading at a very young age, competing in horse riding, playing sports in elementary and middle school, honor roll all the time. Although she was smart and a hard worker, Lana didn't have a lot of friends. Part of the reason was that she was ashamed to have anyone visit her house, but it was also because her life experiences caused her to mature more quickly than her peers.

In fifth grade, Lana's family moved to a 12-acre farm in the countryside. She accepted more responsibility and became a farmhand, lugging 60-pound bales of hay and taking care of the animals. Her grandparents were her role models and they instilled in her an important lesson: "You work hard," she said. "You put your nose in the dirt and you get it done."

A few years later, Lana and Mark, both huge fans of the WWF, decided to build their own ring and host events. "We'd have five, ten girls come over, five, ten guys. We'd put all our names in a paper bag." In their Lanapaloozas you might face off against a boy or a girl, but no one cared. With a huge smile, Lana shook an imaginary bag and said, "Okay, who's going to fight who? It was straight up MMA."

None of the kids understood that WWF wasn't real so the matches got intense. "It wasn't play wrestling, we were trying to tear each other up," Lana said. "It wasn't a martial art, but that was my first fighting experience."

At the start of her freshman year, Lana saw the football team lifting weights and wanted to see how she'd compare. "I was stronger than most of the dudes. So naturally, I'm like 'Whoa, I'm good at this, I might as well get better.'"

Believing that a strong body equaled a strong mind, Lana focused on strength training, instead of bodybuilding or powerlifting. Becoming one of the strongest kids in school was the highlight of Lana's high school years and gave her a sense of much-needed confidence. Her home life had become so violent and out of control that sports fell out of the picture. With her older brother in and out of jail, her parents always fighting, the police banging on their door, Lana often skipped school so she could catch up on sleep at a friend's house.

Her grades suffered because of the absences, so Lana went to a community college to get back on track. When her parents lost their business, Lana returned home to help the family, working in roofing and construction. Throughout this time, she explored martial arts, playing first with Tae Kwon Do and then aikido, but she was not satisfied either would enable her to win a fight. It wasn't the magic bullet she was searching for.

One night while Lana was lifting weights at the gym, a freakishly muscular lady challenged her to a bare knuckles boxing match in the Poconos. "I was like, holy shit, five thousand dollars. That's a lot of money," Lana said. "But then I got offended. Why would she want to fight me? That's just mean, that's just rude. I thought how *bar-attitude*."

Excited about the money and a little pissed off, Lana began training Muay Thai to prepare for the fight set a few months out. The fight fell through, but Lana was already hooked.

During one class a tiny purple belt came in and demonstrated some jiu jitsu armbars, chokes, and other techniques. Lana figured there was no way the moves would work against strength or striking and had thought, "Who would tap? That's just silly." But then it was time to spar and the much smaller purple belt tore through all her teammates, guys Lana considered studs. Not surprisingly, she switched to BJJ, so blown away that she stopped Muay Thai altogether. It wasn't long before Lana and then her brother found their way to Relson Gracie's. She said, "That's how both of our psycho addictions started."

Speaking of jiu jitsu, Lana said, "It's hard and that's how you know it's good." It wasn't like other disciplines that taught simple katas or combinations that gave fighters only an air of confidence. "In here you get humiliated, belittled. You get demoralized by your friends, and by people you don't like," Lana said. "There's no bullshit about it. You either get it or you don't. And you know you got it because you can prove it. With jiu jitsu you can test yourself."

Had jiu jitsu created conflict in the woman who had run away from violence or was this like the Lanapoloozas and the weights, another way to make herself stronger so nothing could harm her?

Lana, who detested boxing and football because they were too violent, didn't feel the same way about the martial arts. She was drawn to the huge element of work and growth. "When you grow up in a violent place, the pain that you feel, the humility you feel, there's no reward for that," Lana said. "You don't get an award for surviving the house I came out of. You don't get an award for having rotten parents. You don't get an award for having a murdering, raping brother." She explained that in practical martial arts like jiu jitsu and Muay Tai, painful lessons made you stronger. They taught you to get back up after defeat. "You might tap today but go on to win World's tomorrow."

I had met some black belts with very little competition experience, some with a ton, but none like Lana, who went undefeated from white to black. As a brand new blue belt, she had her first pro MMA fight in Oakland, the first ever female fight sanctioned by the California State Athletic Commission. Her mom warned Lana that she'd get beat up because she wasn't a fighter, her reasoning being that fighters were all assholes and her daughter was not. Lana understood where her mom was coming from as she used to think the same. "That's the mentality," Lana said. "Fighters are assholes. They're mean, aggressive people."

Her mom flew out for the fight and watched Lana finish her opponent in 50 seconds. After that, her mom came to every fight she could.

Lana's 72-year-old father even began watching MMA, proud that his daughter was finding success.

Their approval meant more than I would have guessed, Lana describing it as being massive. She'd spent her whole life not being recognized by her parents, getting grilled for the occasional B while her brothers were congratulated for getting a C instead of all Ds and Fs. Their praise was something she'd always longed for.

I assumed MMA had been Lana's goal the entire time, but it was just the idea that got her started. "Jiu jitsu was and is my life," Lana said. "MMA was just to pay my bills. In the last fifteen years there's been nothing but jiu jitsu for me."

Lana was good at MMA, winning all 6 pro fights and some titles, but it didn't mean much to her. "I was born for jiu jitsu, and I figure I'm going die in jiu jitsu. You're not born for MMA," she said. "MMA is like a sparkler, but jiu jitsu is the Roman candle that's like thirty feet tall. It's gonna burn as long as you don't blow it out."

Lana said there wasn't much of a difference between competing in BJJ and MMA, but that no fight had been as important to her as any Pan-Am or Abu Dhabi tournament she'd been in. "MMA was just a way for me to show the world my jiu jitsu," Lana said. "It wasn't for me to become famous and the best fighter in the world because I already knew that I was probably the best anyhow. That's not being cocky; that's being real."

Toughness is the trait Lana is most proud of. "I can go through anything. Not come out awesome, but no matter how hard things get, I always get through it." Lana reminded me of Andre Margutti when she said jiu jitsu taught her that. "You're lying on your back, you have a three-hundred pound dude laying on you, crushing, what's the worst that can happen? You're going to break my ribs, you're going to snap my arm, I'm going to pass out, I might tap. That's the worst that's gonna happen," Lana said. "In my life, the worst that can happen has happened."

The last 2 years had been brutal for Lana. On top of an injury she suffered in the police academy that was keeping her off the force and the ending of an eight-year relationship, Lana had spent four months taking care of her mother in Ohio as she slowly died of lung, bone, and brain cancer.

But Lana was a survivor. She would get through it, living and breathing jiu jitsu, sharing it with her students on a Sunday afternoon.

CHAPTER TWENTY-TWO

April 28, 2014

It was Monday afternoon, and Brian Shepard and I were driving from San Jose where I skipped the pro practice at American Kickboxing Academy so I could roll in the no-gi class. I no longer had the interest in striking that I once did, and I was playing it smart by keeping away from lingering temptation, especially in a gym known for hard sparring. Brian sat and offered advice, telling me to get off my back, to stop lying there. After a fairly embarrassing class, I reminded Brian that although I might have given him a run for his money at one point, he'd gone on to earn his brown belt while I'd stopped at blue and still wasn't close to recapturing that.

We were headed to Pleasanton so I could reinterview Leslie "The Peacemaker" Smith. Leslie was one of my favorite fighters and not simply because she shared that same tough-as-nails fighting style and "fuck it" attitude of her teammates. When I had talked to her 16 months before, Leslie had been fighting in Invicta. Just 8 days earlier, she had fought for the UFC, a dream come true although bittersweet losing the decision.

Leslie's background was what I was most interested in. Her father was a United Methodist minister. She came from a nice family, living most her life in South Pasadena, about 15 minutes from where I grew up, but a world of difference. She played soccer and water polo, and seemed to have had a great life.

Then 3 months before graduating from high school she dropped out and spent the next 4 years partying as she traveled across the country.

This interview I wanted to find out why.

We pulled into the parking lot an hour before Leslie would be teaching a kids' class at Cesar Gracie's Academy. The lean and athletic 30-year-old bantamweight greeted us with a huge smile and hugs. I congratulated her on reaching the UFC and we talked a bit about the decision to take the fight on such short notice. It's something hungry fighters often do to get through those doors and something I admire, but such a huge disadvantage.

We quickly went over Leslie's background to see what I'd missed the first time. Although she hadn't been a big fan of church, her parents were supportive, and she had a loving family. But the way she talked about her older brother made me wonder if her idolization of him had turned into perfectionism, one of the problems I had struggled with.

"I spent a lot of time trying to be like my brother and comparing myself to him," Leslie said. "He was always really athletic and bigger than me and better than me." She knew she would never be as good a swimmer or as smart as he was.

Leslie could now recognize that she had been a better player than she'd given herself credit for, and she felt her accomplishments came because of hard work, not natural ability or talent. "I'm not the fastest learner. I don't have ridiculous amounts of agility," she said. "I've always been in the middle of the pack as far as athletic abilities. In water polo, one of the reasons I did better was that I just went for it. I had intensity that nobody else had. That was really the one thing that I brought."

Those unfamiliar with water polo might mistake it for a gentle game, but it is incredibly physical, constant contact with opponents while swimming to stay above water. "We always said that everything's legal as long as the ref didn't see it. So there's punching, kicking, scratching, kicking off of, trying to drown the other person." Players often got kicked out of matches, and in Leslie's experience it was usually because of some gratuitous violence, clubbing someone on the head, yanking them underwater. She said, "It was a violent sport."

The reminiscing seemed to cheer her up. Had Leslie enjoyed the violent side?

"I did take to that part," she admitted with a big grin. "The first nose I broke was in water polo."

Although Leslie enjoyed athletics, she couldn't stand school and preferred partying, upsetting her family who had placed a big emphasis on good grades and a college education. Her last year of high school was painful to remember—friends coming together to do an intervention at her parents' house, being committed to a rehab facility, her father afraid she was going to kill herself. "I was a real problem at that time," Leslie said. "I really put them through hell."

Leslie said she didn't understand why she was so negative, why beautiful South Pasadena seemed like the worst place ever and not a good atmosphere for her. I pushed her a little and asked if she had any idea why she self-destructed.

She thought about it for a moment then revealed a part of her not many people knew. "I get really depressed sometimes," Leslie said. "And it's so hard to break free from that. Nothing makes you feel anything. You don't feel good, everything is bad and it's really hard to look on the bright side, even when you're trying." Leslie recognized that all the self-destructive behavior wasn't about one specific drug or even alcohol. "It was about whatever was there. It was an escaping thing," Leslie said. "It was like what can I do to take myself from reality. Why I hated my reality, I don't know, but I wanted to get away from it."

And get away is exactly what she did, with drinking, drugs, and late nights, 4 packs of cigarettes a day. Leslie spent 4 years selling magazines door to door, living out of motels across the country before settling down in Colorado Springs and becoming a bartender, which only added to the unhealthy lifestyle. Eventually she grew tired of feeling awful and decided she wanted more from life. "I was working on becoming a healthier person with more integrity, and that was when I walked into the gym."

While working as a personal trainer at Bally Total Fitness in Colorado, Leslie came across an MMA practice. After watching for 10 minutes she was ready to sign up, drawn to the idea of hitting someone as hard as she could. She'd trained for a few weeks before taking a fight, landing a first-round knockout that convinced her she was on the right path.

There was little question the reward of pursuing this passion outweighed the risk. "I'm so much healthier for it," Leslie said. "I'm proud of myself. I have a chance to make meaningful relationships with people that I train with or that I coach or have respect for. And that's a big deal and I'm a much happier person."

Leslie reminded me that being happier doesn't just happen. For her sometimes it was hard work. "It was just a choice to be a positive person." Leslie said, "I learned you really have to be in control of how positive you are and I don't think that most people do that."

We wrapped things up when it was time for class to start, and I appreciated the opportunity to watch her teach the kids she'd just talked about, how much she loved seeing them blossom into stronger and more confident children. As Leslie ran them through the warm-up, her words echoed in my head: "I can't help but wonder how differently my life would have been if I did martial arts as a kid."

* * *

Wednesday morning, I hobbled through the doors of Team Alpha Male in Sacramento, my left leg in a new knee brace. Monday night I'd participated in a great no-gi class at El Niño Training Center with Daniel Marks, a BJJ black belt and 5-0 former pro fighter. Tuesday morning's workout had gone smoothly at AKA, as had that night's practice at 10th Planet San Francisco. That is, right up until the final roll, when my partner's weight came down on my leg, and a loud pop sounded from my knee.

The pain had been immediate and excruciating, but after icing up, self-medicating, and putting on the brace, I could put some weight on it. I limped around the massive gym, taking photos of the 40 or so fighters gathered around Duane Ludwig, the former UFC fighter who'd been their head coach but was about to part ways.

After the warm-up, Ludwig walked the team through a series of striking combinations before sparring. I recognized over a dozen of the fighters, but my focus was divided among UFC legend Urijah Faber; contender T.J. Dillashaw; Nico Lozada, who I'd interviewed at Jackson-Wink's; and David Mitchell, who had just fought 4 days before. There was also Paige VanZant who'd just been signed to the UFC, but looked more like a high school cheerleader than a fighter. After practice she was happy to sit down and tell me how she'd been both, and how she'd suffered way more injuries in cheerleading.

Paige had recently turned 20, her first 15 years spent in Oregon, experiencing a good childhood where her father, who'd been a wrestler, loved to roughhouse with her and her older brother. The siblings had a great relationship but often fought with one another. When Paige hit middle school, they amped things up and joined in their neighborhood's backyard boxing matches. She said, "We would just go into the street and beat the crap out of each other. It was fun."

This information was intriguing; I knew that Paige also had a solid dance background, having been brought up dancing ballet, jazz, and hip hop in her parents' dance studio. Dancers aren't generally known for enjoying backyard boxing or even violence in general.

The boxing sounded a lot like Lanapolooza, both Paige and Lana finding enjoyment competing in physical combat at around the same age. I wondered if Paige had had any of the same insecurities and worries about violence as Lana.

"I dealt with a lot of the bullying stuff," she said. "I got jumped a few times. I never actually hit back."

When the family moved to Reno, Paige thought it'd be best if she knew how to defend herself. She went with her dad to an MMA class taught by Ken Shamrock at the Lion's Den and loved it, said it was a huge confidence booster. After a bit, she went to the Reno Academy of Combat and found an amateur fight at 18. The adrenaline rush hooked her; and when Paige was contacted for a pro fight, she figured she might as well get paid for doing something she enjoyed.

The strawweight moved to Vegas for a year in search of a gym with a greater number of professional fighters before moving up to Team Alpha Male. As a 3-1 pro headed for the UFC, Paige was treating fighting as a career while doing it to regulate her abundant energy.

I was glad she brought it up because I was wondering if perhaps her pre-workout drink was still kicking in. Despite having just finished a tough workout, Paige had more energy than anyone else I'd interviewed. Training was a means of handling it.

"I also have a lot of passions outside of fighting, so I make sure I don't make fighting a job where I get tired of it or it becomes something that I *have* to do," Paige said, a very mature response from such a young fighter. Displaying confidence in herself, she explained, "Right now I love to fight and I'm going to keep pursuing that until I get tired of it, and then I'll move on to the next thing."

Up next was David Mitchell, a 34-year-old middleweight who had just won the main event at WFC 9 on Saturday. I scooted in a little closer because the clean-cut fighter with the strong jaw spoke about half as fast and as loud as Paige had.

David described the beautiful ranch he grew up on with his older sister and how they had traveled the world as a family. It seemed like that would lead to a happy childhood, but he shook his head. "Not really," David said. "I was always kind of a dark child, like real serious." He'd been that way since a very young age and said he was prone to depression, something that ran in his family.

I asked if he thought the depression was simply genetics and again he shook his head. David, who had been one of the littlest kids in their small town said, "I got bullied a lot." There had been a group of older neighbor boys that took their anger out on David. "They really gave me hell. They locked me in a trash room one time," he said. "They made fun of me because I was a late bloomer and walked around with an empty stare."

Although David always had the drive to compete, his parents wouldn't let him play football out of fear he'd get hurt. After high school, David was lost. "I remember when I was twenty years old and wanting to join the Army," he said. "A lot of that just came from wanting to do violence."

Construction work presented itself as a better option than the military, but David still felt as if his life had no purpose. That didn't change until he got a DUI at 23 and looked at his peers in the AA meeting, promising himself he could do better. He began working out and was surprised at what a difference just that alone made.

David spoke of the high he got from pushing himself physically. He became addicted to that feeling, better than any drug he'd tried, any high he'd had. Then he saw his first UFC, something he'd always heard high school kids talking about but never watched growing up in the woods with only had one channel on the TV. On watching Chuck Liddell knock out Tito Ortiz, David said, "I remember thinking, I want to do that. I tried getting into Gladiator Challenge with no training, but, luckily, God had other plans and I met up with Dave Terrell."

David dedicated himself to the training and easily defeated his first opponent, but it was that walk to the cage that hooked him. "Everything fell away. I didn't need new socks or drawers. I didn't have girl problems; I didn't have money problems." David said, "You could be depressed. Or you could be upset about this, that, or the other thing, but all that stuff just goes away. You're just trying to survive."

Understanding he could make money doing something he enjoyed, David jumped in with both feet; he'd fought 18 matches over the previous 8 years, winning his first 11 before having a rough time in the UFC, and dropping 4 of 5. When asked who he was in the cage, David explained that that was constantly evolving, something I heard from most experienced fighters. I was surprised when he said what his problem was at the start of his career.

"In the past I had way too much empathy, and didn't really want to hit people," David said. "I just wanted to do my jiu jitsu and submit them, but now I've got to get to the point where I'm the sniper and turn that target into an object, forget about the other person's family and emotions and what you're going to do to them. Just try to destroy."

It sounded as if David was still trying to convince himself, rewire his brain so he could inflict more damage. He was so somber, his voice dull and dark. How much did he still struggle with this? It sounded too fresh and raw to be something of the past.

"Post-traumatic stress disorder every time," David said, no doubting his certainty. "I feel it right now." Since the fight 4 days before, David hadn't really slept, explaining the dark circles under his eyes. Even though he had won with a rear naked choke in the first round, an ideal way to win, he'd punished the guy with strikes before sinking the submission. "I feel like I just killed somebody."

This was the first time I'd heard this. Many fighters struggle with emotions after a fight, but generally winners would have problems with an emotional letdown, riding high for so long only for it all to end. But not David. This was deep.

Although David was fighting a psychological battle due to MMA combat, there was no questioning the positive rewards. It allowed this reserved man with a huge heart to become an inspiration for kids and adults in his community. Martial arts taught him how to stand up for himself and to not take crap from other people, and he passed that on when he worked with anti-bullying groups. He was also in college and thinking about his future, but for the time being it was fighting.

The only thing that mattered for him was the present. Be the sniper or the target.

* * *

Although Brian and I had plenty of time to talk throughout our trip, I saved his filmed interview for the long drive home. I figured it'd be a great way to kill a few hours and get in some laughs. Also a fitting way to celebrate the two-year anniversary of the project.

There were a lot of similarities between us besides our age, birth order, and desire to become professional athletes. I thought I'd had a pretty good childhood, but Brian described his as awesome, something I questioned because he was one of the few black kids living in a predominantly white neighborhood in New York during the '80s.

Brian admitted he'd dealt with plenty of racism, but said it wasn't a big deal. He flashed back to third grade when, for no reason, a kid walked up to him and said, "I hate tall niggers." Brian waved it off and said he was used to hearing stuff like that. "It hurt but you don't grasp it," Brian said. "It was what it was."

Even though we both had the desire to become great athletes, neither of us played team sports until high school and we both struggled the first few years. Brian didn't change until a coach embarrassed him for being out of shape. He promised himself that that would never happen again and he began hitting the weight room religiously, backing up his size with strength.

After high school, Brian played junior college and semi-pro football, making his money bouncing at clubs. At that point, he said, "I just wanted to be the biggest, baddest motherfucker walking the planet. I just wanted to be huge."

I asked about the places where he'd worked, if they had as many fights as the ones I bounced at in LA, where there were several every night. Brian said it'd been bad and he'd been in a lot of fights but not like the kind I had gotten in. I always tried to talk people down, and then restrain and escort them out if had to. Brian escalated situations and often struck patrons instead of subduing them. Part of it was due to him having some stand-up training, but most was due to his temperament. "I got real, real violent after high school." He said, "I just wanted to fight everybody. I was just angry."

Brian attributed this to an overload of testosterone, but I challenged him and said it seemed much of his past would create an enormous amount of anger in a normal person. He brushed it off.

The bigger and "badder" Brian made an impact on the football field and it looked like he'd go to a Division 1 school and then on to the pros. Then things got complicated when his girlfriend became pregnant. Finally, a devastating car accident shattered his leg and any remaining football fantasies.

Brian's dream of becoming a pro athlete was dead. Until he saw a UFC and thought he'd be able to beat most of the guys in there since he'd had an unbeaten record on the streets and in the clubs. The other reason he wanted to give it a shot was to conquer his fear of losing a fight that stemmed from the time a teacher stomped on his chest to break up a fight and hold him down. "It's a fear of failure," he said. "I didn't like that feeling of being dominated."

Brian began training American kickboxing and slowly added other skills, humbled by guys half his size tapping him repeatedly. The training was an outlet and calmed him down. "It gave me purpose again," Brian said.

With fighting illegal in New York, Brian made the move to Vegas, working 2 jobs while training full time at the Las Vegas Combat Club, punching me in the face as only friends can. Another undesirable trait we shared was the willingness to take fights on short notice, and against guys that were heavy favorites. Trying to justify his recklessness, Brian said, "There's always a puncher's chance."

I confided that I now recognized I'd taken these lopsided fights so I'd have an excuse when I lost. The pressure goes away when you're the underdog who is supposed to lose.

Brian said that wasn't true for him. "I just loved the competition. And in the early 2000s you got respected just for stepping into the ring." Brian took pride in it because it was something that nobody else was doing. "It was like a little secret society," he said, talking about fighting before *The*

Ultimate Fighter. With a big grin, he said, "Chicks thought you were hot, too." It was a badge of honor.

Although many fighters, either directly or indirectly, listed identity as one of the reasons for fighting, Brian had another reason I hadn't heard from anyone. "It may sound weird, but I think I did wrong things in my life, I did bad things, and it was kind of like me punishing myself getting beat up," he said. "Because I used to like that feeling."

I flashed back to sparring sessions, how I always needed to be hit first, how I would try to match my opponent's power, but not exceed it. Like David Mitchell, I didn't want to hurt anyone, but a small part of me wondered if I received pleasure from getting hit. Maybe, like Brian, I believed I had deserved it.

Regardless of whether we deserved it, we'd both experienced the results. Brian had sustained a lot of concussions in football and fighting, probably more than I had because he rarely used a mouthpiece for either sport and seldom wore headgear for sparring. There was a four-year period in which he felt very punchy and had trouble getting out the words he wanted to say, often slurring his speech.

His story would have had a happier ending if he'd stopped fighting out of brain health concern like I had. Unfortunately, in 2007, while training judo for a second fight in Japan, he landed incorrectly from a hip toss, compressing and fracturing two vertebras in his low back.

That injury had wrecked his back and body, but it took a long time for him to accept that he'd never fight again. Brian tried telling me that he was fine with that, that the urge finally died a year ago, but I called bullshit. I saw his reactions at Saturday's fights. I asked if he would have been tempted had the promoters asked for a fighter to step up from the audience.

"Oh yeah, I would've, but I'm not actively seeking it out," he said. "I definitely miss it."

This was the first fight I'd attended that I didn't have the urge to get in there. The urge I think most men have deep down. Wanting to test themselves, see how they stack up. I ended the addiction when I realized I no longer had anything to prove.

Brian guessed he wasn't there yet and said he would still do it all over again. "I wouldn't trade it. I have better memories with fighting than football. And I loved football."

After 2 hours we called it quits. We still had another 4 hours on the road, and it was time for Brian to take his pain pills. I wondered how many other mixed martial artists would find themselves in similar places down the road, where their bodies and minds weren't what they used to be. But then I focused on the positive. We were happiest when we were competing, and it had taught us so much about ourselves. Maybe we hadn't conquered all our fears, but at least we'd tried.

CHAPTER TWENTY-THREE

October 15, 2014

I woke early Thursday morning in Providence, RI, anxious about the guest lecture I'd be delivering at Brown University that afternoon. I opened my computer to go over my presentation. An email popped up from the Tri-Force MMA fighter I was planning to interview as the last part of the lecture. There was a miscommunication on dates and he was sorry but couldn't make it.

Damn, that sucked. I was trying to fit 2 and a half years of research into a 2-hour presentation, so surely I could squeeze out another 30 minutes, but I really wanted to do an interview. I figured it was a long shot, but texted Johnny "Cupcakes" Campbell, who lived an hour away. He answered right back, happy to help.

This was perfect, something I should have thought of earlier, but I assumed Johnny would be too busy preparing for his fight in 2 weeks. I had interviewed Johnny on my very first Unlocking trip, just 3 days after his 5-round battle with Tateki Matsuda, the fight that turned me back into a fan of MMA. He'd impressed me as a person, and I appreciated his honesty and the amount of self-reflection he'd done as a 25-year-old. I'd learned a lot about him, but there were plenty of unanswered questions to explore.

I met Johnny outside the Sociology department, both of us a bit uncomfortable being on the campus, 2 brutes surrounded by all these brains.

Fortunately, we had friends to greet us. Adam Aparacio, an amateur fighter I'd interviewed the first time I'd visited Brown's Grappling and Mixed Martial Arts (GAMMA) club had just arrived, and Karl Dominey, my first contact at Brown and a tremendous photographer, was setting up his camera. I introduced everyone and told them how grateful I was that 3 friends I'd made through the project had given up time from their busy schedules to help me out.

After a gracious introduction by Professor Michael Kennedy, I started the slideshow with a few photos of my time at Brown. It was crazy to think that half my life ago I'd been sitting in the same seats the students were. Even crazier was how I followed up my degree by jumping into no-holds-barred fights for little or no money and without any real skill or experience. Why had I done it?

I flipped through the photos of my journey. Getting kicked in the thigh, kneed in the belly, punched in the face, triangle choked, shoulder cranked, ankle locked, heel hooked, electric chaired. Sweaty, old, broken, always on the losing end, trying to play fighter. My one hell of a painful midlife crisis.

My madness had some meaning behind it. I wasn't just embarrassing myself across the country for nothing. I was casting the largest net possible, collecting a much larger sample than any study I had read. Thanks to the help of coaches and my ability to semi-blend into the groups and earn their trust, I felt the group was a solid representation of MMA fighters at large.

But who were these men and women I'd interviewed? I shared the preliminary findings from visiting 95 gyms in 22 states.

I had interviewed 320 fighters, of which only 28 were female.

Of the 320 fighters, 270 had had at least one professional fight.

The fighters had 3,500 fights combined with an average record of 7-3.

Three fourths of them had a winning record, 15% losing, 10% even.

Thirty percent had only fought pro, 20% only amateur, 50% pro and amateur.

Sixty-two had fought in the UFC.

Thirty-six percent had a bachelor's degree; 6% had a master's or above. It is important to remember that many of these fighters were between the ages of 18 and 21, younger than the average age at which people graduate from college.

Only a small number of these men and women made enough money to support themselves strictly through fighting and sponsorships; a large percentage supplemented their incomes by instructing and working at gyms.

Approximately 33% of the fighters had made over $10,000 for one match, but over 50% made less than $2,000.

The fighters worked in a wide range of professions, many of them falling into the expected military, law enforcement, and security fields. But there were also a fair number of businessmen, a couple of lawyers, some preschool teachers, even a porn star.

About 66% of the fighters had been competitive in a high school sport before MMA. Football and wrestling were the top individual sports, but nearly every sport was represented, including water polo, baseball, basketball, track and field, lacrosse, cheerleading, and soccer. The number of fighters who played college sports dropped to 25% with twice as many wrestlers as football players.

About 33% of the fighters had taken some form of martial arts (other than wrestling) before training MMA.

Early childhood heroes and influences were just as varied. Top television programs were boxing, WWE, martial arts movies, and cartoons, but some fighters rarely watched TV. Quite a few of the older fighters were inspired by the first UFC, while the younger group often cited "The Ultimate Fighter" as a prime motivator. There were many that never cared to watch the sport and a few fighters whose first look at MMA was from inside the cage.

They came from all walks of life and had every type fighting experience. Some had been bullied, while some had been the bully. Some had never fought while others had street fights in the double digits.

No one answer would tell me why any of us had become fighters. The factors that could influence the decision to fight were numerous, and each person had varying degrees of each factor. And that's not addressing the biological component and how much genes play a part in reward-seeking behavior, impulsivity, and violence.

I went over some of the reasons a person chooses to compete in mixed martial arts. Often the individual may not be aware of the reasons, and, even if they are, they may not want to admit them to a stranger, especially on camera. That was why I was looking forward to the survey portion of the study which would be anonymous and measurable, each person asked the same questions, unlike my interviews, which often had time constraints and with different answers eliciting different follow-up questions.

The reasons most often reported were competition, livelihood, an outlet for aggression, and the opportunity to represent their school or style and showcase their skills. But discovering these reasons, although still important, took second place to the lessons I was learning from interviewing these fighters and seeing who they were as individuals. These weren't thuggish brutes that lived to hurt others. They were incredibly well-trained athletes dedicating their lives to the one of the hardest tasks possible. They were bettering themselves as people, and often left a positive influence on the lives they touched. None were saints, but they were people I respected.

When it was time for a break, Professor Kennedy took his students out for their weekly Tai Chi session. I changed into my 10th Planet rash guard and shorts for a demonstration when the class returned. I felt a little silly, but thought back to the lecture I'd sat in on the year before, and how my favorite part was the demonstration of moves, not the lineage and philosophy.

The class returned and I talked a bit about the 10th Planet system and how it had been designed for MMA. For the demonstration, Adam, who was a BJJ blue belt, joined me on the carpet since I hadn't arranged for mats. Although I was still a self-demoted white belt, I'd been drilling 2 moves— the electric chair to electric triangle and mission control to gogoplata—

enough to feel confident with them. Maybe I couldn't land them in a live roll, but I could walk through the steps and show what it was doing to the opponent's body. After the demo, I reminded the class about the opportunity they had to train martial arts on campus with GAMMA, and invited them to join us the following night when I'd demonstrate some more 10th Planet technique.

Adam and Johnny switched places while I set up 2 chairs facing each other. The rest of the class circled around, not quite the quiet house where everything had been off the record until Johnny said otherwise. This time I wouldn't be the only one judging him and his answers.

Johnny's young face was hidden behind a neatly-trimmed full beard, no visible bruises like last time. At 5'7" and 130 pounds, with a shirt on, Johnny wasn't an intimidating figure. Plus, he smiled all the time. I doubt many of the students had pegged Johnny for a fighter, unless they noticed his left ear, the cartilage puffing out like a cauliflower.

In our first interview, Johnny had mentioned how much he enjoyed hitting people in hockey. It came up again as he told the class he'd played from seven all the way through high school, and had taken pride in becoming an impact player. He wouldn't call himself a dirty player, but he was one of the edgiest, often angering the other team with hard hits, launching his body, using it as a weapon. "The biggest thing, especially in high school, people just reacted when you smashed into other people," Johnny said. "And I was smaller so that just added to it."

Johnny laughed when I asked whether the crowd's reaction was important. He beamed when he talked of the ooh's and aah's, how other parents would tell his parents how much they loved watching Johnny play. He liked proving to others he was good at what he did, and the recognition helped his admittedly low self-esteem.

During the hockey discussion, Johnny's smaller size had come up several times. I asked if he'd been bullied, but he made it seem like it hadn't been a big deal. He'd always been able to blend in and make friends with most everyone.

Because I was looking for insight into my similar issues, I wanted to know where Johnny's aggressiveness came from and asked if he'd been reckless. Johnny shook his head and mentioned with a bit of regret that he'd been straight edge as a teenager and didn't believe in smoking weed or drinking alcohol. But when asked what he'd been into, Johnny said how important music was to him, especially heavy metal. It helped him vent through a very troubled time.

Besides seeming like one of the nicest and more peaceful fighters I'd come across, I'd been to Johnny's parents' house and seen the area in which he'd grown up. He was a white, upper middle-class, attractive male. I couldn't imagine why he'd been angry.

"Anger in general, that's always been a part of my life," Johnny said. "I was even in an argument with my girlfriend today. I've just always had trouble keeping a lid on emotions sometimes."

Johnny's less-than-stellar grades in school had created conflict with his parents. He rebelled against them and began partying, the drinking mixing with anger and resulting in fights. There was the hint of a smile as he told us of the night he knocked a guy down and mounted him. Johnny rained down imaginary punches and said he beaten the guy's face until it was fractured. Not something he was proud of, despite the fact he'd enjoyed part of it.

This probably wasn't the best story to be telling, and I doubted I'd include it in the YouTube clip. I wondered how many of the students had just changed their opinion about this soft-spoken gentleman.

I realized I was being a hypocrite, judging Johnny for the same emotions I've had. The same emotions I believe most people would experience if they ever ended up in a fight for their life and come out victorious. If someone attacked me or my family, and I managed to get the better of them, I would tell the story with a smile. I believe that's human nature.

Or maybe that's just part of being a fighter: being okay with the fact that you can get just as hurt as the other guy and that you've both agreed to own it.

Regardless of right or wrong, fighting had always been a draw for Johnny. But he said he didn't know where his anger and angst came from, or why he'd ever entertained suicidal tendencies in his senior year of high school.

I'd spent the last few years trying to understand my own reasons for having those same feelings and pinpoint why they'd occurred, and I'd yet to totally figure it out. However, the reasons don't matter when you're struggling with those emotions. Johnny was very fortunate that he'd gone with his buddy to try out an MMA class. In hockey Johnny was a natural, but that wasn't the case with MMA. He stuck with it even though he was terrible, the training and daily beatings fueling his desire to improve.

Johnny referred to his first fight as the craziest 56 seconds of his life, one of the best things he ever experienced. His next 4 amateur fights were all quick finishes, and he was on top of the world. Unfortunately, his first pro fight was a 19 second no contest, and he lost his second fight by rear naked. Not the start of the career that he wanted.

The entire process—the training, the wins, and the losses—is what Johnny needed to break down his powerful ego. He became humble enough to take an honest look at himself and began working to change those things he didn't like. Eventually he changed to a more positive mindset, and everything seemed to fall into place. At the time, his professional record was 8-5, and he was feeling confident about his upcoming fight.

"It's a constant battle all the time," Johnny said, reminding me of Leslie Smith. "I'm trying all the time, to be not just positive, but grateful for life in general."

One of the ways he was appreciating his life was by living it to the fullest, with no regrets. Johnny had recently quit his day job and was now fully focused on fighting with a very ambitious goal.

"I'm fighting for fame and fortune, period. I want to be remembered for decades. I want to accumulate a large amount of wealth, but what I really want is to be considered one of the best UFC fighters, one of America's favorite fighters," he said. "If you put me in front of a million people, three-quarters of those people are going to be like 'who the fuck's that guy' and they're going to tune in again. I can't wait for that."

One student pointed out the interview commodified Johnny, and I seemed more interested in him as a person and not as a fighter. I agreed and said I'd leave that angle to promoters, managers, and the fighters themselves. Although I wanted to see Johnny and all the other fighters succeed, my real goal was to find out who they were and why they were fighting, not speculate how well they were going to do in their next match.

Professor Kennedy shared his thoughts. "One of the things…that I felt between the two of you was that you were helping each other, but you were helping more than each other at the same time. In the following sense that even if this is of commodifying value, which I think it is." He looked at Johnny. "Right? Because you present such a great image. Wow, I'm definitely going to go see this fight."

The class laughed, a couple saying they were going to see the fight as well. Professor Kennedy turned to me and continued. "It's this great image, but on the other hand, you're making an image that's beyond the commodity. It's like you're pulling out the human being behind the fighter," he said. "That kind of dynamic that then leads to the humanization of MMA. It creates a potentially different fan base who appreciates these people not just as blood makers, but as flesh and blood people."

Professor Kennedy ended by saying, "The final part of this whole thing, at least for our class, it extends the whole sense of what the sociology of martial arts can be."

Hopefully, the presentation gave the students something else to think about: that they could find happiness pursuing their passions and not be so concerned with income and material possessions. Class was over, the students off to their studies and dinner. The rest of us were off to train—

Professor Kennedy to his kung fu, Adam to jiu jitsu, Karl and I off to watch Johnny spar at Tri-Force MMA, the perfect way to close out the night.

* * *

It was early November, Tuesday at 10th Planet Headquarters in Los Angeles, a few days after Johnny Campbell knocked out his opponent in the fifth round. I'd been hitting jiu jitsu a little harder since my New England trip, disappointed by my recent performance at the North American Grappling Association tournament, being thoroughly handled by everyone at the Team Santos Fighting Academy, and destroyed by one of the heavyweights in Brown's GAMMA class. The confidence I'd slowly built up had quickly fallen a notch.

I turned to see why everyone on the mat was clapping. The applause was for Ben Saunders, a 17-6-2 middleweight visiting from Florida. Just a few months before, Ben had landed the first omoplata submission in the UFC, Eddie Bravo coaching in his corner. Ben had been a big fan of the 10th Planet system and had taught himself parts of it, but this would be the first time working one-on-one with Eddie.

The classes would be tailored to improve Ben's already dangerous ground game. I looked about the class to see who Eddie would pair with Ben. There weren't any guys Ben's size, and I was probably closest at an inch shorter, but a good 40 pounds heavier. Five weeks out from Ben's next fight, the last thing I wanted to do was ruin his training, but I offered myself anyway before finding out what was planned.

Gogoplatas all class long. Shin under the chin, hands clinched behind head. A gnarly choke often turned into a neck and jaw crank. Most heavy rubber guard days I'd feel like I needed to see my chiropractor to set my jaw back in place, but even with Ben getting all the reps I felt fine at the end of the class. A black belt in BJJ and multiple arts, Ben's a true martial artist with flexibility and body awareness, one that watches out for his partner.

A few days later, Ben came over to my house so we could have an uninterrupted interview then watch the UFC on Fight Pass. It only took a few minutes to learn that Ben knew early on that life wasn't all rainbows and roses. When Ben and his fraternal twin brother were babies, their parents divorced, and Ben's early childhood memories were of them constantly badmouthing each other. Ben's father, a big, aggressive guy, was forced to move them to another city when he lost his high-paying job. Ben was old enough to notice things were different. "I don't want to say we were white trash, but we were definitely on the lower end of the financial spectrum," Ben said. "You see all these people with nice things and nice clothes and you don't have it. You begin to want these things. Maybe it's envy, but it's more like not wanting to feel like the oddling."

On top of the financial problems, Ben had traumatic experiences at home. "My dad had a bad anger problem," Ben said with the kind of chuckle that told me he was sugar coating it. "Not only did I experience that aggression, but I think it was genetically transferred."

Watching his mother deal with extreme bipolar disorder also had a big impact on Ben. "As a kid you're kind of confused, agitated, annoyed, and on top of that I'm aggressive from my dad." Looking on the bright side, he said, "I was brought up understanding psychosis."

In kindergarten, Ben stayed home for his birthday and watched a *Friday the 13th* movie marathon. A few years later, Ben made things worse by watching a graphic zombie movie. "That shit fucked me up bad. For so many years I had nightmares and psychological disorders and fear." Now as an adult, Ben is a fiend for scary stuff and nearly numb to it, but back then he was scared, always worried something bad would happen.

Ben was 8 when his older brother, who'd been training karate, delivered a spinning back kick to Ben's solar plexus. Ben dropped to the floor, his wind knocked out of him. "I literally thought I was going to die," Ben said. "I probably learned something right there, because I survived, realized it wasn't that bad."

Even though Ben's brother beat him up a bit, Ben looked up to him and his idols. "I was all about Ninja Turtles, Bruce Lee, martial arts." One of his favorite memories was watching kung fu movies with his brother while their mom was working. "That was one of the coolest things. It made me believe that superheroes could exist. It made me believe in the chi, the internal energy, ninjas."

Ben began training at home, teaching himself and friends through books and magazines. He was 10 when he saw an ad for the first UFC and vividly remembered watching the event at his friend's house, disgusted by it but also intrigued. He loved the idea of seeing which martial art was the best, but was a little disappointed that no one tried the Dim Mak death touch. There was plenty to be impressed with, though, especially Royce Gracie. The fight against Ken Shamrock blew Ben's mind. "I look at my best friend and say that's what I want to do. Watch, just you wait."

From that moment, Ben had no doubt he would make a living through martial arts, possibly through fighting. With the new goal of becoming a UFC champion, Ben began training harder. Once he had dial-up internet, he spent his time watching videos, printing articles and making books out of them. Eventually he saved enough money to buy a Wavemaster punching bag. With a huge smile, he said, "I beat the shit out of that thing every day."

Middle school was the first time Ben put his martial art skills to the test, standing up to a bully who took Tae Kwon Do. The kid pushed Ben from behind and spit in his face, landed a nice side kick to start the fight. Ben had done pad work and light shadowboxing with his friends, but nothing like this. Fortunately, their fight was all flash, with no significant strikes landing before it was broken up.

They met for a rematch, but a neighbor broke it up before anyone did any damage. Ben stressed to me that he didn't condone street fighting at all, but this was something different. This had turned into a trilogy of matches between 2 martial artists, one of whom was a bully and fought dirty, holding rolls of quarters for their third match.

The kid opened with a punch to the back of Ben's head. Ben kept thinking there should be some martial arts conduct as the guy switched the quarters for a brick and bashed Ben's head. Ben fought through it and got mount, choked the guy until he tapped, and then let him go. "That's where I learned street fighting isn't the same rules as the Octagon," Ben said.

Throughout the fights, Ben stuck to UFC rules and thought of it as training, glad he had that code of ethics. "If I had gouged the guy's eyes out or fish-hooked his cheek in half at age fourteen, it would have been life changing," Ben said. "The martial arts controls who I am. It makes me feel like I have control over myself, and that was a big deal, dealing with my father's anger problems and my mother's psychological problems. Martial arts was a gift."

In what felt like destiny to him, a Jeet Kune Do school opened near Ben's house. JKD was his passion; it made him want to learn all the martial arts and not be close-minded about any of them. "I still believe to this day any martial art, any style you do, works one hundred percent. It's just how much dedication are you putting into the particular moves and techniques that you want to use, and how much speed, power, athleticism; how much of those attributes factor into those techniques that you pick."

Ben chose martial arts as his college and found success testing himself in BJJ and Pancrase. Two weeks after turning 21 and partying like crazy, Ben won 3 divisions in a BJJ tournament. That night, he got a phone call asking if he'd be up to fighting 3 days later in his first pro fight: AFC 8 in Fort Lauderdale, FL.

Armed with confidence from 10 years of training, Ben took the fight. "It doesn't matter that it was only three days' notice and that's what's fucking crazy. No one in their right mind should take that fight. But we're not in our right mind, are we? But all I ever wanted to do was be a fighter since I was ten." Ben said, "This was my moment to prove everyone in the world wrong."

Ben reminded me that we were talking about a sport that was banned on TV at that time. "It was still considered one of the most outrageous things anyone could do, let alone aspire to be, dedicating their life to." Ben said, "If I died in that fight, it didn't matter. This was all I wanted to be, a professional fighter."

The money was also an incentive. "I was broke as hell. I didn't even have the gas money or vehicle to get to this fight." He had to hitchhike to the fight and someone loaned him a pair of shorts.

Despite the big show and his opponent being 10 years older with kickboxing experience, Ben wasn't nervous. He knocked the guy down with a right hand, took his back, and expended himself trying to finish with a rear naked. At the start of the next round his opponent fully recovered, Ben hadn't. "This is what created Ben Saunders, was this fight right here," Ben said, explaining he'd never been to that point of exhaustion. He was drinking his own blood, afraid his teeth had been knocked out, but understood that none of it mattered. If he didn't get his hands up and fight back, he was going to get knocked out.

Ben fought back and the crowd went nuts. The fight ended in a draw, both men earning a modest fight-of-the-night bonus, which Ben quickly partied away with friends.

Ben's next fight was similar, ending in a draw and another fight of the night. Ben considered the draws a nice way to learn from a loss without actually losing, but he had a hard time stomaching being 0-0-2. If Ben wanted to be successful, he needed to train his entire body, something he knew he could not do through individual arts and some MMA sparring.

He made the adjustments and went on to win his next 4 fights and a spot on *The Ultimate Fighter Season 6*. Although Ben didn't win the season title, he earned a spot on the roster and won his next 3 fights in the organization. Ben was cut by the organization after losing 3 of his next 4 UFC fights, but he was determined to return, going 8-3 in Bellator and WEC before he came back with the omoplata victory and $50,000 bonus that went with it.

Making a living as a fighter wasn't easy, but Ben was glad he'd made the choice. He didn't want to think how he would have turned out if he didn't have a martial arts background and embrace the code of conduct. "Things could definitely been dark," Ben said, imagining he might have been a drug dealer or some other kind of criminal. "I'm very fortunate things turned out in a very practical and positive light for me."

Even though Ben's goal all along was to make a livelihood from the sport, he said, "This isn't even a job. I'm bettering myself. I'm bettering my life. Every time I'm learning something new or improving something." He had reset his goal to solidify his legacy, hoping to hone his martial arts proficiency into something others can look up to as he had looked up to Bruce Lee.

* * *

The last 3 months had been busy. I was awarded my blue belt at the end of the year, distributed *Unlocking the Cage* rash guards, fought to a draw in a Gracie Nationals BJJ tournament, and then partially tore my ACL 5 days later. I was enjoying training too much to stop and managed to get by with an air brace, figuring it was just a matter of time before the ligament snapped all the way.

In January, I'd had the pleasure of being Herb Dean's training partner when he dropped by 10th Planet Headquarters. Besides being the most active and respected official in MMA with over 5,000 professional matches around the world, Herb was also a BJJ black belt, a kickboxer and professional MMA fighter. I knew Herb would be the perfect person to talk with; it was just a matter of figuring out a time.

A few weeks later, my wife and I went to the Resurrection Fighting Alliance 23 in Orange County. Herb, one of the refs, sat with us a bit before the fight and we scheduled training and an interview at the Fight Academy, the gym in Pasadena he owned with Savant Young, who had recently ended his 20-fight career with a win at Bellator.

It was my first time stopping by the gym, a clean and spacious facility with everything you need. Savant was busy with a private class and the BJJ class was training in gis, so Herb and I rolled on our own for an hour. It was nice being able to work with someone roughly the same size and age, and with similar goals and approaches to training. I learned a lot about pressure, control, and technique, both on the ground and standing. I also witnessed how Herb treated everyone with kindness and respect, like a true martial artist.

After our workout, we sat on the mat for the interview, Herb explaining what it was like growing up in his area of Pasadena. He is only 2 years older than me, and we grew up about 20 minutes apart. I had known enough to stay out of the area because of gangs, but Herb learned to navigate that on his own.

With 3 older sisters and a much younger brother, the only roughhousing Herb got was with his cousins. He was tall for his age and a good athlete, but team sports didn't interest him. He did play Pop Warner football a year, sticking out the season only because of the money his dad had paid.

"My dad told me I was a timid kid, and so if some of the neighborhood kids beat me up, he wouldn't let me in the house," Herb said. "He made sure I got back out there and defended myself and didn't let people push me around."

In elementary school Herb discovered Bruce Lee, comic books, action movies, and a love for music. When Herb was 10, his dad's friend gave him some karate lessons. Herb absolutely loved the training and jumped at the chance to train kung fu and karate at 13. After a couple of years, Herb replaced those arts with boxing lessons from a friend, sticking with it just long enough to learn the basics. At 18, Herb started kickboxing and began competing in smokers at local gyms, often fighting against grown men.

Herb had been training for a year when his teammate, Zane Frazier, agreed to fight in the first UFC. "Even though I saw the television date, I did not think it was going to happen," Herb said. He remembered that night from that first kick, a tooth flying. Herb had hoped Zane would have better luck, but after a promising start, Zane gassed and got knocked out.

The violence didn't scare Herb away. "Of course I was going to start training that," he said. "It was the natural thing for me to want to do." MMA wasn't that shocking because he'd already competed in boxing and kickboxing, which he considered far more painful sports.

Herb said he enjoyed studying martial arts and that fighting was just a by-product, something he did every so often, taking fights to motivate himself to get in shape. "I would start doing all the other things I didn't like to do back then: run, train, and work out to try to avoid getting a public ass whoopin'."

Herb had a handful of MMA fights over a six-year period, and said, "Each fight made me a better person in so many different ways. I understood more about myself. You put yourself in the cooker, you put yourself under that pressure and you always come out better."

"I wasn't afraid when I first started doing this," Herb said. "I would think about what I was going to do to them, instead of being worried about what they were going to do to me. I was too busy thinking about how much fun I was going to have instead of being afraid."

However, after a long layoff, Herb was a little nervous going into his next fight. "I guess I'd grown up enough to realize, man, something could happen to me." The nerves took their toll. During the match, he realized he was fighting himself as much as he was his opponent. He got hit with a hard shot and asked himself why he was even doing it. A side of him wanted to give up, but he pushed through that weakness. "That's part of the thing I think I miss most about it, is working through that stuff."

But fighting wasn't something Herb could dedicate himself to as a working father who began refereeing under his coach, Larry Landless. "People told me it was a conflict of interest, but they probably just didn't want me embarrassing myself anymore," Herb said with a smile. The urge to compete occasionally came back, but Herb realized the toll training took on his body. "I don't like to train striking anymore since I'm not going to compete. I don't want anyone punching me in the face or kicking me in the legs. It doesn't make me happy."

Submission grappling was a whole other beast though. "So many things I like about it. It's a great sport. It's like playing chess. It's a fun game. It's a workout. It helps my mindset and my philosophy. Just as some people reach enlightenment through meditation, I believe that martial arts, especially the submission martial arts, are a meditation that brings you certain enlightenments. I really believe my approach to things comes from the work I do, the grinding, the meditation. It helps me in life."

When asked why he thought others fought, Herb said, "Anything that people do, there's a lot of different reasons why people do it. It's just the action of what they're doing. Some people are doing this because they want to challenge themselves, because maybe they were a meek type of person. Some people say this is what fits for me. Some people are just aggressive and love getting into confrontation, and they're just happy they can punch people in the face and not go to jail."

Although he's had occasional moments, Herb said he's not an angry person. "I'm not the person who automatically goes to red. I tried to remove myself from that at an early age. My motivation for fighting was to make a beautiful moment. There's guys like that who want to make a moment for the highlight reel."

I thought back to some of the moments from the fights he'd refereed on Saturday and wondered where the line was drawn between beauty and brutality. My wife and I sat in the front row that night, close enough to feel the thuds. I wasn't cut out to be a referee, and wouldn't want the responsibility. I asked if it was difficult to watch a guy take damage, especially if he knows the guy's going to lose.

"Well the thing about it is I don't know if someone is going to lose, and that's the whole point of them getting out there and doing it," Herb said. "Most of these guys are tougher than me, so if I see them going through something that I wouldn't want to go through, doesn't mean I should stop it. For him, he's having the time of his life. It might look horrible, but he's as happy as he can be and doing what he wants to do. So I need to let him go through that. It's balancing that. How do I let him do that so he can have that great moment, so he can have that great comeback that we want to see without allowing too much damage?"

Herb talked about the different safety criteria he uses as a ref to determine if the fight needs to be stopped. His number one concern is the safety of the fighter, and he believes MMA is just as safe as, if not safer than, other combat sports. He also believes it should be in our communities, available to all children.

"I want martial arts to be in the schools," Herb said. "I firmly believe that being involved in full contact martial arts, where you are actually doing it and not just pretending to do it, lessens people from being bullies."

Herb was more than just talk and was making a difference in his community. The martial arts had given Herb so much and now he was striving to pass it on. He encouraged other martial artists to do the same where they live. "I think it's important for people," Herb said. "You develop your mind and soul in so many ways. To develop your body and learn how to defend yourself is also very important."

I couldn't agree more. My daughter had been training jiu jitsu for less than a month, and she was already showing so many signs of growth. If I'd learned anything on this journey, it was that the martial arts are an incredible and underutilized tool, a tool capable of helping individuals and society.

CHAPTER TWENTY-FOUR

September 25, 2015

It was a beautiful Friday morning in Coconut Creek, FL, and I'd just finished a light breakfast with my friend Fortunato Lipari who'd flown out with me Tuesday night. Nato and I been friends since 1998 when I began fighting, and he'd worked my corner a few times. He had been one of my biggest boosters when I was considering starting the project, so I was glad he could experience the last chapter.

Although I didn't feel this trip was necessary to write the book, it was something I'd wanted to do from the start. South Florida was the home of American Top Team (ATT) and their longtime rival, the Blackzilians, located 20 minutes away. Both teams were highly respected powerhouses, but ATT was the gym I'd been most interested in. The visits I'd had with 4 affiliates, and the way Ben Saunders, Carmelo Marrero, Fabiano Silva, and all the other ATT fighters spoke of their main gym and the coaching staff, finalized my decision to fly out.

We pulled into ATT's parking lot and entered the huge industrial building. Steve "The Creepy Weasel" Montgomery, a 24-year-old from South Carolina, greeted us at the front. I'd interviewed Steve via Skype 10 months prior, but a lot had happened since then that I wanted to talk about in person. The day before Nato filmed while I snapped photos of Steve hitting mitts. This morning's workout would be grappling.

Even though we'd been in the gym the day before, I still found it impressive. I'd been to 100 gyms, but only a handful came close to this one.

Everything was clean and professional, painted red and white, the three-story high ceiling a bright blue, a sign that they paid attention to detail and didn't cut costs. Just past the front desk and pro shop was a side room set aside for the kids' program where homework was just as important as training. I followed Steve, the weight area and wrestling mat to our left, striking area to the right. The larger-than-life posters hanging from the rafters held my attention, posters of so many men and women that had gone on to do great things in the sport.

Each of the areas was being used by a different group of fighters. I would be joining the welterweights on the large mat area if I got the go-ahead from former WEC champion and six-time UFC vet Mike Brown, who still looked to be in fighting shape at 40. After promising him I knew enough not to accidentally hurt anyone, Mike welcomed me on the mat and gave Nato permission to shoot photos, but no video, a reminder that MMA is a business; this was their career.

Besides Steve, I recognized 3 other welterweights that had been on *The Ultimate Fighter 21*. I had never sat through an entire episode of the reality TV show previously, but I watched all the 2015 season, American Top Team vs. Blackzilians. Not only was it the first gym versus gym season, it was also the first time the show was filmed outside of Vegas. Plus, it told me a lot about the gym and the fighters that I wouldn't be able to discover on my own on such a short trip.

The ATT captain for the 2015 season, Nathan "Soulforce" Coy, had impressed me on the show; but when I sat down with the 37-year-old in the quiet breakroom the day before, I wasn't sure how the interview would go. It was clear that Nathan wasn't a media type of guy, and the only reason he agreed to do the interview was that Steve Montgomery said it'd be good for the team.

Nathan began the interview with arms crossed, leaning back in his chair, and I couldn't help but feel I was conducting a police interrogation. We began with his birth in Vallejo, CA, relocating often, slowly moving up north, until finally getting to Portland, OR. "My folks were both rolling stones," Nathan gave as an explanation. "They moved where the work was."

I guessed the constant moving must have caused problems, but Nathan smiled and said, "Sure, I think so, but thank God for wrestling." Nathan committed to the sport when he was 8 and said it gave him everything he needed. "It was something to focus on, something to strive for, something to be better at." The father of two swiped the hair from his forehead and said, "There's nothing like competing and training and practicing with your boys, like-minded people. I think at an early age I was able to grasp that. At that point in time, sure playing outside felt great, but nothing else was like this. It made the rest of the day feel great because nothing else made me feel so good. I think that's what inspired me to keep training."

In junior high Nathan got bullied when kids realized he didn't want to fight back. "When I moved to an inner-city high school in Portland, Oregon, I knew that I had to nip that shit in the bud right away," Nathan said. "From freshman year on, if it was time to fight, it was time to go. You take that experience with Tyrone Spong, and I will do that until the day I die. I will always stand up to injustice."

That encounter with Spong, a UFC heavyweight fighter and Blackzilian *TUF* coach, was one of the reasons I wanted to talk with Nathan. When Nathan's teammate, Steve Carl, had to cut nearly 2 pounds in an hour or forfeit the fight, he used the sauna in the Blackzilian's locker room. The Blackzilians weren't happy about this and Spong demanded Carl leave. Nathan stood in front of the locker room door, looked Spong in the eyes, and said they would not move. Nathan refused to be intimidated by the much bigger man, and Carl made his weight cut.

By this point in the interview, Nathan was much more relaxed and seemed to have forgotten the camera. He talked about the Cobra Wrestling Club, one of the best in the country, and how it turned him into a two-time state champion who was awarded an athletic scholarship to Oregon State University. After graduating, the All-American wrestler moved with his wife to the Olympic Training Center (OTC) in Colorado. Unfortunately, the dream of becoming an Olympian didn't materialize, so Nathan began framing houses with his father.

One day at dinner, Nathan's dad asked him to give MMA a try, to train at the nearby Team Quest with Matt Lindland. Nathan had watched the first few UFCs with his dad several years earlier, but hadn't continued to follow the sport as his father had. "It was really that moment there that changed me, that I could do MMA," Nathan said. And the transition had been relatively easy for him as he'd been training with some of the best athletes in the world at the OTC.

It wasn't long before Matt Lindland asked Nathan to fight, but Nathan declined, afraid he'd break his hand. He was framing over 40 hours a week and had a wife and responsibilities. He couldn't justify jumping in a cage simply because he missed competing and wasn't satisfied with what he accomplished with wrestling.

Nathan trained when he could and eventually realized the sport was growing and that athletes could make a living doing it. "Then I saw how awesome of a sport it is," Nathan said. "You wish you had it when you were a kid, 'cause there's nothing like MMA. As much as I love wrestling, MMA is the best sport in the world."

The idea of making money through fighting was more of a rationalization than a reason. Nathan wouldn't make any money fighting as an amateur, and the paydays were small when he began fighting pro in 2007. Nathan, who went 15-5 over the next 7 years, with 3 of those fights in Bellator, said, "It was never about money, but it's slowly become about money." He leaned in with a smile and pretended to whisper. "But it's always been to be the best in the world."

When asked if he considered himself a fighter, Nathan said, "As a kid I would have said, I'm a fighter, you know, no doubt about that. As I grow up and I see the beauty of the sport, I'm a mixed martial artist." Speaking of MMA, he said, "It's a cool thing. You get to perform on everything you've worked on for so long and get to make it happen. It's art."

That was one of the reasons Nathan had been so disappointed with his first performance on *TUF*. He failed to perform to his potential and hadn't shown his true skill. Fortunately, he redeemed himself in the second fight when he escaped a very tight submission attempt and fought to a win that kept ATT in the competition.

At 37, Nathan was one of the older guys hoping to break into the UFC, but his age wasn't stopping him. He was in the best shape of his life and determined to reach his goal, not yet ready to quit and transition to coaching.

When he walked onto the mat Friday morning wearing the Unlocking the Cage rash guard I'd given him after the interview, I was surprised. The UTC rash guard is the brightest thing I've ever worn, and I'm guessing the same was true for Nathan, who seemed fairly reserved. But there he was, leading us in a light warm-up, grinding after his dream. I couldn't help but feel a surge of pride. A martial artist that stood up to injustice and never gave up on himself, exactly the type of person that made the MMA community stronger.

I felt somewhat confident as the warm-ups wound down. I'd done a good job of rehabbing my knee and improving my flexibility by practicing yoga with 10th Planet blue belt and Iraq War veteran Anthony Johnson. His Yoga Lockdown program had made it so I could complete an intense jiu jitsu practice without having to ice everything down afterward. I still had to wear an air brace, but I was just happy to be sharing the mats with these guys.

After a quick stretch, Mike Brown told us to partner up for light takedowns. I hoped I'd be the odd man out so I wouldn't look foolish, but Steve Carl didn't have a partner. Steve, one of the most experienced fighters in our group with a record of 21-4 and the former WSOF welterweight champion, had said his performances on *TUF* were the worst of his career. On top of coming in on short notice and in terrible shape, Steve's house had just been broken into and he'd lost everything, placing him in a poor mental state. After dropping both fights on the show, Steve was hungry for a win.

The last thing I wanted to do was waste Steve's workout, so I told him my takedowns were awful and he should find another partner. He said that was nonsense and walked me through a couple of simple moves, a patient teacher who didn't mind repeating himself.

Next round we were on the ground, starting in a set position then continuing until a tap. The 40 pounds I had on Steve meant nothing. He was strong, fast, and able to control me. My lockdown delayed him for a bit, but I couldn't mount any offense. It was just a matter of time before he got the tap. Then another. And another.

The round ended and I realized I should have skipped that extra piece of toast. There wasn't much rest between the rounds and Mike Brown was next. I got my hopes up that I'd be safe if I used enough strength and size. But Mike worked his way around me, never stopping, always improving position, until he sank a North South choke so deep there was no chance of escape.

I didn't recognize the third guy I went with, but the result was the same. My much smaller opponent dominated me through technique and athletic ability, sweat dripping in my eyes as he applied the head arm choke.

It was a good thing it was my turn to take off a round. I felt as if my breakfast might come up and I sat beside the trashcan just in case. Nato came over and turned on the video camera, asked me how I felt.

Despite the nausea, rapid heartbeat, pouring sweat, and the humbling beating I'd endured, I smiled. "These guys are beasts, but it feels fucking awesome. It was fun. I just wish I could give them more. I wanted to give them a better look."

After the workout, Steve Carl met us in the breakroom for his interview. His tale began 30 years before in the tiny Iowa town where he grew up with 2 sisters and 2 brothers. "Growing up I was real small," Steve said. "I was the runt in school, didn't get bigger until after high school."

At 6' and a ripped 185, it was hard to imagine Steve as a scrawny kid, but the talk had stirred up some painful memories, like being cut from the football team for being too small. Fortunately, his size made him the perfect 103 pounder, and he helped the wrestling team become state champions.

When asked if he was bullied, Steve said, "Oh yeah. And I had a loud-mouth, I'm-not-going-to-take-it attitude, so it was real easy to pick on me." There were times when things got physical and Steve got roughed up a bit, but he never fought back because it would only make things worse.

Steve seemed to have a wild side to him so I asked if he used to be reckless. "Absolutely," he said with a huge grin. "I was the guy that you dare to do something stupid because I was the one who had to prove myself. I would go out there and do anything. I was the crazy kid that everyone talks about." Steve chalked it up to little-man-syndrome, and said he came from a reckless family, feeling like he had to live up to the crazy stories he'd heard about his dad and uncles.

Immediately following high school, Steve joined the Army where he packed on 40 pounds of muscle with a lot of hard work and a late growth spurt. After a scary brawl outside a bar, Steve's friends convinced him he should check out the local MMA gym; they thought he'd be good at it. Steve knew what MMA was but had never been tempted to try it. "I went in simply to gain confidence," he said. "I didn't want to compete."

Wrestling made Steve's transition easy, and with his coach's urging, Steve had his first pro fight after training just 2 months. "I was so terrified," he said, "I can't really remember the fight." Instead of walking to the cage, Steve ran, the whole time asking himself where he messed up in life to end up there. But the first-round knockout washed away any negative thoughts he might have had. "After like the first couple fights, I realized this is what I wanted to do. I was good and I kept beating better and better guys. I realized this was my passion."

Not long after retiring from the Army, Steve flew home for Christmas. The 5-1 pro was involved in a head-on car collision which shattered his leg and broke his hip. "The doctors told me I would never fight again. 'You're not going to play any sports and you're going to walk with a cane.'"

Steve refused to listen and worked his ass off in recovery. After a nearly 2-year break, he returned to the cage, snatching a submission in 59 seconds, the first in a string of 8 wins. Even now when Steve sees doctors, they tell him he should stop training. Steve shook his head and told me, "You can't let other people tell you your limits."

* * *

Friday night we were back at Gracie Barra Fort Lauderdale, the other gym we'd been visiting. Originally, I'd planned on hitting the Blackzilians, but after watching the intense rivalry between the teams I thought it best to focus on ATT. Then I'd seen that my former coach, Ricardo Pires, a fourth-degree black belt, had recently opened Gracie Barra with his 23-year-old son, Victor.

We'd gotten in gi, no-gi, and yoga at their place the last 2 days; Friday night was set aside for interviews. Ricardo taught a class so Victor could go first; the bearded black belt looked nothing like the chubby Brazilian boy who barely spoke any English and used to watch practice at the Las Vegas Combat Club so many years before.

It hadn't been an easy decision for 12-year-old Victor to leave his mother and friends behind in Brazil, but he missed his father, who'd moved to Las Vegas the year before. Victor had also been getting bullied back home and felt like a spoiled rich kid who couldn't defend himself. His confidence was very low.

Each day after school, Ricardo brought Victor to the Combat Club where he would sit and watch Frank Mir, Brian Shepard, and all the other fighters. "So I always looked up to you guys as being that person that I wanted to be," Victor said. "But I didn't know how to get to that point where I was that person."

Ricardo never pressured Victor to train, just made it available. When Victor finally gave up on his dream of becoming a professional soccer player, he put on the gi and began training. First 1 day a week, then 2, then 3.

"I was training more and more until it became a part of me without me even noticing," Victor said.

My daughter had been training for the past year, and my wife and I often had debates about the right approach to training. Victor said he believed many parents were doing it wrong, pushing their kids into the lifestyle. "You've got to be supportive of what they want to do and not try to force them into what you want them to be." If his dad had ever forced him to participate, Victor said he never would have started.

Over the last 3 days, I'd been impressed by Victor's maturity and overall demeanor, on and off the mat. Jiu jitsu had a lot to do with that, but he also gave a lot of the credit to high school wrestling. Wrestling increased Victor's confidence, drive, and determination, and it also made him realize he was meant for jiu jitsu, always thinking how he could peel off for an armbar or sink a choke. "It'd be so much quicker than trying to pin the guy."

This type of thinking was probably one of the reasons Victor decided he'd fight MMA. In jiu jitsu, especially no-gi, there are many techniques and positions that would not work in MMA, and just as many that would end the fight much faster if strikes were allowed. Once someone can do both, it seems it'd be less satisfying applying the tamer version. A martial artist like Victor wanted to show all his skills, not just his grappling.

Victor took his fight camp seriously and trained harder than ever before. Ricardo was nervous but supportive, flying out the day before his son's first fight. Unfortunately, Victor developed a serious staph infection that kept him in the hospital and out of the cage.

Opening the new gym had taken up most of Victor's time and energy, but MMA was still on his mind. "Whenever I compete, I tend not to think about points or merely winning a match. I want to be able to showcase my skills, my abilities and potential," Victor said. Even if it was just once in his life, he was determined to try a MMA fight. "I want to get in there, feel the jitters, the adrenaline, be able to fight through adversity and showcase all my skills, regardless of an outcome. That to me is far more rewarding and exciting than a result."

To Victor, MMA was a small piece of the picture, his true calling still jiu jitsu. "The main thing that really keeps me going, the thing that makes me happy to come here every day is making a positive impact on somebody's life," Victor said. "It's priceless, man, it's the main goal."

Victor wrapped things up by saying, "I just really enjoy each step of the journey. Not only mine, but everybody's. To me that's the biggest reward."

After I removed the mike from his gi, Victor took over the class. Ricardo walked over with a smile, the same smile I'd seen him wear every day we'd been at his gym. Ricardo's positive attitude and good sense of humor were the reasons I'd originally enjoyed training under him. But, to be honest, the way I usually remembered Ricardo was the way he looked after my last fight, which had taken place just 10 minutes away at the War Memorial Auditorium for AFC 7.

I had been sitting upright on a table in the locker room, midsentence, when consciousness returned. Everyone was circled around, Ricardo looking especially concerned.

"What happened?" I asked.

"That's the sixth time you've asked that," Ricardo said. "We're about to take you to the hospital."

Fuck, some of it was coming back to me. The punch. I saw it coming. That's the last thing I remembered.

But the scary part was that punch hadn't knocked me out, it'd just turned off the part of my brain that registered what was happening. I continued to fight for a few minutes before I went down and the ref called the TKO. I had never lost consciousness and walked on my own out of the ring and into the locker room, but that 10 minutes or so of time was completely lost. A CAT scan was ordered. I was done trying to fight. I'd have to live with going out a loser.

Now that Ricardo was sitting across from me, I realized how guilty I'd felt for not being successful. Like so many other fighters, I felt I'd let my coaches down again and again and never lived up to my potential. I believed

I wasted Ricardo's time with fighting, and by disregarding all the jiu jitsu knowledge he had shared.

Ricardo, who had just turned 50, was born in Rio de Janeiro, where his focus was soccer. He tempered that sport with judo and then jiu jitsu as a young teenager because his friends were doing it and it was fun. At the time, he didn't realize why he enjoyed both sports so much, but later he understood that it was because he liked to be surrounded by friends and good people. Being very shy, it was hard for him to make friends. "The part of training I like the most is after the training," Ricardo said, referring to the talks he had with practitioners who hung out after class.

Jiu jitsu helped Ricardo overcome his shyness and develop into a very successful businessman with about 40 retail stores in Brazil and 6 in Miami. When the Brazilian economy tanked and the dollar exchange rate jumped 100%, Ricardo was forced to shut down, his huge overhead and more than 900 employees too much to maintain. He said he went a little crazy but had a breakthrough one day, realizing he'd been missing out on life. He'd been absorbed by his business, neglecting his family, trying to buy their love and happiness.

Ricardo had been a black belt for some time, but he had never thought of coaching before that moment. He decided to exchange his suits and ties for the shorts and flip flops he saw jiu jitsu instructors wearing in the United States. The idea of making a living teaching jiu jitsu was enough incentive to head to Las Vegas and make his way so the family could eventually follow.

Ricardo's first serious student was 18-year-old Frank Mir, a state champion high school wrestler, black belt in Kenpo, and a blue belt in jiu jitsu. Ricardo coached Frank through numerous grappling tournaments in preparation for his pro debut in 2001, belted him to his black belt, and was in Frank's corner when he became the UFC heavyweight champion. Ricardo spoke very highly of Frank, about what a great human being he was and how difficult it was cornering someone you cared about like family.

A moment that stuck with Ricardo was Frank's first loss, at UFC 38. Frank was taking punishment and Ricardo was tempted to throw in the towel, but he explained that, as an athlete, he would never forgive someone who stopped one of his fights. "I started to understand a little more that when you love someone that much you want him to win, but most importantly you want him to perform," Ricardo said. "If you're doing what you love and you're putting your heart into it, I'm with you."

Ricardo never judged Frank if he lost a fight, just as he never judged any of his other fighters. He wanted us to reach our goals because he saw how hard we trained. He wanted us to perform to our potential, something I never did and for which I felt guilty. But now that we were talking about it, I understood a little better.

I wanted to hear Ricardo's thoughts about why I wasn't successful when it came time to perform. He brought up my fight against Travis Wiuff where I reversed the decision because I believed Wiuff had earned the win. "Dude, you did something in Mexico that I'm not sure I would do. I take my hat off to you. It was beautiful, it was nice, but I'm not sure I would do it," Ricardo said. "That says everything about you. You are willing to give up something that you like for someone else to have it."

I didn't completely agree with his last sentence because I honestly believe I gave up the win because of the circumstances. If the judges had awarded me the decision based on performance and not on my willingness to continue fighting past the 3 rounds we'd agreed to, I wouldn't have reversed a thing. But maybe Ricardo had a point.

"Yesterday we were training in the gi and I felt the old Mark," Ricardo said. "You were strong, but you were doing it a little bit slow, you were giving me time. I was getting the positions, but you were okay with it."

The memories rushed back, Ricardo slapping the mat, yelling for me to get off my back. "Move it, move it, get up!" Sometimes it'd be in the shark tank, sometimes individual drills, but all too often I was okay being in a bad position.

"You wouldn't actually explode, Mark. I never saw you mad. Not in the fight, not before the fight, not after the fight, not with the results. I have never seen you mad."

This surprised me. Surely he must have seen me mad. I'd always struggled expressing emotions, but I never thought anger was one of them.

"But when you trained with no gi yesterday you had some flashes, you had some seconds where I went 'oh man, he's trying to hurt me.' That's beautiful. I had never seen that before. Eddie Bravo is doing a great job," Ricardo said. "You have your passion for no-gi."

Passion. That was one of the words I'd been hearing a lot lately. I couldn't deny I had a passion for no-gi jiu jitsu, an urge to learn more and more. I don't know if I ever had that with MMA. It was something I was doing for an identity, to prove I wasn't scared of confrontation, to show I was a man, all while tempering the self-destructive rage eating away inside of me.

Ricardo knew there was more to my problem than lack of passion and being too nice. My confidence had never been there, and it still upset Ricardo when I called myself a mediocre fighter at best. He chastised me like a father. "Don't put yourself down that way," Ricardo admonished. "You should not give up so easy on your dreams, on those things that you want. And if you don't get them, you should get a little bit mad."

Victor's class was over, the noise in the room getting a little loud for recording. "You are one of the reasons why I love this," Ricardo said. He listed all the major fight organizations that had paid him to train guys around the world and said, "I don't even remember their names, but if you call me tomorrow and tell me 'Ricardo, I have a fight in California this weekend but I don't have any money to fly you,' Mark, I would get on a bicycle and ride all the way to California to be in your corner. That's why I think it answers all the questions about 'Why do you like this?'. Because it gave me the opportunity to meet people like you. It gave me the opportunity to be surrounded by people like you. And that's priceless."

I 100% felt the same way about him, Brian Shepard, all my training partners, guys I fought against, most everyone I was coming across in jiu jitsu. I was finally beginning to understand one of the greatest aspects of the martial arts.

* * *

It was Sunday night and we were at Steve Montgomery's apartment recovering from a 90-minute Bikram yoga session, the temperature in the room had been over 100 degrees. It was my first time doing yoga in a studio, but I didn't have any fear about not feeling like a man since Steve, Matt Van Buren, who also fought for the UFC, and Carl Deaton III, another MMA fighter, did the class with us.

Originally, we'd planned to attend the local fights, but we were burned out from the class, and I didn't know any fighters on the card. Plus, the purpose of this trip had been to focus on Steve, who'd been incredibly gracious with his time and hospitality. During the Skype interview we'd had 10 months prior, Steve had taken me through his childhood while I searched for critical events that might have affected his development. He was an only child, very fortunate to have parents who supported him no matter what he wanted to do. Although most of his childhood he was one of the smaller kids, he had a competitive drive that could match anyone's. Whatever he was doing, he wanted to be good at it. Early on it'd been a little bit of karate, then soccer, surfing, and bass guitar.

While telling his story, Steve brushed over how as a young child he'd saved his diabetic father's life by calling 911 more than once. When asked how those intense scenarios had affected him, Steve reminded me it doesn't matter what we go through, it's how we respond. Instead of seeing it as a negative, Steve saw it readied him to handle extreme situations, including those he'd later face as a fighter.

As a child, Steve had an appreciation for martial arts in the movies, but there weren't many martial art schools in his hometown of Florence, SC, and the one he'd tried as a kid had been underwhelming. Having lived there in 2006, I could testify to that. It was so bad that I had run a small MMA class at the local fitness center. There weren't many of us, and I wasn't offering much as a rusty blue belt, but it reminded me that even though I'd said I was done fighting, I still had the urge to train.

While I'd been trying to teach from a book and a battered memory, Steve was a 15-year-old butchering a bass guitar in a band. The 21-year-old guitarist was always telling Steve about MMA, but Steve didn't think much of it, imagining something fake like WWE. One day the guitarist brought in a tape of the UFC, Robbie Lawler smashing someone. This was not fake.

The guitarist introduced Steve to his trainer, who held privates at his house. Steve was hooked from the first class. While his friends were out having fun, Steve was training. Over the next seven months he sprouted from 5'7" to 6'1" and put on a lot of muscle from exercising. He watched Season 3 of *The Ultimate Fighter* and set his intention that he would become a professional mixed martial artist. Steve said, "I jump in with two feet. If I'm going to do something, I'm gonna do it."

Besides the huge draw of the friendships he formed with training partners, Steve listed several other reasons he immediately loved training. "The excitement of catching a submission and the excitement of getting out. And all those fears you might have—what it's like to get hit in the face, getting crossfaced, getting choked, getting choked out, getting kicked in the head, getting rocked and sent to your knees. All those fears just become your friends." Steve said, "I think it's the right way to feed your ego. You keep your ego in a cage and leave it there."

Steve admitted that initially a big part of why he trained was his ego, but that evolved to just wanting to train and have a good time. "I like the grittiness of being in long grappling sessions and escaping tight chokes. You just like that toughness," Steve said. "You really feel yourself become a superhero. Compared to what you used to be, you're a superhero that you dreamed you want to be. It's a way to bring your imagination into reality."

The initial training helped Steve understand that he was somewhat tough, but he wanted to test himself. He heard the guys at the Florence Fight Farm could help him.

The first time I visited the FFF, I was more than a little skeptical. The directions were sketchy but accurate, a series of turns on unpaved roads until you turned past a broken-down barn and drove through a field where there was a small room with a makeshift cage beside it, a tin roof to keep out the rain. The owner of the property and coach of the team, Eric Lee, was a big man who'd welcomed me into their group as they trained using videos, magazines, and the internet. I had enjoyed training there, but it was probably less than a dozen times. At least one of those times I'd shared the mat with a young Steve Montgomery.

Steve loved the FFF and Eric became a second dad to him. Eric understood Steve's desire and told him if he wanted to be a fighter, he would have to be prepared. Eric began taking Steve to local MMA events, a couple of UFCs, seminars, and training sessions at other gyms. He entered Steve in a dozen grappling tournaments over a period of six months to give him experience competing. "If I wasn't working or at school, I was training. I really stopped hanging out with my friends, who were slowly transitioning to partying," Steve said.

MMA was illegal in South Carolina, and Georgia's restrictive rules didn't appeal to Steve, so he went on *The UnderGround* forum and found himself a fight in North Carolina. Steve was expected to lose against a tough wrestler, but he managed to make it through all 3 rounds and win the decision, the most difficult thing he had ever put himself through. He had exerted himself so much in the fight that he couldn't stand at the end, puking in the corner, unable to appreciate the victory.

Most 18-year-olds probably would have decided that fighting wasn't worth that. Why put your body through hell and fight another man for no pay? Why not focus on school and girls like other seniors?

But the difficulty only motivated Steve to train harder for the next fight, which Steve accepted before realizing it was the same night as his prom. Steve wanted to back out, but Eric made him understand that he had given his word. If Steve wanted his word to mean anything, he had to stand by it.

What most people probably could not understand, especially in South Carolina where no one cared about the sport, was that Steve was looking at MMA as a career, not a hobby. He was a smart kid and had been accepted at the University of Alabama. Then Eric took him to a seminar at ATT, and Steve was impressed by how gracious and pleasant everyone was. "I was thinking I was going to go to college," Steve said. "That's what everyone wants me to do, that's what I'm supposed to do. And then I walked in there and I just got this feeling. When you just see all the fighters. You saw it today."

Skipping the prom cost Steve his girlfriend, but he never questioned he'd made the right decision. "The universe starts to point out the right path. So I went and trained really hard for the kid. I TKO'd him. And that was the first time I had like that euphoria of winning and finishing, and that was amazing."

The next fight landed on Steve's high school graduation day. There was no backing out because Steve wanted to prove to himself and ATT that he was worthy of being part of such a great team. "I cut weight in the morning, walked across the stage and got my diploma, drove three hours." He weighed in at six o'clock and got another first-round win a few hours later. The next week he moved to Florida so he could join ATT.

Steve devised a somewhat manipulative plan to work his way to ATT, enrolling in a nearby junior college so his parents would help foot the bill. The ploy didn't last long; he soon dropped out, realizing he was wasting his time and his parents' money. He understood that whether or not he became a fighter, he could make a living through the martial arts. "American Top Team was the university I choose."

Down in Florida, Steve stayed busy with 3 first-round wins before the end of 2009. Sitting at 6-0 as an amateur, Steve felt ready for his pro debut, but he was submitted late in the third round of his first pro fight. Not wanting to risk losing his second fight, Steve focused on improving his skills over the next year and a half.

His patience paid off and Steve won with 3 finishes in his next 3 bouts, dropping the fourth in a close decision. Steve went on to win his next 5 fights and went into 2015 and the filming of *TUF* with high expectations. "Whenever I go into an adventure, I think of the best situations possible," Steve said. "If I'm not the hero on the show, I'm going to win two fights, at the very least one. I'm going to do sick, I'm going to kill it and help my team."

ATT had dropped the first 3 fights and the team was desperate for a win. The coaches selected Steve, the stage set for the heroic moment he'd envisioned. It was a quiet afternoon at the fighter's house before weigh-ins, when someone upstairs yelled for help. Steve was seizing on his bed, his muscles locked, mouth foaming, his teammates trying to keep him from harming himself.

This was Steve's first seizure, which he said was a result of drinking too much water without ingesting any electrolytes with it. Although Steve felt fine, the UFC played it safe and released him from the show, Dana White promising Steve a shot if he could successfully cut weight and win a fight.

Steve was demoralized by the seizure and felt awful that he'd let down both himself and his team. "Now it wasn't necessarily harder things that I expected from the fights, it was like, 'alright, life's throwing you a new turn, you got to figure this out,'" Steve said. "I stayed positive. The people from ATT, I knew they were my family, but I didn't realize they were my lifeline. They really came through for me on so many levels."

Instead of feeling sorry for himself or second guessing his career choice, Steve went after it harder than ever before, begging his managers to find him a fight. Fights were scheduled but fell through. Then the UFC offered a fight in June, just 2 weeks out.

The fight did not go Steve's way, and he got knocked out by a punch in the first round. "So now I feel more mature. I feel pretty humble in the sense that if I'm fighting a 125-pound chick, I'm going out there to do it like a prison murder," Steve said. There could be no worries about being flashy.

All it takes is one punch, one kick, one mistake. "You got to go in there and as efficiently as possible silence them."

At the time of our interview, Steve had just found out he would be fighting in Australia against Daniel Kelly, a 10-1 MMA fighter who competed in judo for Australia in 4 Olympic Games. The fight was 7 weeks away, a solid camp, plenty of time to prepare. Steve knew it was going to be a tough fight, but he was going in to win. "I want some redemption."

I wondered if Steve's goals were much different from the goals when he'd been the high school senior slugging it out on graduation day. Steve shook his head. "I think I've reached the goal. It's my living," Steve said. "Meeting all the different people and getting knowledge. Just being on so many adventures and meeting so many new faces. This is the goal; living here by the beach and training."

When asked if he was a martial artist or a fighter, Steve said he was a combination of both. "The fighter is more on the ego side. I'm definitely a martial artist in the sense that if you put me in a country where I didn't know anybody at all and all I could do is train all day and I didn't get to tell anyone about it or put it on social media, I'd be happy. The martial artist does it for the love of the sport, but the fighter does it just to say he's a fighter. Even some of the good ones. I'm sure there are guys that are sixty percent martial artist and forty percent fighter. I'm probably one of those." Steve said, "I'm not going to lie, I like telling people I'm a fighter, and if they want to talk about it, of course I'm flattered."

Steve was a free-thinker who questioned himself and others, not some brutish thug that wanted to inflict damage. Speaking of MMA, Steve said, "It's a brotherhood. A very dysfunctional brotherhood in the sense that at the end of the day it's a business." He said, "It allows us to live a comfortable life and people (spectators) get to have a greater appreciation. No matter how corporate it becomes, it's still *Fight Club*. It is still two dudes. Once you get through all the picture taking, all the camp, all the social media posts," he said, "you're in a cage naked, standing with the other person and you got to try and kill him until someone tries to stop you."

To Steve, the martial arts weren't about fighting people; they were about working against yourself, thus making yourself a better athlete, fighter, and person. "You're really competing against yourself. And so is everybody else. That's what I love about it. No matter how violent it gets, it lets people appreciate the beauty in the violence."

In pursuing their passions, Steve and the others became martial artists striving to find the positive in every situation and overcoming whatever obstacle was in front of them. Steve suffering a stroke and then a knockout, bouncing back stronger and hungrier than before. Nathan, momentarily stalled by his disappointing loss on *TUF,* only to regroup and battle to a win, giving his team life. Steve Carl refusing to listen to the doctors who told him he'd never fight and would walk with a cane, rubbing each of his subsequent 20 fights right in their faces. Ricardo losing his fortune but finding himself, and giving his family a healthier and happier way to live through jiu jitsu. Each of them incredibly grateful for the gift of martial arts and planning on practicing and spreading their knowledge until they die.

CHAPTER TWENTY-FIVE

December 18, 2016

A lot has happened over the past year as I've gathered thoughts, rewatched interviews, and followed the careers of these athletes, many who I now consider my friends. Every weekend it's another rush of wins and a wave of crushing defeats, crammed with cuts and concussions, blood and bruises.

In the 4 and a half years I'd been working on this project, there have been many mixed martial art events held around the world. Except for the smaller organizations putting on fights at the local level, most of the events have been televised. Between pay per view, Fox, Fox Sports, Fox Sports 1, and the UFC Fight Pass, there have been 9 seasons of *The Ultimate Fighter* and 181 UFC fights (of 384 total). All of Bellator's 103 fights were televised on Spike TV and 45 RFA fights were on AXS TV, and NBC is the home of World Series of Fighting. Viacom, the fourth largest media conglomerate in the world, owns Bellator and in July of this year, the UFC was sold to the WME-IMG group for $4 billion, the biggest transaction in history for a sports organization.

The sport has been legitimized through mainstream TV and is skyrocketing with all the exposure. It's not quite there, but close to reclaiming the glory of the Roman Empire's gladiator games, where crowds filled coliseums to see which man would survive. Although the average professional fighter can't support himself on fighting purses alone, the superstars are bringing in tremendous paydays. In just salary and disclosed bonuses, Connor McGregor has earned just under 10 million in his 10 fights for the UFC, and probably double that with his pay-per-view shares. Brock Lesnar, Georges St. Pierre, Michael Bisping, Anderson Silva, Vitor Belfort, and Dan Henderson have all made over $4 million in salaries from the organization. Close to a hundred other competitors have made more than a million.

The competition in MMA becomes steeper every day as the market is flooded with incredible athletes crossing over from other sports and new blood joins the fold at an increasingly younger age. To become the best and bring home huge financial bonuses, they train harder and smarter and become increasingly more proficient at the art of dismantling another person. There's never a shortage of men and women who are willing to fight. There never will be.

With the seemingly unbalanced risk versus reward, especially in the early stages of a career, it can be difficult staying dedicated to the sport. 75% fighters I interviewed have winning records, but only 3 remained undefeated in 7 or more fights. Jakes Mapes from The Arena ended his career 8-0 and is satisfied teaching jiu jitsu. Joe Lowry, a young fighter out of Daddis Mixed Martial Arts in Philly that has won all 10 of his bouts. The last is John Johnston from Sityodtong, who won all 7 pro fights while in his 40s, finishing all but one of the fights in the first round, and became the heavyweight champion for CES. More importantly, Big John opened IronClad Martial Arts Center where he now passes on all he has learned.

Andre Soukhamthath, the fiery young man from Tri-Force MMA whose 9-month-old son had passed away from a rare blood disease, moved to Florida to train with the Blackzilians. Andre is now the father of 2 healthy boys and is 11-3 as a pro, finishing all but one of his wins, both losses by decision. He should get his shot soon.

Up at the other end of the coast at Young's MMA in Bangor, MN, Bruce Boyington went 11-4 over the last 3 years, including 2 WSOF wins, while his teammate, Ryan Sanders, earned a big win in front of Dana White at an NEF fight. Head coach and former fighter Chris Young is very proud of how well his team has done, especially his wife, Angela, a nurse and mother, who has fought 3 times as an amateur, loving the challenge.

In Fresno, CA, Chris Honeycutt went 7-1 as a pro with 5 of those fights in Bellator. Troy Lamson graduated from Michigan State and went 7-2 as a pro. In New Mexico, Steve Garcia went from 1-0 to 7-1, and 2-0 Landon Vannata snatched 6 more finishes before stepping up on short notice to fight in the UFC against 20-3 Tony Ferguson, a top-ranked UFC lightweight contender. Although Landon got caught in the second round, the match was such a brilliant display that it was awarded the Fight of the Night, earning each fighter a $50,000 bonus, more than Landon's previous earnings. He returned to the Octagon at UFC 206 last week and more than doubled his $20,000 salary, collecting another $50,000 bonus with a tremendous head kick knockout in the first round.

Another fighter who entered the UFC with a bang was 22-year-old Paige VanZant. There was a lot of speculation that Paige had only been signed by the organization because of her looks, but she silenced critics with a third-round knockout and Fight of the Night bonus. From there she went 3-1, earning a Performance of the Night after an 8-month layoff, during which she took second place on the TV show *Dancing with the Stars.* Some were surprised Paige would put her fight career on hold, but that's what had impressed me the most about her interview. She had made it clear that MMA was simply one of her passions and she'd only fight as long as it continued to make her happy.

This past weekend, Paige headlined *UFC on Fox* against Michelle "The Karate Hottie" Waterson, and it was obvious Paige was still enjoying herself. She and Michelle had a fun dance-off at the weigh-ins, and Paige was all smiles as 4.8 million viewers watched her head to the cage. Both fighters looked confident as the round started, but Michelle, the former Invicta FC atomweight champion, used her experience and took control, ending the fight in the first round with an incredible throw to set up a deep rear-naked choke that put Paige to sleep and earned Michelle the Submission of the Night.

The card's Fight of the Night bonus went to Leslie Smith, one of my favorite fighters. Leslie, who once argued with the doctor to let her continue to fight despite the giant bloody hole where her cauliflower ear exploded, had a tremendous win and broke the $100,000-per-fight payday, something only 20 of the fighters I interviewed had accomplished. I'm happy for her success because she's a true warrior in and out of the cage and isn't afraid to voice her opinion regardless of what her employer, or anyone else, might think. Whether it's her stance on a fighters' union or protesting the Dakota Access Pipeline, Leslie will always fight for what she believes in.

Beneil Dariush is another fighter I've enjoyed watching rise through the ranks. When we first talked 4 years ago, Beneil was 3-0 and deciding whether he would devote himself to BJJ or MMA. He's gone 11-2 since with eight impressive wins in the UFC. This year Beneil opened a beautiful facility with Kings MMA Anaheim, and, like Leslie, he uses his celebrity for good causes, speaking out on injustices.

It's always exciting when fighters get the call to the big show, but disheartening when they get cut soon after. If new fighters aren't winning their first 2 fights or competing in an exciting fashion, they'll be lucky to get to a third fight. Just like in any professional sport, if you don't make it in the big leagues, you go back to the minors to sharpen up.

That doesn't make it any easier to watch when you know how hard someone has worked to get to that point. With Steve Montgomery, one takedown in the last round against Daniel Kelly cost Steve the decision and a place on the UFC roster. Some athletes like Steve continue grinding, determined to get back to the UFC. Many, however, have become discouraged and hung up the gloves. It's humbling to take the step backward, and it can be hard to justify sticking with the selfish sport to oneself, family and friends. Why put in all that blood, sweat, and tears, sacrificing so much for 1 or 2 fights in an organization, especially when the pay is less than they'd make at a regular job?

Getting cut from the UFC or any large organization can trigger or amplify depression in fighters, just as any loss can. Although Ben Saunders suffered silently, he had a very difficult time following his loss to Patrick Cote. Ben wasn't cut by the UFC, but essentially removed himself by turning down fights because he wasn't mentally ready. After an 8-month break, Ben focused himself and returned to the cage, beating a very tough and experienced Jacob Volkmann in 17 seconds. Displaying his prowess as a martial artist. Improving his stats. Cementing his legacy.

And then there are the injuries. Nico Lozada, from Team Alpha Male, had his orbital bone crushed in his pro debut but bounced back and won his next 2. Zach Freeman from St. Charles MMA looked great going into the RFA championship bout at 7-1 but suffered a broken hand in the second round and a fractured shin and torn ankle ligament in a later round. Yet somehow, Zach fought all 5 rounds, immediately asking for a rematch when he lost the decision.

Although Zach will return to fighting, injuries often end careers, especially when it's the same injury over and over or the fighter just can't stay healthy. Dominick Cruz has been plagued with injuries since a torn ankle ligament ended his dreams of college wrestling, but his desire to compete pushed him to became the final WEC bantamweight titleholder and then UFC bantamweight champion. After two brilliant defenses of his belt, ACL and groin injuries sidelined Dominick for nearly 3 years, and he was stripped of his title.

Instead of accepting his reign was over and being content with his position as a UFC color commentator, Dominick did everything possible to recover. Eager to prove he was still the best in the world, he came back strong, earning Performance of the Night honors, but the celebration was short lived when another injury forced Dominick back into rehab. After a year of recovery, Dominick stole his belt back from T.J. Dillashaw in an exceptional five-round battle that earned them Fight of the Night. His defense of the belt against Urijah Faber occurred 5 months later, Cruz winning every round, in a comeback most didn't think possible. Dominick will go down as one of the top pound-for-pound fighters of all time and a true champion on and off the mat.

As much as I enjoy watching MMA events and appreciate the talent and skill involved, I'm still more interested in the person than I am the fighter. Through social media, I've watched these athletes be parents, siblings, sons and daughters, enjoying life's beauty, dealing with everyday struggles, and some incredible challenges.

Not long after I interviewed Eddy Rolon, a former fighter and the head coach of Endgame Sports Academy in New Jersey, he confided he was struggling with chronic inflammatory demyelinating polyneuropathy (CIDP), a rare disorder of the peripheral nerves characterized by gradually increasing weakness of the legs and, to a lesser extent, the arms. It is very similar to multiple sclerosis and the symptoms are at times severe. Since August 2013, Eddy has been receiving a nurse-administered IV infusion for about 15 hours over 3 days every 3 weeks. This was seriously affecting not only Eddy's personal life, but also his business. The support of his family, friends, and the martial arts community helped him get through each obstacle and daily ordeal. He has adjusted his life schedule but still gets on the mat and puts on gloves a few times each week. Training others and getting some sparring in have been both physical and mental therapy. Eddy continues to make a difference in his community and was elected to serve on the Rutherford, NJ, Board of Education.

In January of 2014, just a few weeks after Joe Lauzon's 23rd win as a pro, his son, Joey, was born. Instead of being one of the most joyous experiences a young couple could have, Joe and his fiancée, Katie, learned that their baby boy was born with cancer, the odds not in his favor. Little Joey began chemotherapy at 6 days old, his parents right by his side, helping him battle through 3 rounds. After hearing Joey was cancer free, Joe began breathing a little easier, still enjoying every moment with his son but allowing MMA back in his mind. He returned to the UFC a few months later and earned a huge knockout and Fight of the Night bonus. In his next 5 fights, Joe earned another 2 bonuses and currently holds the record for the most post-fight bonus awards with 15.

A little over a year after I interviewed Oklahoma City Police Department officer Matt Grice, his car was rear-ended at a red light by a van going 65 mph. The crash nearly killed Matt, and he was rushed to emergency surgery for a traumatic brain injury. Doctor's didn't give Matt very good odds of surviving or coming out of his coma, but after a month Matt awoke, a large portion of his skull removed, unable to recognize his wife or two daughters. Through incredible hard work and determination, and the constant support of his family, Matt relearned who he was, how to talk, how to live. And although Matt won't be able to return to the cage like he wishes, he returned to work as a police officer, risking his safety to help others.

I'm impressed and inspired by these stories, but not surprised. I've watched these men and women dedicate themselves to becoming stronger, tougher, more resilient every single day. Sharing the mat with them gave me an opportunity to see their character and some of the ways they built it. Although many had no idea I was a writer, not one person asked me to get out of the way, stop wasting their round, or discouraged me in any form from training. They all pushed me and gave pointers, acting like true martial artists, recommending other gyms and friends to interview. Their encouragement was priceless.

By sharing their dreams, regrets, and philosophies, these athletes have given me a blueprint for my own life. I took note of who are the happiest and their habits. I've been shown the importance of finding balance and been given the belief you can learn anything if you put in the time. By asking what it means to be a man and a father, I've refined my definition and strive to achieve it. I take Tom Murphy's pillow test each night and am ever so slowly increasing the number of days I'm satisfied with my day's efforts.

Following their example, I've adopted a much healthier lifestyle and continue to train jiu jitsu and yoga. 2016 had been frustrating for me as a competitor with most of my matches ending in a draw or defeat. I kept at it and at Gracie Nationals I managed to submit both opponents and win gold in front of Eddie Bravo, who belted me to purple at the next night's promotions.

This is one of the few accomplishments I'm proud of. It wasn't easy taking myself from being the joke of the gym, getting submitted by hundreds of different individuals each year to holding my own against guys half my age. But I'm even more grateful that we helped pro fighter Jonathan Santa Maria open the 10th Planet Youth Center in Whittier, the first 10th Planet focused on women and children. My 3-year-old son loves riding piggyback with his rear naked choke sunk in and has great body awareness. My 8-year-old Olivia has gained great confidence from training and competing. My wife, Jen, has become obsessed with learning and just had her first competition.

Jen hadn't competed in any sport since high school softball, and, although she runs a successful law firm and is under constant pressure, the month leading to the jiu jitsu tournament caused her a lot of anxiety. She looked for an escape everywhere she could but overcame the fear and self-doubt and won her match in a lower age bracket. The competition had a powerful effect because it was so far out of Jen's comfort zone. It was the hardest thing possible that she knew how to do. That challenge is one of the big reasons MMA fighters often say they compete.

Ashlee Evans-Smith who's now 5-1 as a pro (2-1 UFC) nailed it when she said, "Nothing else feels this fun. Nothing else feels this rewarding. I just know that if I picked another sport, I wouldn't feel as happy with myself because I know it wouldn't be as tough of a sport. I really like to challenge myself in every aspect of my life. I think the reason I fight is because it's the hardest thing I can think of doing, on an athletic level at least."

I often worry about the future of some of these individuals, but less than I do about those of football players or boxers. I also keep in mind Matt Horwich, who laughed about people questioning why he would risk his body and brain fighting. Thanks to MMA, Matt has become addicted to positive choices. He gets plenty of rest, eats incredibly clean, and trains his ass off, all to stay at a maximum health level. He said he happily accepted the bruises that'd come with his 53-fight career.

Even considering the risk of traumatic brain injuries, most MMA athletes would probably argue that it was still well worth it. For many of these athletes, MMA has transformed them into a better version of themselves, giving them confidence in everyday life and the cage. Usually the biggest regret these men and women have is that they didn't get involved in the martial arts at a much younger age. Not because it would make them a better fighter, but because it would have sped up their growth as a person.

Most of the individuals I interviewed won't make a fortune fighting, but they've learned material possessions won't bring happiness. And maybe fighting will take years off their lives, like football and boxing, but what good are those years if a person is unfulfilled?

But what about a guy like me who had a losing record, made nearly nothing, didn't travel to any cool locations, only to walk away with a spotty memory and damaged ego? One who worked graveyard shifts to fit in training and burned up vacation days to fight for a few hundred dollars. One who got a tooth knocked sideways, a broken nose, slurred his speech. What kind of idiot does that?

That question was one of the main reasons I started the project. By asking everyone else, I was presented with a giant list of reasons to choose from. Motivators included money, fame, therapy, identity, competition, a test of wit and skills. For some it might be the desire to be good at something, overcoming a fear, or a spiritual calling. Sometimes it's as simple as Steve Montgomery's idea that *it's a chance to become that superhero you wanted to be since you were a kid.*

Going down the list, I could agree most were applicable for me, some more than I wanted to admit, but I wasn't satisfied. My memory is unreliable and I'm constantly warping my past by blending it into my fiction, so it's difficult to say who I had been at that point in my life. Deep introspection, along with talking to friends and family who knew me then helped, but the answer to why I had fought seemed too intellectual for what I was feeling.

But then everything began adding up. Not like an "aha moment" but an accumulation. Adding up as in stress on my body, mind, and personal life. The days spent away from my family, the miles driven, the lack of sleep, the terrible food, trips to the chiropractor, the cost of each trip. The bumps and bruises, aches and pains, busted ribs, torn ligaments, and concussions, my ego shredded on the mat, built back up then humbled again.

My question went from, "Why did that angry young man try to fight?" to "Why the hell am I seriously considering trying to fight at 40-something, when I have absolutely nothing to gain but so much to lose?" Why did I allow myself to take punishment by Babalu and Werdum and all the other fighters I risked sparring with? Why bother with any of it, when the project was taking so much time away from writing fiction? Why not go back to being happy and content on the couch, my kids cuddled next to my bulky body?

Throughout this process, I was forced to take a good look at myself, past and present, and all too often I was disappointed with what I saw. Instead of turning a blind eye and letting it slide, I decided to work on changing those things that no longer benefited me. The time invested in training made me mentally stronger, and surrounding myself with positive and inspiring individuals kept me coming back.

Maybe it's a bit romantic, but I now look at my failed attempt at fighting in a different light. Instead of focusing on my low self-esteem or my desperate search for an identity, I understand how much of a release it served, and that without it, I never would have started this project or had the willpower to see it through to completion. It allowed me to understand to some degree, the emotions these men and women experience in training and competition. And maybe it wasn't necessary, and perhaps it was a bit foolish, but I believe my willingness to get on the mat helped convince these men and women to open up to a stranger and share their souls: fears and mistakes, dreams and accomplishments. If I could trust them on the mat, they could trust me off it.

Everyone else's story has influenced mine and lead me to commit to being a better father, husband, and human being. Even though it's cliché, I'd like to say I've unlocked my cage, that I understand myself more fully, but that's an on-going process that should never end.

As human beings, we should continually be exploring who we are, and pushing past our limitations. Forcing ourselves out of our comfort zone. Doing the toughest thing we know how. Pursuing our passions.

FROM THE FIGHTERS

One of the hardest things about writing this book was not being able to include everyone I interviewed. One of my favorite parts of the project has been watching these men and women progress through life. This section is a combination of those two ideas - an opportunity for the fighters to share an update, reasons for fighting, or personal messages.

Zach Maslany

When I first met Mark I was living in the back of my newly opened jiu-jitsu/MMA school, and sleeping on a futon or sometimes the mats themselves. I had begun the business a year and a half prior with my long-time training partner and friend, JM Holland, who at the time had been fighting as an amateur. We were two broke purple belts trying to make a living teaching martial arts in our hometown, repping our own brand Finishers MMA, and flying the 10th Planet banner ranked under Eddie Bravo himself. When I chatted with Mark I had no intention of fighting again and putting myself at risk. I was older and more mature, and felt secure about what I was trying to do in the jiu-jitsu community. I wanted to build a team, start a tournament, compete, and give back to the community.

Fast forward another year and I completely changed my tune. I wanted to lead my students from the front, and let these guys know what it was like to prepare for a fight. I thought if I stepped back into MMA after 11 years behind the scenes, it would hype up the academy. I also believed my jiu-jitsu training gave me an advantage. I ended up fighting in CFFC and losing a three-round decision; I had some chances to finish submissions but couldn't seal the deal. I was satisfied for the moment because I'd done what I said I was going to do. Follow through is what my dad taught me. Finish the job.

Looking back at this story I realized that I can't worry too much about the future. Things can change so fast and your life can take all types of funky

317

directions. Martial arts and MMA have taught me to live in the moment. When you're out there at a competition or rolling at the school, you can't help but think only of the task at hand, which is usually trying not to get knocked out or submitted. I am grateful that Mark decided to stop by that time; I don't know if I would have been able to reflect on my past experiences as I am able to now.

Evan Scott

Five years ago, when Mark interviewed me, I was ambitious, full of energy and confusion. These feelings fueled and interwove into my martial arts training. In the interview, I had mentioned that fighting is full of possibilities, and to predict what would happen is like rolling the dice, unpredictable. My prediction was that I would be learning, fighting, and basically completely consumed by mixed martial arts. I've been in thirteen competitions, consistently trained, studied, and travelled to new gyms. I was given the opportunity to teach at Lauzon MMA and this last year welcomed my first-born baby girl. The aftermath? I am still ambitious, and full of energy and confusion, which is all still very much a part of my martial arts training. I've won and I've lost, smiled and picked my shots. I've never been knocked out or hurt by anyone other than myself. The twenty-six-year-old version of Evan Scott had some tricks up his sleeve, but was too polite and cautious to hustle. This thirty-year-old version has confidence and rigged dice. Four years from now, I'll still be full of ambition and energy, which will remain connected with my martial arts training up until the end. Fighting is a calculated risk but I'm very lucky; lucky to be involved in something so f**kin awesome.

Matt Perry

The fighters you see in the UFC are amazing athletes and martial artists, but they don't realistically represent the MMA community. Most of us are just regular people who recognized that we needed something to elevate our lives. For many of us, martial arts is a religion, a foundation, a crucible, a place to belong. For me it was fight club; a way to learn about myself and to become strong enough to live the way I wanted to live, to empower myself to do all the things that scared the hell out of me.

Matt Hamilton

First of all, I want to thank Mark for honoring me with inclusion in this project. The interview actually helped me figure out why I have dedicated my life to this sport, besides simply avoiding a "real job." I have to say that I wouldn't change anything about my career. I'd like to have performed a little better for sure. But I did get to be in on the ground floor of this sport and see it from its infancy. I got to compete in three MMA Tournaments and won two of them. I got to see athletic commissions come in and regulate the sport (some for better, some for worse). And now I get to pass on knowledge and guide young fighters. I couldn't have asked for anything more. I do what I love and I love what I do. Thanks to Mark, I have a concrete way to express that.

Peter Jeffrey

Martial arts has been an extension of my musical arts life for years. For the first many years as a martial artist, I thought the two disciplines were worlds apart. It took about six years to find the training parallels. Realizing how the study, application, and practice were the same was mind blowing to me. I was using martial arts as an escape from long hours and the burn-out factor that comes with teaching 12-15 private music lessons a day. One day during one of my striking classes a particular song came on while we were sparring in the gym. I had transcribed this song for one of my students and knew the rhythms very well. I thought it would be funny to try to strike these rhythms on my training partner. He didn't think it was very funny; it was the most accurate I had been against this particular partner to date. Realizing that I was using rhythm to figure out where to strike was a monumental breakthrough for me. After this I tried this same application with Jiu Jitsu ... amazing! It worked! For years the two had been completely separate arts in my mind. This became a huge factor in my teaching. I have seen great results and have gotten very positive feedback from many students when I teach this concept in class. I have my music training to thank for the breakthrough.

319

Martial arts I believe is for everyone. You just have to apply the things in your life that make you unique, and use them to help you understand the fighting arts. Everyone has a story to tell. Most stories have not been written yet. You have to open your mind and explore who you are. Finally, be humble and try to learn something every day. In this sport nobody knows when to say someone is too old to train and compete. In my opinion you're only old when you close your mind and stop learning. Thank you to Mark Tullius for opening people's minds with this book, to my family for all their support, to the teachers who have guided me, and to my students who everyday push me to be a better person and artist.

Rudy Morales

I became the 1st Guatemalan in history to fight (and win) in Bellator MMA. I started a world class (Amateur) MMA organization called Real MMA and I created the motto "Believe 2 Believe" which has been adopted by UFC fighters like Heather Jo Clark. I still have the dream to one day be in the UFC, but for now I am proud of my kids and have come to the realization that I'm not just a fighter. Life without risk is not life.

Eddy Rolon

The most common thing I have said since 1998 is, "Don't break your toys; you'll have nothing to play with." This reminds training partners to keep each other safe when striking and especially employing joint and bone submissions. Having become physically diminished so quickly due to my Autoimmune/Neurological Disorder of CIDP has given me a huge reaffirmation in the power of technique. There is always someone stronger, faster, better conditioned and more aggressive out there. We all age (or in my case, experience aging type limitations), and I find solace in being calmer, more technical, more aware, and using a good strategy against any potential opponent. Technique doesn't get tired anywhere near as quickly as unfocused aggression.

Elaina Maxwell

Both of my parents died in 2006, so after that tough experience, I really needed a change in scenery, so I moved to Vegas after that for a couple years to pursue my fighting career only to move back 2 the Bay Area 2 years later 2 join Gracie Fighter in the East Bay, along with CSA Gym My only regret is fighting in the wrong weight class my entire career because I never found the proper dieting guidance until I met my current Muay Thai trainer, Kirian Fitzgibbons. I always waited until the last minute to cut weight, and now I have irreversible damage to my thyroid. I wonder how different my career would have been if I had committed to fighting at 135 from the beginning, instead of 145. Despite that one regret, I had such an awesome experience, traveling and fighting around the world.

I haven't fought since 2012. I met my husband during a fight camp in Thailand in 2011, and we have a one-year-old son. To date, I still train at Combat Sports Academy in Muay Thai and BJJ, as well as Cross Fit. In November, I'll be inducted into the HOF, with my husband and son in attendance. I work in law enforcement. (As I did before my first fight.) I'm grateful for my martial arts mentality, as I know it helps me in my everyday routine.

IG: @elaina_maxwell Twitter: @elainamaxwell

Derek Shorey, Team Kaos/Shatterproof Combat Club

Fighting for me has never been about winning or losing, or even really had much to do with my opponent. Fighting was and is a way for me to discover truths about myself, and have no choice but to accept them. I've come to find more success coaching than I did actually competing, but I think I may have a few fights left in me.

Darryl MarcAurele Jr.

It's interesting to think back to being 21 and struggling, when I'm now 31 with a great career. Without the confidence and control I developed through training and fighting, I'd never have made it to where I am. I hired on at a nuclear power plant with no degree, and within a year and a half I was promoted to supervisor, bypassing 14 other applicants who'd been there for 15 or more years. My success is due to the work ethic and portraying confidence beaten into me in the gym. Nothing is harder than that one more round of training, one more minute in the cage, landing one more punch. If you can do that, everything else is easy.

Joseph LeVasseur

When I did the interview for *UTC* with Mark, I had no idea what to say. I just wanted to be interviewed. Since then I've really thought a lot about why I fight. I realized that I did it for more reasons than just because I enjoyed it. There are many reasons, too many to list, but I think I can put my finger on the biggest ones. Since the interview, I've gone through a divorce and moved from Tri-Force MMA gym in the Providence, RI, area to Gracie Barra in Portland, OR. GB Portland formed under black belt Fabiano Scherner with a bunch of people who left other gyms in the Portland area. It's a great place to train with many world class fighters on the mats all the time. I've been back in the cage and have had two wins and two losses since restarting MMA. I've also taken home many gold medals in the advanced divisions of regional jiu-jitsu tournaments. People used to say to me, "You're tall. You should play basketball." I tried, but I always had a hard time remaining focused in team sports. I would not be paying attention and the other team would rack up points while I was watching something on the other side of the court. Everyone would be mad at me and I'd go home feeling bad about myself. It's likely that I was never diagnosed with ADHD, because I've noticed I have a problem remaining focused in routine situations. Combat sports and some other solo sports are really the only sports I can remain focused on. I make improvements, I remain productive. It does a lot for the self-esteem to know what you're good at. I have never been as happy as I am when I am training and competing.

Scott McQuary

What motivates fighters to fight is usually fear or desire. The definition of motivate is, move to action. What inspires them to step into the arena of combat can be insightful, the reason to fight is what moves you. Fighting is a very individual sport, in victory as well as loss, how you conduct yourself with either gives a real reflection of character. Understanding motivation and character of oneself thru fighting is profound.

Steve Dunn

I started wrestling with my twin brother, Rich Dunn, when we were eight years old. We competed for over 20 years, and we both won multiple New England freestyle championships and many state titles. I was always fighting in the streets and local bar scene. I started watching the UFC from its very beginning. I lost interest because there were no weight classes. I got back into watching because of Randy Couture and Matt Hughes. I would never watch the local scene because I knew I'd be tempted to fight, but I was eventually talked into going to watch a friend compete. It felt like a wrestling tournament; I caught the fight bug and had my first fight three months later. After nine professional fights I have a 7-2 record. My last fight was June 25, 2017, just two months shy of my 51st birthday. I haven't officially retired; I figure I'll just walk off into the sunset when I'm ready.

MMA saved me from the streets. Since I started training and fighting I've really chilled out as far as bar/street fighting. I'm much better off due to the time I've spent training and coaching MMA. I've met a lot of good people and I train kids in wrestling and MMA. I even opened a gym, Wai Kru, located in Brockton, MA.

Rob Emerson

If there is one thing I could teach to other fighters, or even athletes in general, it would be for them to BELIEVE in themselves. The power of belief and the power of visualization are all things that I am learning about in the latter part of my career, and it is truly the most powerful and performance enhancing part of the game. I have spoken to multiple sports psychologists, people with PHD's in the field, experts who have worked with combative athletes. The one thing they all had in common was their emphasis on VISUALIZING and practicing the FEELING of being victorious. The body physically performs better when it has "rehearsed" the live action mentally.

Dave Rosky

I am 48 years old, and I live in Rahway, New Jersey. I own Rosky Combat Sports, and I am the inventor of the Rosky MMA SnapBack focus mitts.

I have been a lifelong martial artist and plan on continuing that tradition until I take my last breath. My journey in martial arts has always focused on sport combat. In school I struggled with intense dyslexia and it seemed I could never get anything right. Even in my martial arts endeavors, doing KATA or any memory based drills, I would always go the wrong way or in the wrong sequence. In live combat I always felt like the right and wrong had to do with winning and losing, not memorizing moves or following patterns, but in seizing opportunities and performing ad lib rather than memorizing. And that was something I could do.

I have always felt indebted to my opponents for helping me open doors that I couldn't have opened without them. Fighting has never been something I've done out of anger or rage, but more out of a desire to outplay, outthink, and outwork my opponents. Fighting is the only place I have ever felt smart.

Kevin Green

I've been a local and federal cop, and been in two wars...Brazilian Jiu Jitsu/MMA are the only arts I've seen and trained in that test you physically and mentally. You can't hide on the mats. It's helped me through a divorce and fighting for custody of my kids. Now, at 42, these arts are another mental and physical tool I'm taking in my kit bag to combat.

George Zuniga

I made my professional debut in May 2013 and currently have a 3-1 professional record. MMA has given me a different outlook on life; everyday problems don't seem to faze me the way they did before competing in the cage. At work I keep my poise in the roughest conditions. I explain to my son how to control emotions and breathe in competition and in real life situations. MMA teaches discipline and understanding on different situations that call for different skills, and that's what makes it such an amazing sport.

Instagram: @GAZuniga Twitter: @zuniga_george

Jessica Martinez

I began my martial arts career in 2007 after moving to Virginia. My boyfriend, who was a Tae Kwan Do instructor, encouraged me to begin training. Within two years I took my first of eight amateur fights. After my third fight I learned that I could take some wicked hard punches and not get knocked out, that I needed to prepare better, and that I could become friends with a woman who had kicked my ass.

My last fight was four years ago for the Las Vegas promotion, Tuff-N-Uff, for their vacant 135 title, and, to be honest, I could have used about another month of fine tuning. Losing that fight was very tough, and hit me emotionally in a way I had never experienced before.

I had two choices after that fight: get back to training, learn from it, and go back out there to win like I knew deep down that I could or fuck off. I did the latter. From there life has been a mix of crazy ups and incredible lows like I'd never experienced before. I'm slowly beginning to rise again from this crazy journey, and am discovering who I am.

There are many times I find myself missing fighting. Then the little devil on my shoulder whispers in my ear "You're too old. You don't train enough. You work too much. Are you really even any good? It's been too long." I cannot say with certainty that I would never step in the ring again. As a matter of fact, I miss competing in Jiu-Jitsu and have actually had a few dreams about it recently. Who knows, maybe I still have it in me to get out there and prove to myself that I still have what it takes, not only to be challenged, but to be talented enough to win.

John Esposito

I am no longer competing in MMA due to starting a family and my current job. As much as I would love to compete, it requires devoting not only 100% to the sport, but your life. Fighters today are so good the risk versus reward doesn't make sense unless MMA is your life.

Zach Lee

The martial arts have helped me learn how to cope with everyday life and face the reality of things on a different level. Nothing is perfect and even the best at what they do still have to practice and sharpen their tools. I keep an open mind thanks to martial arts. It's helped me keep calm in bad situations and to think fast in other situations. My years of doing martial arts has taught me that you're always learning and you are never master at anything completely; that's why being humble is a great tool for any martial artist. It's helped me overcome obstacles, do things people thought I could never do, and accomplish things that I thought I could never accomplish.

Since I retired from fighting I have focused on jiu jitsu where I still compete at a world level and just earned my black belt. I love being able to teach people how to better themselves by learning something new.

John Raio

My training, competing, and coaching in MMA has brought me closer to God and brought me closer to people. I have developed relationships with incredible people that I would have never met working a typical 9-5 job and going straight home to my family every night. I have met some of the most humble, caring, and genuine people in this sport. For that I will be forever thankful.

Connor Matthews

When I started MMA in my sophomore year of high school, I had no way of knowing what an incredible impact it would have on my life. I originally started training as a means to channel my teenage aggression. I was almost immediately becoming addicted to the sport and before long I was training almost every day and when I wasn't doing MMA I was working out with a boxing or kickboxing coach. I was fighting every opportunity whether it was MMA, kickboxing matches or Golden Glove matches. I loved the physicality of the sport, I love the strategy and I loved the comradery with my fellow fighters. I didn't realize it at the time but this multi-discipline training was going to lead me into a great job. A couple of years after I graduated I decided to try to become an Air Force Combat Controller. Not many people know who they are, but Combat Controllers are battlefield airmen that are part of the Air Force Special Operations. They are certified air traffic controllers that deploy into combat and hostile environments to establish assault zones or airfields, while simultaneously conducting air traffic control, fire support and command and control activities. When I found out about this small group of extraordinary individuals I knew I wanted to be one. But the odds were against me because it requires the most rigorous training of any military job. All in all it was about a three year long pipeline of training. It was the discipline that I learned in my MMA training that made the difference. Many of the guys trying out for this job were former college athletes. They all seemed to be bigger, stronger, and smarter than me, but what I had was the ability to get punched in the head and not quit. I have attained the goal that I sought for many years. I still do MMA training several times a week; it is still my passion. Last year I even had the great honor of boxing in London representing U.S. Special Forces against British Special Forces. I still love the sport and I know I will continue to train and fight for the rest of my life. Hopefully that will involve an even bigger comeback in getting back in the cage.

Steve Montgomery

Martial arts changed my life. During my senior year of high school, I toured colleges looking for a place that felt like home. I was simultaneously an aspiring fighter, and when I walked into American Top Team, I knew what college I wanted to go to. I wanted to major in martial arts. Martial arts is all about passion. If you are doing it for some ulterior motive like ego, or to be a bully you will get burned out and lose interest. To stay involved in the fighting arts for a lifetime takes a true connection to the lifestyle. The lifestyle is all about camaraderie, learning and evolving. Training in any fighting style almost always helps to develop a person's character for the better. Mark's book, *Unlocking the Cage*, is brilliant because it shows what fighting is behind all of the cameras and social media posts. He shows a fighter, or a martial artist, for who they are as a human being. To me that is exciting because the people I have met through MMA have all been very interesting people! This book is going to be revolutionary for our sport and one of a kind.

Roli Delgado

When it's all said and done, whether you got out of the sport on top (albeit rare), or stayed too long and got beaten out, what you're really left with are relationships: old coaches, teammates, competitors, their coaches, etc. I couldn't care less about being lucky enough to catch a win in the UFC, Bellator and have coached a student to a Black Belt world championship. What I care about are all the connections that I made through those successes. I've been so fortunate in this regard, having made so many amazing friends across the globe.

Kenneth Degenhardt

I think it's important to realize that just because you had a fucked up life or upbringing, doesn't mean you will be fucked up. You are in charge of yourself and how you act. I grew up in some of the most fucked up family situations you can imagine. It wasn't always bad, but definitely less than ideal, so I was proud when I opened my first company at 18 and began a successful MMA career.

At the request of my fiancée, I sold my company and moved us from Tennessee to Sacramento where I decided to train and fight full time with Team Alpha Male. While it is amazing to be part of such a welcoming team, shortly after moving our relationship ended and I went from being a millionaire to working for $15 an hour doing construction just to get by.

Even with all the misfortune and I still smile at everyone I meet. I keep my head up and push forward. I know I'll be back on top, because that's who I am. The only person who can stop me is me. When people have a problem, they call me. When people are down they call me. Life is not about money or possessions. It's about the experience. It's about the people you meet; the ones you share your life with along the way. It's about being in the moment.

I have not fought with anger or need for validation. I fight because it's the truest form of testing myself, the truest form of competition. It's you vs the other guy. No one can help you. You are going to do it or you aren't.

That's it. So that's what MMA has done for me. It's helped me to constantly learn who I am. It's been a way to keep myself in check and at the same time better myself. It is my balance in an often fucked up life.

Jason Skip Libby

We created The Shop MMA to give myself, Bill Jones, and other fighters a place to train and beat each other up. It evolved into something much more, and we have had people from all walks of life join, including young kids finding themselves, older mature clients looking to get back into shape, and full-fledged fighters looking for other fighters to train with. We were one of the last true "fighter" gyms and loved every bit of it!

I would like to thank the following people for our success inside and outside the cage: Dan Langdon, Troy Pickering, Adam Rivera, Tammy Jones, Celina Libby, Dana Hall, and the rest of The Shop MMA family!

Michael D'Urso

Since my interview, I have become a teacher's aide at a special education school and am pursuing my teacher's certification and special ed certification, while also pursuing my Master's in Education. I have continued training BJJ where I am now a purple belt (I believe I was a white belt when we spoke) under Black Belt Marcos Duarte and Brown Belt Abraham Awad at SubforceBJJ. I volunteer as an assistant some days at Subforce in Lyndhurst for the kids' BJJ classes. I still have the desire to fight and may step into the cage again at a later time, but my focus now is continuing to progress in Jiu Jitsu and my education. I have no regrets with how my training or fighting has gone. I have fallen back in love with BJJ and train as much as possible. Marcos and Abe have lit the fire under me to develop not just as a BJJ practitioner, but also as a person. I live 50 minutes away from the gym and there are gyms that are a lot closer, but there is a reason I keep going to them and will always go to them. I hope one day that I can influence lives in the classroom and gym like they have for me. I am always reminded of the quote from Robin Hood: "Rise and rise again, until lambs become lions."

Jonny Wester

You interviewed me at a very pivotal moment in my career. The day you interviewed me I hopped on a flight to Brazil for the first time. Later I turned pro as an MMA fighter and went 5-3 but more importantly have been fortunate enough to travel all over the country training with some of the best in the world and made one more trip to Brazil. I opened up my own gym, Gravitas MMA , received my brown belt in BJJ under Danny Dring and have continued to utilize the sport to travel all over and meet some of the most inspiring people. Recently I had the humbling experience of hosting a BJJ black belt from Maceio, Brazil, to teach at my gym and live with me for several months. My accomplishments in this sport will never be able to stack up in comparison to the experiences I have had and the lessons I have learned.

Jonathan Gary

My name is Jonathan Gary, professional Ronin, and here's what I've taken from fighting: 1. Be level-headed and keep your eyes on the mission at hand. 2. You will always have to make some type of sacrifice, especially in regards to time spent with loved ones. This is time you won't get back, so make sure your support system is grand and make sure you prepare yourself for some resentment; no one will truly understand what you go through. 3. Last but not least, free your mind.

The gods have blessed me with the gift of being combative and possessing the mindset for it. I feel truly blessed that I have MMA in my life.

John Salter

I'm on a six-fight win streak and have also qualified for the 2017 ADCC World Championship where I will be competing in Finland. I have earned my black belt in BJJ. I am from Gardendale AL. My IG page is Johnsalter_mma.

Adam Aparicio

I'm a brown belt in Brazilian Jiu-Jitsu under Tim Burrill and currently train at Unity Jiu-Jitsu in New York City. It's been almost a decade since embarking on my journey in Brazilian Jiu-Jitsu, MMA, and combat sports.

Mark has generously given me the opportunity to contribute to *Unlocking the Cage* and share some words of wisdom. I have three sentiments I'd like to share. First, pursue your passion and don't get discouraged, because you never know where it will take you unless you try. Second, keep an open mind and always remain a hungry student to your craft. And finally, pay it forward — because we've all been flailing white belts in something at one point or another, until someone took the time to teach us.

I've learned a lot about myself, and have met some incredible people and made lifelong friends along the way. I believe we are all products of the people we meet and surround ourselves with. With that being said, I want to take this chance to thank some of those people. There's too many people to thank, but here we go:

Special thanks to Ryan Parker, Bobby Dias, Mike Littlefield and everyone at the Boneyard for teaching me right at the beginning and cornering me in my MMA fights; the late Don Banville for introducing me to the leg lock game early; Andrew Tenneson and all of the awesome training partners between Jackson's and Gracie Barra in Albuquerque; Tim Burrill for changing my perspective on how I learn Jiu-Jitsu; Pete Jeffrey for welcoming me to assistant coach at Brown University's GAMMA and always having the doors at Tri Force MMA open for me; all of the incredible training partners between Tim's, GAMMA, and Tri Force MMA in Providence; and thank you Murilo Santana and everyone at Unity Jiu-Jitsu for welcoming me to your school.

Maurice Jackson (Hulk)

I'm 7-1 and training in Albuquerque, MN at Jackson/Winks.

Andrew Tenneson

The inner workings of a martial artist are probably not that different from any other profession, that or it is totally different. The reason I can say both those seemingly contradictory things is because of the constant flow back and forth that is going on inside my own head as I write this; and still probably as you are reading this. The conflict is that I feel alone in my contemplations, but mirrors everyone else. Therefore, we are not really alone. A writer struggling with fleshing out a character, or an engineer trying to fix a design flaw are working on the same level as I've seen great coaches and martial artists deal with an opponent or situation. Deeper still they are struggling or ignoring the great contradictions inside their souls.

"Who am I really?" "Am I good enough?" "Is this the right path?"

Even when there seems to be a strong sense of consistency and purpose on the inside, the outside world has a tendency to bring things crashing down.

The single mindedness and commitment needed to become a champion is the same obsession that makes fighters fight long past their prime or even when they lack the abilities to really compete in the first place. That means you end up with people who dared greatly and fell further than if they never tried at all.

Financially broke and physically broken fighters who have a few old VHS tapes or YouTube clips of greatness to show for it are far outnumbered by those with even less. The same goes for writers, politicians, bus drivers and anyone else that dared to love someone or something and make themselves vulnerable in the process.

What MMA has done for me has not been the ability to exit these absurd realities or take charge of my destiny like some mythological hero. Instead, the work put into the gym, the camaraderie of those I train with, the competition, the proverbial blood sweat and tears are just my way of giving witness to these realities. I know I'm not the best fighter in the world but hell if I don't try to fight like I am. I know there are better ways to make money, but there are ways to make money that leave me emotionally broke. My choices don't dictate the future, but I make my best predictions and own those choices. I've chosen to be a martial artist and use what I know to help myself grow and help other people. My glory is in the struggle, the process, the grind. I embrace it because in the end life is the same thing.

Will Kerr

Fighting never gave me fame or fortune, but it's given me things that I think are greater than those. It's given me skills I'll hopefully never have to use outside of a cage. It's revealed parts of my character that I don't think I would have learned any other way. But, most importantly, fighting has given me earned friendships; friendships that weren't dependent on being from the same town, going to the same school, or working the same job. Friendships made by great sacrifice of time and well-being to help one another succeed. No matter how infrequently we see each other now, those friendships will always be something I'm grateful for.

Jonathan Escalona

I'm now a full-time tattoo artist, but I feel like in some way I owe it to combat sports (pankration) more than anything. I also feel like a more complete artist because of my training.

Francisco Salguero

I need to first thank my coaches and advocates that helped pave the way for me into MMA. Starting with my high school wrestling Coach Gary Embrey, good friend MMA coach, mentor, and legend Yves Edwards, Fernando Yamasaki, Francisco Diaz Neto, Joe Cunningham, Rene Rodriguez, and all the Yamasaki Academy family. My strongest advocate and supporter has always been and continues to be my partner and love of my life, Linda Salguero. My son, Dominic Salguero, is my inspiration, and I always work hard to make him proud. MMA is not only a sport but a way of life that has introduced me to many great people that I am glad to say have become family and friends.

Dominic Warr

I became a fighter to be the alpha and was so hooked on the action that I didn't care if I was winning or losing I fought enough to know that I couldn't make a career out of it and seriously considered joining the military before having my son. I now have as a machine operator and can easily have a happy life without wanting that aggression. I will keep the animal in me quiet for now, because my wife and son are what matters now. If I ever learn how to control my excitement then I'll come back. I need meditation and quiet for now, I need peace. That's me the Hawk

Lenon Ford

I have a different perspective now because I was forced to stop training due to potentially deadly heart disease. I fought my last fight a day after being told I could die and had to retire; I just had to get my last fight and pro debut. It was with RFA fight of the night and I lost, robbed by ignorance, but I didn't care I was glad to have a war. I've coached ever since, from amateur to UFC fighters.

Jared Carlsten

A fighter only trains and fights as long as his career, a martial artist does this it for life.

Ana Carolina

A lot has changed since my interview. I'm not an MMA fighter any more. Of course I have learned big lessons from my 15 years of jiu jitsu and a year of MMA, but now I'm following another path, doing groups of meditation and getting my Reiki (energy healer) certification.

Miguel Santos

I am currently a Purple Belt under Nova Uniao Black belt. I am still training and competing in grappling tournaments. I no longer fight professionally in MMA due to my family life schedule and working in my career.

Jesse Veltri

Corporal Andrew Grenon kept a group of outcasts together, without him we all split ways. His words led me down the direction of learning and educating myself in Martial Arts. With him I'd be a soldier, without him I became a fighter.

Cpl Andrew Grenon Birth: Jan. 19, 1985, Canada Death: Sep. 3, 2008, Afghanistan

Desmond Walker

When, I got into MMA it was never to become a fighter. It was merely to add to my football talent and self-defense because I was a bouncer at a night club in high school. My skills rapidly developed, and I gave a football scholarship up to chase a newfound dream. My family was pissed, said I blew my shot at possibly playing pro ball to basically do human cock fighting. My mother eventually said to me, "If you're going to do this, you gotta go hard." My third amateur fight was a title fight, and I destroyed the guy in 32 seconds. I felt like telling everyone to go fuck themselves for doubting me. But I didn't. I just kept pushing, training, making great friends, becoming a top prospect. MMA became hard for me once I became a single father with full custody of my now 9-year-old daughter. I tried to balance both worlds, but that didn't really work out. So I did what any standup man would do: I helped train other fighters and took care of my responsibility. But I've had my opportunities on the pro level. Hell, I fought UFC contender Azunna Anyanwu in my pro debut in what was not your standard, boring heavyweight fight. We've become great friends and I've helped him train at several fight camps. One way or another I will always be in MMA. I may never fight again but I won't rule it out. I'll train and continue to meet and build friendships with the great people of this community.

Adam Rivera

I finally made it the UFC as a coach, and that's been a dream I'd been shooting for.

Kurt Chase-Patrick

Is a writer for CombatDocket.com and co-hosts the podcast Combat Docket Radio. Be sure to check out Episode 11 where Kurt and Mark catch up five years after their *Unlocking the Cage* interview.

ACKNOWLEDGEMENTS

Sincere thanks to all the men and women who shared their stories with me and encouraged this project. Rest in peace to the three men that passed.

Joe "JC Plentee of Skills" Camacho
1972-2013

Walter "Pops" Carvalho
1934 – 2017

Thomas Mac Truex
Captain United States Army
Persian Gulf, Iraq
1984 – 2017

Kelsey Adkins	Heather Clark	Shaun Durfee
Andy Aiello	Jeff Clark	Anthony Ellison
Brandon Alderman	Carlos Cline	Tim Elliot
Magno Aleimida	Jina Cole	Kyle Ellsworth
Armond Allen	Brock Combs	Rob Emerson
Marco Alvan	Anthony Cordoza	Jonathan Escalona
Wes Anderson	Randy Costas	John Esposito
Reese Andy	Brandon Cottrell	Ashlee Evans-Smith
Joey Angelo	Kim Couture	Tony Ferguson
Adam Aparicio	Ryan Couture	Alessandro Ferreira
Dylan Atkinson	Nathan Coy	Jon Fitch
Saad Awad	Dan Cormier	Brandon Fleming
Nathaniel Baker	Dominick Cruz	Felipe Fogolin
Nick Banks	Ashley Cummins	Lenon Ford
Phil Baroni	Joseph Cushman	Chris Foster
Lance Benoist	Sarah D'Alelio	Zach Freeman
Fernando Bettega	Mike D'Urso	Alan Fried
Corey Bleaken	Beneil Dariush	Tyree Freshner
David Bollea	Sean Daugherty	Ricardo Funch
Justin Bonitatis	Brian Davidson	Steven Garcia
Rodrigo Botti	Alexis Davis	Marcelo Garcia
Bruce Boyington	Danny Davis	Diego Garijo
Paul Bradley	James Davis	Jonathan Gary
Diego Brandao	Marcus Davis	Christopher Gates
Roger Brito	Germaine de	Dmitry Gerasimov
Amber Brown	Randamie	Christos Giagos
TJ Brown	Herb Dean	Nick Gilardi
Brandon Brugman	Carl Deaton III	Mikey Gomez
Josh Bryant	Kenneth Degenhardt	Kevin Green
Mikey Burnett	Roli Delgado	Matt Grice
John Campbell	Michael DeLouisa	Joe Guernsey
Steve Carl	Charles Dera	John Gunderson
Carsten Carlsen	John Dodson III	Javier Guzman
Jared Carlsten	Davis Dos Santos	John Hahn
Ana Carolina	Joe Duarte	Dasha Hamilton
Owen Carr	J.A. Dudley	Matt Hamilton
George Castro	Alexis Du Fresne	Brad Hannah
Michael Chandler Jr.	Evan Dunham	Ako Harper
Kurt Chase-Patrick	Steve Dunn	Jeff Harwell
Todd Chattelle	Robert Durant	Scott Heckman

David Heath
Curtis Hembroff
Joseph Henle
Jason High
Ty Holder
Cleon Hoggard III
Jon Holland
Chris Honeycutt
Keegan Hornstra
Matt Horwich
John Howard
Toby Imada
Eric Irvin
Cody Isaacson
Jay Isip
Maurice "The Gorilla" Jackson
Maurice "The Hulk" Jackson
Ricky Jackson
Nate James
Rick James
Mike Jasper
Keith Jeffery
Pete Jeffery
Kirik Jenness
Chris Johnson
John Johnston
Brandon Jones
William Jones
Julie Kedzie
Kory Kelley
William Kerr
Josh Key
Josh Koscheck
Kody Kramer
James Krause
Shane Kruchten
Joshua LaBossiere
Joe Lauzon

Justin Lawrence
Tim Lajcik
Troy Lamson
Lionel Lanham
Robert Larson
Justin Lawrence
Zach Lee
Tommy Leisman
Roberto Lerma
Joseph LeVasseur
Jason Libby
Jeremy Libiszewski
Cody Lightfoot
Matt Lindland
Scott Lockhart
Kristi Lopez
Joe Lowry
Nico Lozada
Duane Ludwig
Luis Luna
Bill Mahoney
Andy Main
Damon Malon
Michael Malvesti
Jason Manly
Chase Mann
Jake Mapes
Darryl MarcAurele
Darryl MarcAurele Jr.
Andre Margutti
Daniel Marks
Carmelo Marrero
Brett Martinez
Danny Martinez
Jessica Martinez
Richard Martinez
Zach Maslany
Dan Matala
AJ Matthews
Connor Matthews

Elaina Maxwell
Bubba McDaniel Jr.
Bryan McMillan
Scott McQuary
James Meals
Gilbert Melendez
Marcus Mendoza
Joe Merritt
Daniel Meuse
Casey Milliken
David Mitchell
Jacob Mitchell
Steve Montgomery
Rudy Morales
Anthony Morrison
Quinn Mulhern
Pedro Munhoz
Nathan Murdock
Kyle Murphy
Joe Murphy
Tom Murphy
Arash Nadershahi
John Naples
Rafael Natal
Marcio Navarro
Paul Nischo
Jacob Noe
Kyle Noke
Tim O'Connell
Bobby Oller
Joshua Oppenheimer
Benjamin Ortiz Jr.
Damon Owens
Alp Ozkilic
Fredson Paixao
Chris Palmquist
Ian Park
Jamal Patterson
Jeff Paulson
Andy Paves

339

Kurt Pellegrino
Matthew Perry
Jessica Philippus
Wayne Phillips
Chuck Pieritz
Brandon Pitts
Lew Polley
Michael Polvere
Joe Pomfret
Van Wyk Povey
Joe Proctor
Mike Pyle
Andres Quintana
John Raio
Luiz Pedro Ribeiro
Matt Ricehouse
Aaron Riley
Andy Riley
Falon Ring
Art Rivas
Adam Rivera
Jorge Rivera
Clint Roberts
Denis Roberts
John Robles
Jose Rodriguez
Eddy Rolon
Dave Rosky
Marvin Rowell
Casey Ryan
Francisco Salguero
John Salter
Josh Sampo
Andrew Sanchez
Mateo Sanchez
Jonathan Santa Maria
Ryan Sanders
Mat Santos
Miguel Santos
Sean Santella

Jeimeson Saudino
Ben Saunders
Stacey Scapeccia
Colleen Schneider
Ryan Scope
Evan Scott
Hannah Scott
Maurice Senters
Dustin Severs
Brian Shepard
Simon Masaki Shiota
Derek Shorey
Brad Simpers
Fabiano Silva
Marcus Silveira
Robert Slade
Leonard Smith Jr.
Leslie Smith
Tyler Smith
Andre Soukhamthath
Paul Song
Pat Speight
Matthew Spencer
Lana Stefanac
Jeremy Stephens
Alexandria Stobbe
Houston Stout
Jacob Swinney
Brad Tavares
Justin Tenedora
Andrew Tenneson
David Terrel
Courtney Thomas
Jesse Tobar
Jason Trevino
Jon Tuck
Ron Turner
Ryan Vaccaro
Matt Van Buren
Landon Vannata

Paige VanZant
Roberto Vargas
Jesse Veltri
Desmond Walker
Dominic Warr
Michelle Waterson
Andria Wawroa
Jonavin Webb
Stephanie Webber
Christian Wellisch
Cassio Werneck
Jonny Wester
Alex White
John White
Curt Wilson
James Wilson
Aaron Wise
Tyler Wombles
John Wood
Robin Woods
Christopher Young
Lionel Young

Thank you to the coaches, MMA hopefuls, jiu jitsu practitioners, kickboxers, other athletes, and friends that were interviewed and helped along the way.

Danny Acosta
Al Alejandro
Joshua Aragon
Doug Balzarini
Frank Barca
Todd Barselow
Jimmy Binns Jr.
Kris Bowers
Eddie Bravo
Evan Brooks
Dan Bruce
Alex Canders
Cynthia Cavillo
Rob Cipriano
Bob "Crazy Bob" Cook
Rafael Cordeiro
Daniel Cormier
Joe Cunningham
Jeremy Fields
Eric Del Fierro
Randall Dolf
Sevan Donoian
Dan Faggella
Matt Frazier
Giulliano Gallupi
Jose Garcia
Marcelo Garcia
Dawna Gonzales
Ben Greenfield
Ian Harris
Johnny Ho
Joe Hughes
Eugene Inozemcev
Chuck Isen
Anthony Johnson
Peter Kerantzas
Kipp Kollar
Knuckle Junkies
Eric Lee
Miles Lee

Elizabeth Levesque
Rob Levesque
Roland Levesque
Brandie Light
Russell Longo
Dan Luttrell
Thomas M
Geo Martinez
Tara McClure
Adrian Melendrez
Igor Mendelevich
Javier Mendez
Ricardo Migliarese
Frank Mir
Mark Munoz
Robert Navone
Billy Padden
Kerry Phan
Ricardo Pires
Victor Pires
Derek Rayfield
Jon Roberts
Mike Rogers
Ivan Salaverry
Paul Santiago
Sam Sheridan
Dr. Mike Simpson
Prof. R. Tyson Smith
Renato "Babalu"
Sobral
Brandt Stebbins
Anthony Szpak
Jasper Tayaba
Tyler Turner
Frank Ursino
Cain Velasquez
April Vergara
Fabricio Werdum
Cole Williams
Heather Winkeljohn

Mike Winkeljohn
Wes Wolfe
Joe Wooster
Joe Worden
Fernando Yamasaki

Thank you to all the chiropractors that made training possible.
Dr. Steve Tullius of Center for Health and Human Potential, San Diego, CA
Dr. John Holland of Holland Chiropractic, La Habra, CA
Dr. John Taylor Holland of Holland Chiropractic, La Habra, CA
Dr. Zandall Carpenter of Carpenter Chiropractic, Albuquerque, NM
Dr. Dale Johnston of Wilsonville Chiropractic Clinic, Wilsonville, OR
Dr. Marc Saulnier of Saulnier Family Chiropractic, Norwood, MA
Dr. Brandon Mills of Mills Chiropractic, Oklahoma City, OK

GYMS VISITED

Thank you to all the gyms and their staff for making me feel so welcome.

AKA
Alive MMA
Alliance MMA
Allstar BJJ
Alpha Male
AMA
American Top Team
Coconut Creek
American Top Team
Danbury
American Top Team
OKC
American Top Team
Orlando
American Top Team
Steel City
American Top Team
Temecula
Athletics MMA
Babalu's Iron Gym
Balance Studios
Bas Rutten's Elite
MMA
Black Diamond Mixed
Martial Arts
Body Architecture
Brown University
GAMMA
Cassio Werneck Jiu
Jitsu
Cesar Gracie Jiu Jitsu
Combat Fitness
Combat Sports
Academy
Combat Training
Center
Costa Mesa Training
Center
Cung Le Kickboxing

Daddis Mixed Martial
Arts Academy
Destruction MMA
Dethrone MMA -
Bullard
Dethrone MMA -
Kings Canyon
El Niño Training
Center
Endgame Combat
Sports Academy
Fight Academy
Fight Ugly
Fighting Arts
Academy
FIT NHB
Glendale Fighting
Club
Grindhouse MMA
HD MMA
Inferno MMA
Ivan Salaverry MMA
Jackson-Winkeljohn
King's MMA
Kurt Pellegrino's
Mixed Martial Arts
Academy
Las Vegas Combat
Club
Laselva MMA
Lauzon MMA
Mean 1 MMA
Mephis Judo & JJ
Mikey's Gym
Millennia MMA
MMAFC
Nashville MMA
New England
Submission Fighting
Pure MMA

R1
Railroad City MMA
Rebel Fighting System
Reign Training Center
Renzo Gracie Jiu Jitsu
- NYC
Renzo Gracie Jiu Jitsu
- Philadelphia
Rivera Athletics
Rosky Combat Sports
Sityodtong Boston
Sityodtong LA
South Shore
Sportfighting
St. Charles MMA
Stefanac BJJ
Strike Zone MMA
Syndicate MMA
Systems Training
Center
Team Irish
Team Link
Team Quest Gresham
Team Quest Olympia
Team Quest Tualatin
Team Santos Fighting
Academy
The Academy
The Arena MMA
The Factory
The Shop MMA
Tri-Force MMA
Triple Threat Combat
Sports
Tristar
Triunfo Jiu Jitsu &
MMA
Undisputed Boxing
Wai Kru South Shore
Warriors Garage

West Coast Fight
Team
Westside MMA
Wink's Gym
Xtreme Couture MMA
Yamasaki Rockville
Yamasaki Woodbridge
Youngs MMA
10th Planet
Bethlehem
10th Planet Buena
Park
10th Planet Burbank
10th Planet Corona
10th Planet Costa
Mesa
10th Planet HQ Los
Angeles
10th Planet Orange
10th Planet Riverside
10th Planet San Diego
10th Planet San
Francisco
10th Planet Vista

Thanks to the promoters from each of the different events I attended:

UFC
Bellator
Resurrection Fighting Alliance
Cage Titans FC
New England Fights
Samurai MMA 3
Rumble at the Roseland
Rhino Fights
West Coast Fighting Championship

SINCERE THANKS

I owe special thanks to the following people:

My wife, Jennifer Tullius, for believing in me when I did not and for making this journey possible.

My father, Michael Tullius, for all his love, guidance, and red ink used in editing this book.

My sister, Mary Nyeholt Tullius for her assistance with the editing, transcribing, and general help seeing this to completion.

Todd Barselow, for being the extra set of trusted eyes.

Fortunato Lipari, Glenn Cantillo, Marc Saenz, and Richard King for their encouragement and constant push.

Brian Esquivel and Ken Kanenbley for assisting with filming, editing, and transcribing the interviews.

Karl Dominey helping me see the greater picture and Professor Michael Kennedy for his encouragement and guidance.

And finally, thank you to all who I've had the pleasure of training with. It's each of you that's helped me realize what the martial arts can mean.

ENDNOTES

The records and other information about these athletes have been verified using a combination of www.MixedMartialArts.com and www.Sherdog.com Some of the facts on pages 305-306 were taken from this article by Jeff Fox at The Sports Daily website:

http://thesportsdaily.com/mma-manifesto/ufc-fighter-salary-database-salary-main-ufc-career-fighter-earnings-html/

OUT NOW

Brightside

Across the nation, telepaths are rounded up and sent to the beautiful town of Brightside. They're told it's just like everywhere else, probably even nicer. As long as they follow the rules and don't ever think about leaving. Joe Nolan is one of the accused, a man who spent his life hearing things people left unsaid. And now he's paying for it on his hundredth day in Brightside, fighting to keep hold of his secret in a town where no thought is safe.

Twisted Reunion

"Time-honored frights with innovation infused throughout."- *Kirkus Reviews*

Plunge deep into darkness with 28 terrifying tales. Explore heartache, happiness, and horror in this collection of all the stories in *Each Dawn I Die*, *Every One's Lethal*, and *Repackaged Presents*, plus two bonus stories.

25 Perfect Days: Plus 5 More

A totalitarian state doesn't just happen overnight. It's a slow, dangerous slide. *25 Perfect Days Plus 5 More* chronicles the path into a hellish future of food shortages, contaminated water, sweeping incarceration, an ultra-radical religion, and the extreme measures taken to reduce the population. Through 25 interlinked stories, each written from a different character's point of view, *25 Perfect Days* captures the sacrifice, courage, and love needed to survive and eventually overcome this dystopian nightmare.

Try Not to Die: At Grandma's House

It's Grandma's house – quiet, cozy, nestled on a little mountain in West Virginia. What could possibly go wrong? A lot, actually.

So watch your back. Choose wisely. One misstep will get you and your little sister killed.

To survive, you'll battle creatures, beasts, and even your grandparents as you unravel the mystery of your older brother's death in this interactive, graphic novel.

Triple S Agency: Puzzle at the Preschool

The first children's book written by Mark and his daughter, Olivia. In this book, Lena and Marie are best friends and Super Secret Spies. For their first case they try to solve the mystery of the missing puzzle piece.

COMING SOON

Ain't No Messiah
"God has chosen Joshua to bring forth his new kingdom on Earth."
From the day he was born, Joshua has found himself the recipient of death-defying miracles. His earliest memories include his own father proclaiming him the second coming of Christ. However, Joshua has wrestled with serious doubts about the validity of this claim all his life. How could he not, having survived a childhood filled with physical and emotional abuse at the hands of his earthly father.

Now, one way or another, Joshua is going to show the world who he really is. Out Feb. 5, 2019

The Bridge
The second book in the Messiah pentalogy scheduled for release in 2020.

Beyond Brightside
The sequel to Brightside scheduled for release late 2020.

Try Not to Die: In Brightside
Mark and jiujitsu teammate Dawna Gonzales continue the Brightside saga, this time from the eyes of a female teenage telepath. Scheduled for release mid-2019.

Try Not to Die: Hard Road
Mark teamed up with poet and former MMA fighter Tim Lajcik for this installment in the Try Not to Die Series.

In 1979, following his mother's death, Samo Poutnik sets out from his North Oakland neighborhood to Tucson, where his incarcerated father is scheduled for release. Through railyards, over mountain passes, surviving by his wits and fists, Samo travels the Hard Road.

Try Not to Die: In Dixie
Mark and MMA fighter Steve Montgomery coauthor this installment in the Try Not to Die Series.

Try Not to Die: At Deathfest

Mark and Glenn Hedden join forces to bring you the deadliest heavy metal festival.

VICIOUS WHISPERS
PODCAST

To hear free audiobooks and listen to Mark's weekly rant, be sure to look for his new podcast, *Vicious Whispers with Mark Tullius* which you can find on YouTube, iTunes, Stitcher and other places podcasts are played.

https://viciouswhispers.podbean.com

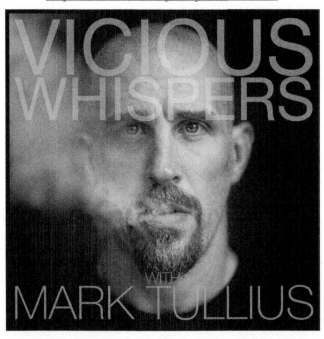

ABOUT THE AUTHOR

Mark Tullius is the author of *Unlocking the Cage, Twisted Reunion, 25 Perfect Days, Brightside,* and the co-author of *Try Not to Die: At Grandma's House.* Mark resides in Southern California with his wife and two children.

For more information about Mark's work, he invites you to connect with him on Facebook, Twitter, and Instagram.

And if you'd like to listen to Mark, please check out his weekly podcast, *Vicious Whispers with Mark Tullius,* which you can find on YouTube, iTunes and Stitcher.

REVIEW

If you enjoyed this book I hope you'll take a moment to write a quick review. As an independent author, I find word of mouth and reviews incredibly helpful. Whether you leave one star or five, honest feedback is truly appreciated. And, if it is a one-star review, be sure to leave your address so I can send one of my friends to visit you. Thanks!

CONNECT ONLINE

Instagram - @author_mark_tullius
Facebook – http://www.facebook.com/AuthorMarkTullius
Twitter - https://twitter.com/MarkTullius
Youtube – http://www.youtube.com/MarkTullius
Podcast - https://unlockingthepodcast.squarespace.com

Printed in Great Britain
by Amazon

22076126R00209